The

LOST ROCKS

—— The Dare Stones and the ——
Unsolved Mystery
of
Sir Walter Raleigh's Lost Colony

by

David La Vere

First Edition 2010 by Dram Tree Books
This edition 2011 by Burnt Mill Press.

Publisher's Cataloging-in-Publication Data
(Provided by DRT Press)

La Vere, David.
    The lost rocks : the Dare stones and the unsolved mystery of Sir Walter Raleigh's lost colony / David La Vere.
    p. cm.
    Includes bibliographical references and index.
    ISBN 978-0-9835236-0-4

1. Roanoke colony. 2. North Carolina —History —Colonial period, ca. 1600-1775. 3.
Roanoke Island (N.C.) –History—16th century. I. Title.

F229 .L3 2010
975.6/175—dc22

10 9 8 7 6 5 4 3 21

Call for volume and educator discounts

Burnt Mill Press

1520 Chestnut Street
Wilmington, N.C. 28401
910-264-5007 burntmillpress@yahoo.com

FOR JACK AND CAROL MILLS

Best in-laws ever

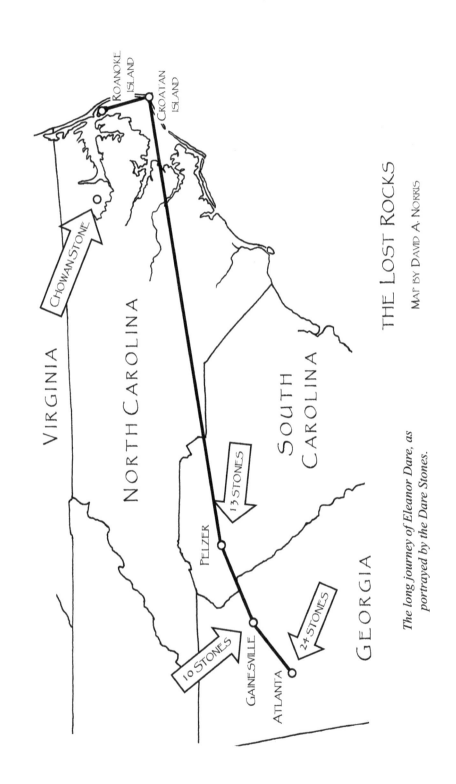

THE LOST ROCKS

MAP BY DAVID A. NORRIS

*The long journey of Eleanor Dare, as
portrayed by the Dare Stones.*

CONTENTS

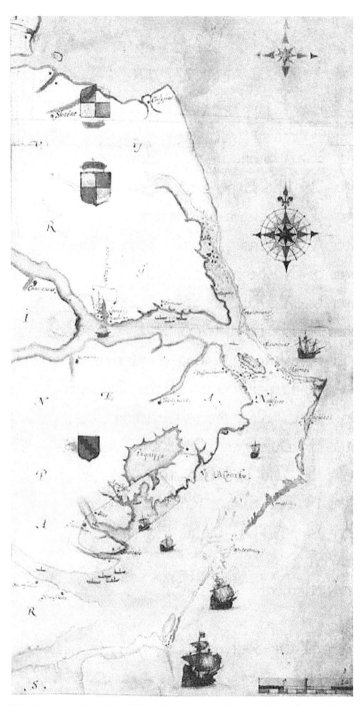

John White's map of the North Carolina coast, showing Roanoke and Haterask (Hatteras) Island.

A Colony Lost

From the deck of the Hopewell, *Governor John White spied the column of smoke rising far off to the northwest. He was ecstatic. It seemed directly over Roanoke Island, right where he'd left his colony three years earlier in 1587. It was obvious. His people had spotted the* Hopewell *and the* Moonlight *anchored off the coast and were signaling them. While it was too late in the day to make a landing, White figured that by this time tomorrow he would be reunited with his daughter, Eleanor, her husband, Ananias Dare, and best of all, his granddaughter, Virginia. He tried to imagine how she'd grown. At three, she would surely be walking and talking—though it was too much to hope that she would remember him.*

The next morning, the sixteenth of August, 1590, Governor White, Captain Abraham Cocke of the Hopewell, *Captain Edward Spicer of the* Moonlight, *and a crew of sailors set out in a couple of landing boats for Roanoke. The Island was a long ways off as it sat sheltered from the Atlantic behind a string of sandy barrier islands. The master gunner on the* Hopewell *was ordered to fire signal cannons at intervals to alert the colonists to the governor's arrival. But as the two small boats neared the gap between barrier islands, White saw another column of smoke rising from the large sand dunes on Hatarask Island* just to the south. He directed Captain Cocke to make for Hatarask instead.

It was all a waste of time. The column of smoke was much further away from where their boats came ashore. The search party spent hours trudging through deep sand, and when they finally reached the fire, they found no evidence that it had been a signal intended for them . "We found no man nor signe that any had bene there lately, nor yet any fresh water in all this way to drink," a dejected White wrote. And then, thirsty and exhausted, they had to march all the way back to their boats. By that time, it was again too late in the day to make for Roanoke. Fortunately, they found a source of fresh water among the beach dunes. The boats headed back to the Hopewell and Moonlight to try again the next day.

By the morning of August 17, the bad luck that had been dogging John White for the past three years caught up with him again. Instead of getting an early start, Captain Edward Spicer of the Moonlight used his landing boats to ferry casks to Hatarask Island for fresh water. It wasn't until ten o'clock that White, Captain Cocke, and their boat managed to make for Roanoke Island. Even then, the most dangerous part of the whole voyage lay before them: getting through the gap between the barrier islands. It was dicey work trying to pass over a barely submerged sand bar while fast-running currents and breaking waves tossed the boats around like driftwood. Roughening seas and a freshening wind foretold the approach of a nor'easter. White's boat had just gotten into the breach when a huge wave broke over the boat, almost capsizing it and half filling it with seawater. White claimed it was only "by the will of God and carefull styrage of Captaine Cocke we came safe ashore, saving only that our furniture, victuals, match and powder were much wet and spoyled."

Captain Spicer of the Moonlight was not so fortunate. Spicer's landing boat followed into the breach but was halfway through when a great wave hit the boat and overturned it. A few sailors were thrown overboard but managed to hold on to the boat's side. Then the next wave crashed on top of it, driving the boat down into the sandbar, breaking their grip. Now the sailors swirled in the surf, struggling to stay afloat. Another wave and then another pounded them. Some tried to wade ashore, while others clung to the twisting boat. White witnessed it all from the beach, watching the waves beat them down "so that they could neither stand nor swimme, and the boat twice or thrise was turned the *keele upward." Captain Cocke and other sailors immediately went to their rescue. Of the boat's eleven men, they managed to save four, but seven, including Captain Spicer, were drowned. Their deaths put such a cloud over the sailors in Cocke's boat that many refused to go any further. Only by Captain Cocke's commands and Governor White's persuasiveness were the sailors convinced to row on to Roanoke Island and the rescue of White's colonists.*

It was dark by the time the landing boat reached Roanoke. As the weary men rowed around the northern tip of the island, they caught sight of a large fire in the woods. Unsure of its origin and unwilling to stumble around in the dark, White ordered the boat anchored just off the island's shore. In hopes again that their settlers had set the fire as a signal, the men "sounded with a trumpet Call & afterwards many familiar English tunes of Songs, and called to them friendly; but we had no answere." The sailors spent a cramped night in the boat and at daybreak landed to investigate the fire. Again White was disappointed. It had been just a wildfire of grass and rotten trees with no one about.

From there, the landing party made their way through the woods to the western side of Roanoke, the part of the island that faced the gentler waters of a large sound, where White had left his colonists three years earlier. Where he hoped he might come upon a bustling colony and reunite with his granddaughter Virginia, Governor White found the site completely deserted. In August of 1587 he had left 117 men, women and children here. Now there was not a single person to be found. A few prints of bare feet indicated not the leather-shod English, but Indians. The settlers' fort was overgrown and in disrepair. A nagging dread inched up White's spine. It was clear no one had lived here for some time.

Gone were the colonists' houses, but there was no evidence the buildings had been burned or destroyed. The structures appeared to have been dismantled and moved elsewhere.

Signs of activity presented a strange and disturbing puzzle. About the fort lay four iron fowling pieces, some iron shot, as well as heavy bars of iron and lead. White believed these had been left because they were too heavy. His own personal belongings, which he had stored in trunks and buried for safekeeping, had been dug up. His maps, papers, books, picture frames, pieces of now-rusted armor all lay strewn across the ground. He blamed this on the Indians. But his people, his daughter and granddaughter, his colonists, all of them, their effects, and the small boat they had for navigating the sounds were gone. Vanished like a forest mist under a hot sun. Still, he was somewhat relieved. If his colony was missing, at least there was no sign of war or destruction. They had not been attacked and overwhelmed, but had made an orderly relocation away from Roanoke. That gave him hope.

As White saw it, the colonists must have put into motion their plan to move away from the inhospitable Roanoke. That meant they must have left clues to their whereabouts. A quick search found them. Carved on one of the large posts next to the fort's entrance was the word CROATOAN — the name of an Algonquian village on a nearby barrier island. As if to emphasize the signal, the letters CRO were carved on a tree closeby. In neither case was there a cross carved above, the agreed-upon sign if they had been attacked. White took comfort that his English had not been driven from the Island. To the governor the message was clear. "I had safely found a certaine token of their safe being at Croatoan, which is the place where Manteo was born, and the Savages of the island our friends."

Back on the Hopewell, *White convinced Captain Cocke to sail to Croatoan, about a day's run to the south, where he expected to find his colonists. But bad luck clung hard to John White. That evening was stormy. Fierce waves forced them to abandon the ship's freshwater cask on the beach.*

By the next morning, the weather was a little better and the wind favorable. Cocke's plan was to hurry south to Croatoan, rescue the colonists, then return for the water cask, a job well done. But as the sailors were hauling in the anchor, the cable broke and they lost the anchor — the second one lost on the voyage. Even worse, without the anchor's tension, the Hopewell *now shot toward the shore. Racing toward destruction, Captain Cocke ordered another anchor dropped. It caught just in time to prevent the ship from running aground. Cocke was just able to maneuver the ship into a deeper channel, saving his command but losing a third anchor in the process.*

Cocke knew when to cut his losses. With three of the ship's four anchors gone, Captain Spicer and six others from the Moonlight *drowned, food scarce, the freshwater cask left behind, and the weather shaping up into a hurricane, Cocke explained to White that they could not continue to Croatoan. Instead, they would make for the Caribbean to resupply and then return to the island next year. White had no choice but to agree with his captain's expert recommendation. But as the weather* worsened, the backup plan proved unworkable and Cocke steered east toward the Azores and home. White would not reach Plymouth, England, until October 24.

John White would never see his family again. But he thought of them every day. Others thought about them, too. England wanted to find her lost people or at least learn what happened to them. And though several efforts were made to locate them, firm answers eluded the searchers. The fate of the Lost Colonists of Roanoke remained a mystery. Then, in 1937, exactly 350 years after their landing on Roanoke, a stone was found that seemed to record the terrible and tragic destiny of White's Lost Colony.

*The front of the original Dare Stone, found by Louis Hammond off Highway 17
near Edenton, N.C. in 1937. It is often called the Chowan Stone because it was
found near that river. Brenau University Archives.*

CHAPTER 1

A Stone on the Chowan

L ouis Hammond was walking around lucky that day. Here it was August of 1937, the Great Depression draped over the country like a shroud, millions out of work, out of money, out of food, but he and his wife were on a leisurely vacation on the opposite side of the country. The couple from Alameda, California, across Oakland Bay from San Francisco, had been touring the South by car for more than a month. Retired from the produce business — or so he said — the forty-year-old Hammond had the time and means to travel.

Today found the Hammonds just outside Edenton, North Carolina, cruising the newly opened stretch of U.S. 17, the two-lane hardtop Ocean Highway that had been designed to promote tourism from Florida to New York City. The region they traveled was rich in history and rural beauty. Edenton, a speck of a town on the north bank of Albemarle Sound named for royal governor Charles Eden, was one of the oldest permanent settlements in North Carolina. It served as the colony's capital from 1722 to 1743. Its Georgian courthouse and stately eighteenth- and nineteenth-century homes along the waterfront, picture-postcard parks, white picket fences, and tree-lined streets drew visitors to its quiet sidewalks. Situated only thirteen feet above sea level, it was surrounded by dense cypress and tupleo swamps and drained farmlands. Just three or four miles away, the Chowan River, wide as the Mississippi and named for the long absent Choanoac Indians, emptied into the Albemarle.

The back of the Chowan River Dare Stone. Brenau University Archives.

Automobile traffic was sparse on the isolated ribbon of road, which was built up from the low-lying bottomlands. In many places the shoulder was too narrow for a car to pull off; narrow bridges crossed numerous creeks and swamps. Tall hardwoods and pines formed a canopy that dappled sunlight along the route. Insects buzzed in the summer heat. Hammond decided to pull over to look for hickory nuts, he later said. Or maybe it was to stretch his legs. Could've been a bathroom break.

Whatever the case, it was a stroke of luck and one of the great coincidences of history when Hammond eased the car over on the shoulder at that particular spot. He estimated he was about fifty miles west of Roanoke Island and North Carolina's Outer Banks, those sandy barrier islands made famous about three decades earlier when Orville and Wilbur Wright flew the first powered aircraft off the dunes at Kitty Hawk.

Hammond stepped off the grassy shoulder into the soggy woods. The August sun was broiling and the hot breath of the forest nearly took his away. Nonetheless he strolled around a bit, nudging aside ferns, chokeberry, and myrtle, hopping over watery places. Then he spotted a dark stone the size of a large platter jutting from the damp earth.

His first thought was that it was an old, forgotten tombstone. But he quickly dismissed the idea. It didn't appear purposely set in the ground, and the mass of faded words chiseled into the rock seemed more of a statement than a grave marker. His mind raced to other possibilities. Indians had once lived in the area. Did it have something to do with them? Maybe it marked buried pirate treasure. Back in the early 1700s, Blackbeard and his

A model of Blackbeard's ship,
Queen Anne's Revenge.

buccaneers of the *Queen Anne's Revenge* had prowled North Carolina waters. The legendary pirate was no stranger to the sounds and for a while used the nearby town of Bath as headquarters.

Hammond stooped for a closer look. It was a moderately-sized flat piece of dark vein quartzite, almost fourteen inches long and about ten inches wide. It would weigh out at twenty-one pounds. The stone was somewhat oval, but looked more like a battered shield tapering to a blunt point at the bottom. Hammond's curiosity got the better of him. He picked up the stone and carried it back to his car.

Still parked alongside U.S. 17, Hammond showed the stone to his wife. He brushed the dirt away, hoping to read the inscription. He could barely make out lines of words, all small and crabbed together, clotted with grime. Hammond pulled out a wire brush and went at it, scraping off any moss or lichen to help him get a better look. In the process, he destroyed evidence that might've helped a scientist date the artifact. Still, the words remained too faded and too strange for him to make out. He wrapped the stone in an old cloth, tossed it into the back seat of the car, and the Hammonds resumed their trip.

For the next three months, as summer gave way to fall, the Hammonds continued their tour of the South. Nothing is known of their itinerary or plans. Every now and again Louis pulled out the stone and tried to decipher it. He went over the inscription to better make out the words, first with a pencil, then with a nail, but could make no sense of them.

Dr. James G. Lester.
Emory University Archives.

Louis Hammond and his wife were themselves a mystery. No details are known today of their physical appearance, where they resided, what car they drove, what they saw, whom they met. Their unexplained motives and background, their apparent aimless wanderings in a time when few Americans had the resources to travel extensively, would raise serious questions.

On Monday morning, November 8, Hammond appeared on the campus of Emory University in Atlanta, the stone, still wrapped in cloth, tucked under his arm. He wandered about the campus awhile, usure of what he was looking for, before he happened into the Alumni Relations office. There he met Alumni Director R. F. Whitaker and told him that he had a rock he'd like someone to look at. There was writing on it, Hammond said, but he couldn't make it out.

Professor James G. Lester had gone to the Alumni Office telephone exchange to make a call into downtown Atlanta. The lanky geologist was one of the most popular professors on the Emory campus. When Lester was finished, around 11:30, Director Whitaker caught his attention and told him there was a gentleman with a rock that needed looking at. It wasn't unusual for folks to stop by unannounced with some strange rock, insect, or arrowhead to show a member of the faculty. Lester and Whitaker took Hammond out into the corridor to see what he had.

In the hall Hammond unwrapped the stone, saying he'd found it not far from the North Carolina-Virginia border. Lester propped it on a radiator for a closer look. About that time Dr. Thomas H. English — aptly, a professor of English — strolled by. English spotted the stone, became interested, and edged in on the conversation. Finally, he grabbed the rock from off the radiator and sat down right in the hallway to take a closer look. The sight of a respected professor sitting on the floor engrossed in examining a large rock was indeed an unusual occurrence, so a crowd of students soon gathered. All the while, Lester and English tried to decipher the wording. They could make out a cross and were astonished to read the name "Ananias." Everyone was getting excited. "Newshawks among the students crowded and pushed forward snatching at phrases spoken concerning the Lost Colony," James Lester would recall.

To escape the crush of curiosity seekers, the men retreated back into the Alumni Office. Lester found a magnifying glass to aid in the translating. Physics professor J. Harris Purks popped in and got interested as well. Soon the Alumni Office was packed with people and no one was getting any work done. So Lester, English, Purks and Hammond carried the stone down to the building's basement, where Purks had his biophysics lab. There the professors again turned their attention to the inscription. Hammond stood aside and let them work. He "did not contribute a single suggestion for a single word," Lester said.

Word of the stone traveled fast across the Emory campus. Within minutes Professor Haywood Pearce Jr. of the Department of History, Professor J. M. Steadman of the Department of English, and Jeff Davis McCord, professor of physical education, barged in to get a look. They were brought up to speed on what was happening, joined the investigation, and offered their ideas on the stone and inscription. The men, all immersed in deciphering the find, worked well into the night and all the next day. It would take the team of professors Lester, Pearce, Purks, Steadman, English, and McCord almost a week to completely transcribe the message carved in the rock.

Founded as a Methodist college in Oxford, Georgia, in 1834, Emory University by the 1930s had become one of the South's preeiminent institutions of higher learning, with a growing national reputation. With the help of Asa Candler, the founder of the Coca-Cola Company, in 1914 the university moved from its original site to an elegant campus in the Druid Hills suburb, not far from downtown Atlanta.

As a top-flight university, Emory also attracted a top-flight faculty. And the professors now studying Hammond's stone were all men highly regarded in their fields. Geologist Lester, a Navy veteran of

Emory is one of the nation's finest universities.

World War I, joined the Emory faculty in 1919 and was founder and first chair of the university's geology department. He would teach at Emory for fifty years. Professor Haywood Pearce Jr. was a respected historian and rising star in the field of American History. His book *Benjamin H. Hill*, a biography of the Georgia secessionist and Confederate Senator, had won the very first Dunning Prize in 1929, awarded by the American Historical Association to a young scholar for the best book on American History. Dr. J. Harris Purks had joined the Emory faculty in 1923 and for years taught physics at the university. But not long after the Dare Stone arrived at Emory, Purks moved into academic administration, becoming dean of Emory College. In the mid-1950s he served as provost of the University of North Carolina and briefly its acting president. Thomas H. English, also a World War I veteran, received his Ph.D. in English from Princton University in 1924. He came to Emory in 1925 where he taught literature and poetry until 1965. He retired in 1980 as Emory's special collections librarian. Jeff Davis McCord not only taught physical education at Emory, but was also the university's Athletic Director. English professor J. M. Steadman had written books on grammar and vocabulary and was a member of the South Atlantic Modern Language Association. Overall, it was not a bad collection of scholars to initiate an investigation of the stone.

As the words revealed themselves, the professors realized what they had was big. Really big. Here, sitting right in front of them, was a historical bombshell that answered one of the great mysteries of American history — what happened to Sir Walter Raleigh's Lost Colony of Roanoke. Furthermore, the inscription hinted at a second stone bearing more of the story.

Naturally their professional training led them to suspect a hoax. They quizzed Hammond hard about his discovery, pressing him for details. Hammond told them his story of how he had just happened to spot the rock in the woods near Edenton. It was a great coincidence, but the story seemed plausible enough for the time being.

The group agreed that further investigation was warranted immediately. The following day the Emory professors determined to make a trip to the Chowan River in North Carolina, in hopes of locating the exact spot where Hammond found the rock. Hammond agreed to lead them to the place and drew a crude map for the investigators on the back of a paper bag. Prof. Pearce cleared the trip with Emory president Dr. Harvey Warren Cox. So Lester, McCord, Pearce, and Purks, accompanied by Hammond, embarked that week on a trip of five hundred fifty miles, in search of a swamp near Edenton, North Carolina.

During the long hours in the car, with only the hum of the tires to keep them company, the professors had plenty of time to quiz Hammond about himself and his find. The Californian's answers and demeanor only reconfirmed to Lester, Pearce, and the others that Hammond was on the up and up. Lester figured that if Hammond was a hoaxer, then he had "no business carrying a piece of stone around showing it to college men; he should be selling gold bricks to the hardboiled bankers of America." The Emory faculty were apparently satisfied with Hammond and his story. During the ensuing weeks, while the professors conducted a thorough investigation of the stone, they welcomed Hammond and his wife as guests of the campus. Throughout Hammond's time there, Lester said, the Californian "conducted himself with persistence and fidelity which to my mind was beyond the reach of the most perfect actor. Everyone with whom he came in contact was favorably impressed with his simplicity, and his naturalness." As he told his colleagues in the Faculty Club the following spring, "Frankly, I believe the man was what he said he was."

The North Carolina trip, however, revealed nothing new. The delegation found no more stones. They were not even certain they had identified the exact spot where Hammond had found the rock. Disappointed, the team raced back to Emory to finish up the translation.

On November 14, 1937, less than a week after the stone had created such a sensation on the Emory campus, the professors announced that they had deciphered the words carved into it. On the stone's smoother side was carved a rough cross mark, beneath which were the words, styled in capital letters maybe a half inch to an inch tall:

ANANIAS DARE &
VIRGINIA WENT HENCE
VNTO HEAVEN 1591

Then below that, toward the bottom, on the same side:

ANYE ENGLISHMAN SHEW
JOHN WHITE GOVR VIA

On the rougher reverse side were seventeen unpunctuated lines of crowded words, in what appeared to be Elizabethan English, and a signature of initials. (Punctuation has been supplied in this transcription for ease of reading.)

FATHER SOONE AFTER YOV
GOE FOR ENGLANDE WEE CAM
HITHER(.) ONLIE MISARIE & WARRE
TOW YEERE(.) ABOVE HALFE DEADE ERE TOW
YEERE MORE FROM SICKENES BEINE FOVRE & TWENTIE(.)
SALVAGE WITH MESSAGE OF SHIPP VNTO US(.) SMAL
SPACE OF TIME THEY AFFRITE OF REVENGE RANN
AL AWAYE(.) WEE BLEEVE YT NOTT YOV(.) SOONE AFTER
YE SALVAGES FAINE SPIRTS ANGRIE(.) SVDDIANE
MVRTHER AL SAVE SEAVEN(.) MINE CHILDE
ANANIAS TO SLAINE WTH MVCH MISARIE(.)
BVRIE AL NEERE FOVRE MYLES EASTE THIS RIVER
VPPON SMAL HIL(.) NAMES WRIT AL THER
ON ROCKE(.) PVTT THIS THER ALSOE(.) SALVAGE
SHEW THIS VNTO YOV & HITHER WEE
PROMISE YOV TO GIVE GREATE
PLENTIE PRESENTS
EWD

Updated and expanded for modern readers, the smooth side of the stone reads: "Ananias Dare & Virginia went to Heaven, 1591" / "Any Englishman show [this rock to] John White, Governor of Virginia."

The reverse leaves a telling and plaintive message. "Father, soon after you go for England, we came here. Only misery and war [for] two years. Above half dead these two years, more from sickness, being twenty-four. [A] Savage with [a] message of a ship came to us. [Within a] small space of time, they [became] frightened of revenge [and] ran all away. We believe it [was] not you. Soon after, the savages said spirits [were] angry. Suddenly [they] murdered all save seven. My child [and] Ananias, too, [were] slain with much misery. Buried all near four miles east [of] this river, upon [a] small hill. Names [were] written all there on [a] rock. Put this there also. [If a] Savage shows this to you, we promised you [would] give [them] great plenty presents. EWD." To any schoolchild who'd studied the history of the first English settlement in the Americas, the closing initials could only stand for Eleanor White Dare, daughter of Governor John White who had made the futile search for them.

Here was the discovery of the century — plausible and final evidence of the fate of the 117 men, women, and children of Sir Walter Raleigh's Lost Colony. The colonists' disappearance from Roanoke Island in 1587 had captivated the world for three and a half centuries. It had become an American legend, raising a question that begged an answer. Now, here it was, carved in stone.

Over those three and a half centuries, the Lost Colony had become a pillar of North Carolina history. While Virginia could boast of Jamestown on Chesapeake Bay as the first *permanent* English settlement in America, North Carolina consoled itself with Raleigh's failed attempts on Roanoke Island. The Lost Colony might have disappeared, but it had done so in the state where England had chosen to make its first stand at American colonization.

In the 1930s as the three hundred and fiftieth anniversary of the colony approached, the citizens of North Carolina began to promote Roanoke Island, the last known site of the Lost Colony, as a heritage tourism destination. Plans were in the works for a Fort Raleigh Park on Roanoke Island with a museum dedicated to this first English settlement. But North Carolina boosters had even bigger ideas. Community leaders on Roanoke approached Pulitzer Prize–winning North Carolina

An enlargement of a John White map showing Roanoke and surrounding Indian lands.

playwright Paul Green with a commission to create an outdoor drama celebrating the Roanoke colony. Though initially they had hoped to stage a production in 1934 on the anniversary of the first English expedition to the island, the economic fallout from the Great Depression caused the Roanokers to delay the project for three years.

As Green's play was coming together, with locals as cast members and crew, plans were being laid for a gala night to coincide with the 350th birthday of Virginia Dare on August 18, 1937. State and national dignitaries were expected to attend. An amphitheatre overlooking Albemarle Sound was being constructed to accommodate nightly crowds. A postal stamp honoring Virginia Dare would be issued in conjunction with the festivities.

That spring, the publicity machine for *The Lost Colony* cranked out news features that were picked up througout the South and, eventually, nationwide. In April 1937 the *Atlanta Journal* ran an article on the Works Progress Administration's efforts to restore the Fort Raleigh site. By summertime the entire country could hardly have missed the highly anticipated events on remote Ronaoke Island. The July 4 premiere was covered enthusiastically by popular North Carolina newsman Ben Dixon MacNeill. President Franklin Roosevelt attended the August 18 gala, establishing the play not only as a hit in its inaugural season but a summer tradition ever since. There is no record whether Louis Hammond and his wife attended any of the performances or the August 18 extravaganza. Roanoke was big that summer—some 50,000 visitors saw Green's *Lost Colony* between July 4 and its Labor Day closing—and it's likely that any tourist in the area would probably found their way to the Island and seen the play.

Green's play told the story of the Lost Colony with a patriotic emphasis on how the colonists had come to North Carolina to secure liberty in a new land. America was born here on Roanoke Island, North Carolina. As Green wrote, "the coming of Eleanor Dare to this country, as she did, would suggest a daring mind. . . . There was something noble and tremendous in them and they felt that their hardships in the New World had meaning."

The Dare stamp.

No matter how freedom-loving the play cast the colonists, the story ended with the colonists being forced off Roanoke Island by the untimely arrival of a Spanish ship. According to Green's version, the colonists headed to Croatoan Island, where they were never seen again. Audiences left the play brimming with patriotism but pondering the colony's unknown fate.

Poignantly, they were left also to ponder the fate of Virginia Dare, the first English child born in America. If the English had tried and failed in North Carolina, Virginia Dare nonetheless signaled the birth of the American people — in North Carolina. Virginia Dare was a symbol of state pride. She was every North Carolinian's mother and their daughter, the missing child, the unredeemed captive. They carved statues of her, wrote poems about her, created myths in which she turned into a white doe. Wines and other products were named after her. A postage stamp now bore her likeness. The state even issued her a birth certificate in 1937, with the "Citie of Raleigh in Virginia" given as her place of birth.

Disappearing into the woods, Virginia Dare took on a sort of immortality. She has often been portrayed as an adult, as if she lived a long life in the forest though she was just an infant when the colony disappeared. But now this rock shattered the legend. Virginia Dare was dead, killed, along with her father, by Indians near the Chowan River in 1591. Her widowed and now childless mother was left alone in the wilderness. Hammond's stone had the ability to change history, to make or break a state's entire identity. If authentic, it was a powerful artifact indeed.

The highly trained team of Emory faculty knew that the stone, which they had started to call the Dare Stone, needed much more careful investigation. As college professors they understood the rules of evidence.

With a reliable transcription settled, they now focused on the text of the inscription. Were the words consistent with late-sixteenth-century English? Were they in use at the time? Would a woman of Eleanor Dare's age and class know and use them? Just about everything checked out. In an era of inconsistent orthography and punctuation, "miserie" for "misery" was common enough; "beine" and "bleeve" seemed plausible, as did of the spelling of "spirits" as "spirts." The ampersand (&) and other abbreviations were regularly employed to save space. Arabic numerals had come into wide use in England by the fifteenth century. And the cross was among the most ancient of symbols.

Some things were more problematic. The researchers could find no usage of the word "affrite." And while they could find instances of women signing with only two initials, they could find no historical precedent for three, as in "EWD." These might be chalked up to misspellings, the nebulousness of the English language in the sixteenth century, or just the fact that the Colonists had been separated from the language for four years. Nevertheless, there was nothing in the inscription, to their lights, that did not seem authentically Elizabethan English. Nothing conclusively ruled it a forgery.

They also took a much closer look at the Dare Stone and the technique used to inscribe it. The Stone itself was easily identified as vein quartz, a rock common to the Piedmont of the American Southeast, but also found in England. Oxidation had left brown stains on the Stone, which was a dark gray overall. However, this type of stone was not native to the coastal plain where Hammond had found it. Lester, the geologist, would have known that quartz did not occur in the region, and in fact noted that when the team had gone back to the North Carolina site they had seen no rocks at all other than isolated fragments in stream bottoms. One intriguing possibility was that the piece of stone had arrived as ballast in the ship's hold, as many rocks from the British Isles had made their way to North American shores.

How, the investigators asked, had the inscription on the Dare Stone been made? Whoever carved it had done a very good job as there were no hesitation marks where the carver made an aiming mark and then struck. There were no scratched over letters, where the carver started, made a mistake, and then tried to correct it. There were no marks on the edges to indicate that it might have been held in a vice. The Emory team now took similar stones, coated them with paraffin, cut words into the wax layer, applied hydrofluoric acid in the exposed areas, and let the rocks sit for sixty hours. The acid left only very light marks, none of which looked anything like the Dare Stone carvings. In a granite workshop they coated a rock with rubber, carved in comparable letters, and had it sandblasted by an expert. While sandblasting could produce somewhat similar letterforms, it yielded differently shaped grooves and left a "delicate frosting" on the rock.

Team members attempted a variety of chisels on similar stones. Stoneworkers at the McNeal Granite and Marble Works in Marietta, Georgia, were asked to take a look. The experts offered different opinions. A few said the inscription was made by sandblasting, but most thought a chisel had been used. One worker even showed how easily the letters could be made with a chisel, replicating the dots that appeared frequently for the "a" and "o." "He held the bit on the rock and with the handle vertical between his hands rotated the bit by rubbing his hands back and forth," Lester explained. "The process was similar to the friction principle of starting a fire without a match. The chief cutter at the McNeal Works insisted that he could reproduce the Dare stone in a few days (48 hrs) if he had nothing else to do and a suitable piece of quartz."

After weeks of testing, the Emory team could find nothing on the rock or inscription to prove or disprove the Stone's authenticity. Surely they were dismayed that Hammond had removed the Stone from its natural environment, where an archaeologist might have been able to determine when it was buried. When in due time the group would make its findings public, they unequivocally urged anyone else making such a discovery to "leave the evidence INTACT and AS FOUND until it may be viewed by reputable historical groups."

Lacking definitive evidence for all their time and effort, the Emory University investigative team was in a real quandary. These were university men putting their reputations on the line. Had they tapped into the historical find of the century — or the makings of an elaborate hoax? If they wound up backing a fake they'd be laughed out of every faculty lounge on the continent.They had to consider it a distinct possibility.

* * *

Here was the New World, all lush green trees and bright promises. On that hot July day in 1587, the three small ships edged as close as was safe to the narrow strip of sand that formed a barrier between ocean and mainland. The men and women aboard the boats must have imagined those promises. Wealth, land of their own, fame, vices to be satisfied, adventures made so they could be recounted back in England. A man could drink for the rest of his days if he had a good story to tell. All seemed within reach.

But darker possibilities also haunted their minds. The tangled islands and surging waters were unknown to all but a few, and that terrified them. Eleanor must have become jittery when her father, Governor John White, explained how just last year the colony here on Roanoke Island had to be evacuated because of angry Indians. It was, however, the known risks that held even more horror: shipwreck, abandonment, starvation, thirst, torture, or painful death in any one of a thousand forms. So when Master Simon Fernandez of the Lion *ordered the anchors dropped, it was with relief and apprehension that Eleanor, Governor White, and 115 other men, women, and children began clambering into the ship boats. Those on the smaller pinnace and flyboat did the same.*

It fell to Edward Spicer, captain of the two-masted flyboat—the same Captain Spicer who three years hence would drown at almost this exact spot—to ferry Eleanor and her fellow passengers from the ships to the beach. These English townfolk had been at sea for three months now, on a voyage that took them from Portsmouth on the southeast coast of England, across the Atlantic, down to the Caribbean for fresh water,

then up the Gulf Stream to what would become known as the Outer
Banks of North Carolina

Their wobbly sea-legs made it a precarious venture just
climbing into the bobbing ship boats, even with the help of the sailors
manning the oars. It must have been especially hard on the nineteen-
year-old Eleanor Dare, not only the governor's daughter but also wife of
Ananias Dare, one of Governor White's right-hand men. She was big
with child, in her last weeks of pregnancy. So was Margery Harvie, wife
of Dyonis Harvie, another of White's assistants. Women and children
were needed to make this into a real English colony that could grow and
thrive and turn a profit. This venture was to be a transplanted English
farming village, and not just a soldier's fort like Colonel Ralph Lane's
outpost the year before.

Once settled in the boat, Eleanor and Margery took a wild ride
through the crashing waves and over the barely submerged sandbar at
the mouth of the inlet. It must have been difficult for any of the company
to keep down their fear, and their breakfast as well. Making it from ship
to shore was no easy task. It was in fact dangerous work, the risks of
losing supplies or even lives all too real. But once they made it through
the shallow inlet, it was easy rowing to Roanoke, a small, forested island
amid that great inland sea formed by the banks and the mighty
Albemarle and Pamlico sounds.

As the first small boat neared Roanoke Island, the men yelled
and hallooed to announce their arrival. The colonists were only to be
here for a day or so, to stretch their legs and pick up the few men left on
Roanoke the year before. Fifteen English soldiers had been ordered to
hold the colony that Ralph Lane had abandoned. But the fifteen were
nowhere to be seen. White expected them to come rushing down to the
water's edge, overjoyed to see their countrymen. But there was no one to
greet them, neither Englishman nor Indian; nothing except the sounds of
the birds and the oars slapping the water.

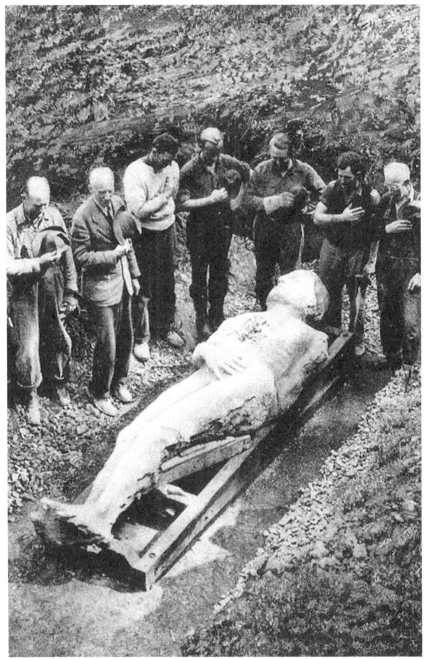

The Cardiff Giant, pictured here, was a hoax that captured the imagination of the country.

CHAPTER 2

The Experts at Emory

oax: An act intended to deceive or trick, says the dictionary. Hoaxes come in all shapes and sizes. At their most base, they are blatant forgeries with a profit motive—counterfeit coins or currency, confidence games, Ponzi schemes. In America during the 1930s, a sizeable forgery business had also grown up around American Indian relics. Fake pipes and celts, forged masks and effigies cobbled together in some craftsman's garage or workshop were attributed to ancient Indian civilizations. Many were quite convincing, and some of the top museums in the country fell for them. The same thing had been happening in Europe for centuries. No telling how many churches or unsuspecting tourists shucked out good money for forged religious relics. Mark Twain himself complained in his *Innocents Abroad* that "we find a piece of the true cross in every old church we go into, and some of the nails that held it together. I would not like to be positive, but I think we have seen as much as a keg of these nails."

But it was P. T. Barnum who popularized the word "humbug." No less a forgery, and while money was often made from them, the humbug was bigger in spirit. Before the Civil War, Barnum challenged visitors to his American Museum in New York to view the "Feejee Mermaid" — a specimen that was nothing more than a dried upper half of a monkey and the lower half of a fish sewn together – and decide for themselves if it was real. The Cardiff Giant, a ten-foot tall "petrified" man found in 1869 in Cardiff, New York, was eventually revealed to be a hoax, merely a rough sculpture hacked from a block of stone. And even as the Emory team worked on the Dare Stone, a debate over the authenticity of another recently discovered Elizabethan artifact was roiling the academic world. A brass plate attributed to Sir Francis Drake had been found in northern California the year before. Supposedly left behind in 1579, the plate's inscription claimed the Pacific coast for Queen Elizabeth I and England. Most scholars thought it authentic. Only years later was it determined to be a hoax. Of course, the Emory men didn't know this at the time. Still, they couldn't afford to let themselves be hoodwinked by a humbug.

Now they took a much closer look at Louis Hammond. Emory was considering purchasing the stone. If the stone proved authentic, then the university had a valuable relic of American history in its lap. But university officials wanted to know for sure what they had. They contracted with the Pinkerton's National Detective Agency and the Oakland, California office of the Retail Credit Company to dig into the Californian's background.

Drake's Brass Plate, thought authentic until proven fake in the 1970s.

The Pinkertons turned first to Oakland-area fruit and vegetable dealers and warehouses. They checked with coastal California police departments, chambers of commerce, and a host of directories in the Los Angeles–Pasadena area. Their efforts turned up several unlikely matches. A Leonard E. Hammond, a hardware store clerk, and his wife, Hattie, lived on Hermosa Avenue in Los Angeles. A Lawrence C. Hammond was a Los Angeles bank clerk. The Pinkertons investigated both men and ruled them out as the Dare Stone finder. Lacking access to the wealth of public records available today, they overlooked a Louis Hammond listed in the 1930 census as a fifty-five-year-old boarding-house lodger in Santa Barbara, California in 1937.

The flesh-and-blood Louis Hammond, by this time gone from Emory and returned home, proved elusive. Hammond had given his address as General Delivery, Alameda, California—while not an uncommon custom for the time, a dead end for locating a person. The Retail Credit Company picked up a thin trail in Alameda: other than the general delivery address, they found no mention of him with the United States Post Office or in San Francisco Bay Area telephone or street directories, police departments or banks.

Nor could they find anyone, with the exception of the one man Hammond had given Emory as a personal reference, who knew of him. Mr. Dove, who ran a second-hand jewelry store in Alameda, said that he didn't know Hammond all that well, but described him as about forty years old, no children, with a wife and a pension, living somewhere in east Oakland. He was, Dove claimed, a "regular fellow." The investigator duly checked out Dove, reporting that he was "not particularly well educated, has no known connections or information on North Carolina history, is not a publicity seeker and has nothing to do with the finding of the plate supposedly left by one of Drake's ships." The investigator added, "We do not learn that Mr. Hammond himself has any of these attributes."

Where the Pinkertons provided a considerable list of other Hammonds in Los Angeles, in the Bay Area the Retail Credit Company zeroed in on "L. E. Hammond" and so overlooked some other leads. Over on Santa Clara Street lived William A. Hammond and his wife, Annie. William, a partner with his father in the successful real estate firm of Hammond and Hammond, would have been 61 years old in 1937. William and Annie had no children, or at least no children who lived with them. As a young man, William had spent five years in the wholesale grocery business before joining his father in real estate. Of course, there is no way to confirm whether William A. Hammond was actually Louis E. Hammond, finder of the Dare Stone. Maybe the Credit Company checked and ruled out any connection between William A. Hammond and Louis E. Hammond, finder of the Dare Stone. If so, it does not appear in the report the company provided to Emory University.

The hazy details of Hammond's life rattled nerves back at Emory and have aroused suspicions ever since. It would have been much better for all involved if Hammond had been a solid citizen with a well documented life. But this was the Depression '30s, when millions of Tom Joads were on the move searching for work; when Social Security numbers were only just being introduced; and long before computers or the Internet. It wasn't hard for a person to disappear, be overlooked, or fall between the cracks. Of course, that also made it all the easier to pull a hoax.

But did this sketchy information on Hammond make him a huckster? The Emory professors, many of whom had spent considerable time quizzing him, could find no fault with him. Lester gave Hammond his seal of approval. "Conversation and correspondence with Mr. Hammond indicate that he is utterly incapable of writing such a message," Lester said. "For the most casual student of the Dare Stone must soon come to realize that it was written, if a fraud, by the highest type of learned individual. One capable of carrying on research along several lines – history, language, (Elizabethan writings), cartography, geology, and stone carvings. I doubt seriously if there is any one individual in the United States capable of such a performance."

Hammond's innocence seemed verified when he willingly left the Dare Stone with the Emory investigators upon his return to California. The November 9, 1937, contract between Emory and Hammond stipulated that Hammond was to receive one dollar in cash, while Emory was to take temporary custody of the Stone and generally maintain safekeeping responsibilities, such as keeping it in the University Treasurer's vault when not being studied. Emory also got "exclusive right to publish under its own name any and all historical discoveries which may arise from the research and study of the said stone, its inscriptions and the surrounding territory from which it came."

The Emory professors certainly thought the Stone was the real deal when not even a week later, on November 15, Professors Lester,

Pearce, McCord, and Purks formed a partnership with Hammond. Ownership of the Stone remained with Hammond, but at any point when he might decide to sell the Stone, because of all the effort and expense the four had put in, they would have the right of first refusal by submitting a competitive bid. They could not prevent Hammond from selling it to whomever he chose. But when the Stone did sell, the four Emory men would share ten percent of the proceeds. Hammond would keep ninety percent. So these respected Emory professors from several different disciplines believed the Stone was authentic and Hammond nothing more guilty than being a fortunate tourist who stumbled across the find of the century.

Still, uncertainty nagged at Lester the geologist. Not so much about Hammond; he felt the man was legitimate. But he wondered if the retired produce dealer had stumbled across a humbug. Lester voiced doubts that bother researchers to this day. Why would Eleanor Dare use a stone to leave her message, as this would mean she would have to dictate it to a stonecutter? If she wanted to send a message to her father, whom she expected back in the near future, then Lester wondered why she didn't use "a part of her petticoat, or even a part of her dress, a piece of baked pottery, a fragment of soapstone pot or other cooking vessel, or even a piece of parchment which she could have easily carried with her when she was taken into captivity by the Indians." Others had similar reservations. Did Eleanor Dare really believe that an Indian would carry a twenty-one pound stone fifty miles or more to Roanoke or Croatoan in search of John White? Carrying burdens was women's work in Algonquian Indian society, not men's. But she did promise presents of valuable English merchandise to any who would carry the stone. That might be enough to persuade a woman, maybe even a man, to make the effort.

If the Dare Stone was a hoax, the professors wondered, then who set it up? Questions about the authenticity of Drake's Plate of Brass rang in their heads. Some wondered if Hammond had been involved in that. Later revelations about the Brass Plate showed that he evidently was not. But why devise a hoax at all? Money? At this time, Hammond had only received one dollar for the Stone. That was a point in his favor. Still, he stood to gain more if Emory bought it. Fame? Hammond did not want any of that, and at first refused to have his name publicly connected with the Stone. That in itself seemed suspicious. But the Emory team had already investigated him, and while there was an aura of mystery about the Californian, their own experiences with the retired produce dealer ruled him out as a hoaxer. So who would undertake such a scheme, and to what end? Lester felt it might have been "planted by a person possession [sic] a warped mentality which delights in the puzzling and befuddling of the so-called 'learned group' or professionals." Then again, maybe the Stone was innocuous, possibly a prop made for some long-ago pageant about the Lost Colony. Or could it have been an advertising stunt "desiring to start a real estate boom, or to obtain publicity of a fashion for a certain town or community?"

Maybe it was a group of folks who just wanted to publicize Virginia Dare. Or advertise *The Lost Colony* on Roanoke Island. Or maybe it really was a full-blown hoax by some crazed history buff. No less than President Franklin Roosevelt had predicted, after attending Paul Green's play, that someday someone would find something that would provide evidence of the Lost Colony's fate. Now just weeks after the President's speech, here it was.

If the Dare Stone was a hoax, then whoever pulled it off, Lester believed, had to be pretty amazing in their own right. The creator of the Stone had to be smart, know a lot about a host of different things, and be able to keep ahead of the fools who would fall for it. If a hoax, then the person who made the Stone surely knew of the 350th anniversary of the Lost Colony. As Lester admitted, the one true thing about the rock was that "its authenticity can never be established in the laboratory. It must be corroborated by further findings in the field." That meant going back to North Carolina.

But North Carolina was not going to be so accommodating. Within days of the Emory Team's deciphering the transcription, on November 22, 1937, the *Raleigh News and Observer* ran a wild story with the headline, "Grave of Virginia Dare Believed Found in the State." From the start, the *News and Observer* writer, G. deR. Hamilton Jr., had details and dates incorrect. The story reported that Dr. "Pierce," the Emory historian, had actually found the Dare Stone with the help of an unnamed California archaeologist. The Dare Stone itself showed "that Virginia Dare, born in 1585, had died in 1589, at the age of four years."

As for Hammond taking the professors back to North Carolina, the newspaper mistakenly reported it as a full-blown archaeological excavation. Not only were the professors looking for Lost Colony information, the paper said, they also were seeking "evidences of an ancient and highly cultured, but long ago extinct civilization supposed to have existed in this area some 500 or more years ahead of the superlatively cultured Aztecs and Incas of Central and Southern America." The paper believed this ancient North Carolina Indian culture was just as advanced as the Aztecs and Incas and was the ancestor to the Choanoacs, Tuscaroras, Cherokees, and other North Carolina Indians. However, the paper said, Dr. Pearce was not commenting on any of it and reasoned that Pearce's silence was because the planned Chowan River archaeological expedition was being funded by newspaper baron William Randolph Hearst, who wanted "a smashing scoop for Hearst papers."

When asked about the article, Pearce denied the newspaper's claims and stated the story had its facts wrong on just about all counts. They had certainly not found Virginia Dare's grave or tombstone. Still, the Emory team did not want to make the Dare Stone's inscription public until they had it fully translated.

Up in Raleigh, North Carolina, the story was spotted by C. Christopher Crittenden, secretary of the North Carolina Historical Commission and director of the state Department of Archives and History. Tall,

William Randolph Hearst

balding, nattily dressed, Chris Crittenden was a Wake Forest graduate with a Ph.D. in History from Yale. Appointed to the commission in 1935, Crittenden took an eager interest in anything concerned with North Carolina history. Word of the Dare Stone reached him in mid-November 1937, even before the newspapers reported it. But if what was being rumored about the Stone was true, then Crittenden knew he needed to get involved. He quickly penned a letter to Professor Haywood Pearce Jr., who had emerged as the spokesperson for the Emory investigation team. "I understand that you have at your disposal some very interesting information connected with the fate of Virginia

Dare and the 'Lost Colony,'" wrote Crittenden. "And I will greatly appreciate your telling me anything you are at liberty to divulge."

Pearce replied cordially that he regretted "the premature publicity given to the matter, the utterly garbled quotation attributed to me and the false impression left by the Raleigh news releases." But he

strongly denied that they had found Virginia Dare's grave and certainly had not made off with a tombstone. Still, while they were only now studying the Stone, it did appear connected to the Lost Colony and its fate. Crittenden reminded Pearce that the North Carolina Historical Commission owned the Fort Raleigh tract on Roanoke Island, "on which the 'Lost Colony' is thought to have settled, and for many years has been desirous of solving the mystery of the fate of the colony." He urged Pearce and his Emory colleagues to work with North Carolina historical officials.

Pearce ignored him.

* * *

Christopher Crittenden.

John White's plan to situate his colony on Roanoke Island in 1587 was England's third attempt in as many years to establish a settlement in what they called Virginia in honor of Elizabeth I, the mother country's Virgin Queen. Throughout the sixteenth century, England had jealously watched Spain conquer the Indian peoples of Central and South America as well as those of the American Southeast. From these places, Spain shipped back untold amounts of gold, silver, gems, and other precious items. Some Englishmen, like Sir Walter Raleigh, believed that if only England could plant a colony in the Americas, it too would be able to tap into these riches.

So in 1584, with Queen Elizabeth's blessing, Raleigh sent two small ships on a scouting mission to Virginia. Captained by Philip Amadas and Arthur Barlowe, in July the two barks reached the narrow

Sir Walter Raleigh (left) was a favorite of Queen Elizabeth I (right). It was with her blessing and support that Raleigh dispatched colonists to settle at Roanoke.

barrier islands that lie off the middle Atlantic capes. The ships sailed up the coast, threaded their way through one of the inlets into Pamlico Sound, then anchored on the inland side of one of the islands. It was not long before they were discovered by the Roanokes, an Algonquian Indian people who lived on Roanoke Island to the north. Barlowe, Amadas, and the crews spent a happy month and a half trading with the Roanokes and exploring the sounds.

The Indians seemed fascinated with the manufactured goods brought by the English – swords, guns, metal plates, brass kettles, glass beads, linen and woolen cloth. They gladly exchanged shells, beads, copper, baskets, dressed hides, and fish for what the English would give. It was a profitable and peaceful time for both peoples. After six weeks, in August 1584, the two ships sailed back to England, taking two Indian emissaries with them: Wanchese of Roanoke and Manteo of Croatoan. Sir Walter Raleigh considered this reconnaissance a success and determined to send a much larger colony to Roanoke Island the following year.

For Wingina, the wiroans, or "king" of the Roanokes, contact with the English was no less hopeful. He had risen to govern several towns, including Roanoke on Roanoke Island, Dasemunkepeuc on the mainland directly west across the sound from Roanoke Island, which served as his capital, and possibly the town of Croatoan to the south on what is today Hatteras Island. There may have been other towns as well. The scope of Wingina's chiefdom was not unusual; Thomas Hariot, one of the English scientists on the 1585 expedition, observed that "in some places of the countrey one onely towne belongeth to the government of a

Wiróans or chiefe Lorde; in others some two or three, in some sixe, eight, & more."

Certainly Wingina believed that a strong relationship with his new English allies would increase his power in the region. Wingina and his towns maintained friendly relations with two other major chiefdoms in the area, the Weapemeocs and the Choanoacs, Algonquian peoples with a similar culture, language, and economy to Wingina's own. The Weapemeocs, governed by their wiroans, *Okisko, lived on the north bank of the Albemarle Sound. Up the Chowan River lay the Choanoac chiefdom, the area's largest, governed by Menatonon, an old man crippled in body. Menatonon governed eighteen towns spread along the Chowan, the largest being Choanoke, which served as his capital.*

Wingina's Algonquians were also part of a vibrant regional trade network. They exchanged seashells, pearls, and peake — tiny beads drilled out of seashells — with inland peoples for copper. The name Roanoke itself seemed to mean people who made these tiny shell beads the English later called wampum. But copper was the most highly desired commodity. Wassador, *Wingina, called it, and he coveted it more than anything, as did the Weapemeocs, the Choanoacs, and just about every other people in the area.*

Unfortunately for Wingina, copper only came from the west, and the Mangoak Indians had a stranglehold on any supply that might reach Wingina and his towns. Even worse, Mangoak territory blocked Wingina, the Weapemeocs, and the Choanoacs from reaching the Indian trading town of Occaneechi, which sat on an island far up the Roanoke River, at its confluence with the Dan and Staunton rivers (in present-day southern Virginia). Occaneechi town lay across the Great Indian Trading Path and so was a major Indian exchange entrepot in the region where copper, shells, and other valuable commodities might be found. But the Mangoak middlemen, who reportedly had houses draped in copper, jealously guarded eastern access to Occaneechi and the copper-producing towns further west.

Wingina surely hoped the English would help him break the Mangoak trade monopoly and make him the most powerful wiroans *in the area. The goods the English brought conveyed powerful status, unlike anything the Algonquians possessed. The Roanokes quickly saw the potential of English metal weapons — swords, knives, and firearms — and asked the English for some, a request Amadas and Barlowe declined. But they were willing to offer other things. A tin plate,* something of low value to the English sailors, had high value to the Algonquian leaders, who saw it in the same light as a copper gorget indicating high status and prestige. Glass beads rivaled shell beads. Mirrors and broken glass made better hide scrapers and arrow points than native stone. Brass kettles held up better and longer than clay pots. Woolen and linen cloth provided a whole new type of clothing, warmer in winter and cooler in summer. Even English baby dolls delighted Roanoke children, who had made theirs from corn shucks. The Indians also saw something spiritual in these items, a sort of mystical power. So once Barlowe and Amadas sailed back to England in September 1584, Wingina and his people anxiously awaited their return, expecting even more merchandise from their new friends.

Wingina probably hoped for another small English trading expedition like that of Barlowe and Amadas: a few ships, a few sailors who would stay a few weeks, exchange goods, and then sail away, leaving Wingina and his people all the more powerful and wealthy. What he got was much worse.

Dr. Haywood Pearce Jr. championed the authenticity of the Dare Stones.
Emory University Archives.

CHAPTER 3

Pearce on a Mission

By early 1938, Prof. Haywood J. Pearce Jr. had become the Dare Stone's strongest champion. Almost from the first moment he held it in the physics lab, the wavy-haired history professor believed the Stone was the last word on the fate of Raleigh's Lost Colony. It just had to be authentic.

Pearce was no Georgia rube, but an award-winning history professor teaching at one of the South's most prestigious universities. Forty-four years old in 1937, Pearce had a solid career in the field of American history. He had been one of the first graduates of Riverside Military Academy, the Gainesville, Georgia prepatory school co-founded by his father. He earned the master of arts in history from Emory in 1915 while also teaching there as an assistant professor. When the United States entered World War I, he'd served as a lieutenant in the army but remained stateside. In October 1917, Pearce married Anna Sue Bonnell, whose father was one of Emory's first science professors when it was still located in Oxford, Georgia. After the war, Pearce taught history and Latin at Brenau College, another private institution owned by his father, who appointed him vice president. Then in 1932, Emory hired him as a full-time history professor. If the academic community held any reservations about the scholarly rigor of a small private institution like Brenau, it surely had no such compunction about Emory. In joining its elite faculty, Pearce found his position in academia fully validated.

Now, with the Dare Stone as his guide, Pearce was ready to tackle the fate of the Lost Colony. He just needed the evidence to back up the Stone. Finding that second stone, the one inscribed with the names of the dead colonists, buried "neere foure myles easte this river uppon smal hil," would do nicely. The Second Stone, he hoped, would lead him to a mass grave and the solution to the mystery of the Lost Colony. Though he and his Emory colleagues had not found anything when Hammond took them to North Carolina back in early November, that just meant he'd have to search harder.

By the end of fall semester 1937, Pearce was ready to search for the Second Stone. He'd drawn up maps and had been in contact with landowners along the Chowan River. He had permits prepared, which he hoped landowners would sign, giving Emory University permission to dig on their property. According to the document, the Emory team would not injure crops or buildings and would not remove any valuable minerals, but wanted permission to "photograph, measure, survey . . . search for, collect and preserve permanently in its museum any fragment, relics, and remains of historical, ethnological or archaeological interest." The permit also authorized Emory to "accept as gifts, purchase or otherwise acquire such fragments, relics or remains which may be or may have been discovered on my lands by others."

Christopher Crittenden soon learned of Pearce's plans to excavate North Carolina sites. Hoping to steer him off, Crittenden warned that the Emory historian could dig within the state only if his staff were qualified archaeologists. He even mailed Pearce some archaeological excavation permit forms from the National Park Service. Though promising cooperation, Pearce again snubbed Crittenden and the North Carolina Historical Commission when he made several more trips back to North Carolina during the winter of 1938.

Up near where Hammond had found the Stone, Pearce met with Capt. J. P. Wiggins, a former mayor of nearby Edenton. Wiggins told Pearce about seeing a large moss-covered stone in the woods when he was a boy and invited him to come look. The former mayor and the professor wandered into the swamps and after a couple days of searching located the large rock. It bore no inscription. Nevertheless, Pearce returned during the summer and dug beneath the rock in hopes of finding human remains. But Pearce's North Carolina forays that year yielded nothing but a handful of ballast stones, a few fragments of stones used as land boundary markers, and some river pebbles. Undaunted, he planned broader searches for 1939.

Up in Raleigh, his overtures continually rebuffed, Crittenden was irked. He complained that Pearce had "telegraphed me twice, promising full co-operation with the North Carolina Historical Commission, but he has never let me know just how he proposes to co-operate or what his plans are." Whether it was Pearce's willingness to dismiss him or just his natural protectiveness toward his home state, Crittenden was developing bad feelings about the Dare Stone as well as a not-so-subtle antagonism toward its advocate. The Director of the North Carolina Historical Commission now turned to friends in the history profession. He hoped to find information to discredit Pearce, something he could use to stop the inquisitive professor. But word came back that Pearce's reputation was above question. Crittenden could only wonder whether the good professor had not "become the victim of a hoax."

Crittenden put out inquiries. Some residents of coastal Carolina recalled a hoax having to do with a brick above the door at the old St. Thomas Church at Bath, North Carolina, which was inscribed with the date 1734. Others remembered some Indian pottery found on Roanoke

St. Thomas Church at Bath is one of the oldest colonial buildings in N.C.

Island that turned out to be a cheap forgery made of sand. Other rumors drifted in at second- and third-hand. Renowned North Carolina newspaperman Ben Dixon MacNeill, then the state publicist for Paul Green's *The Lost Colony*, told a story that eventually made its way to Crittenden and up to Paul Green in New York.

MacNeill heard that a couple of years earlier someone had approached State Senator Bradford Fearing, a Roanoke Island businessman, with a promotional scheme. At that time, Fearing was also

Sen. D. Bradford Fearing.

executive director of the Roanoke Island Historical Association and in the process of preparing for the Lost Colony's 350th anniversary in 1937. The unidentified promoter had offered to "plant an old metal chest and a stone on which there was a lengthy inscription. It was the man's idea to plant these two articles and then later have them accidentally discovered with subsequent startling publicity." MacNeill said he'd heard that Fearing would have none of it. Now he wondered if there was a connection with Hammond's find.

Adding more fuel to the controversy, MacNeill also offered that there was an "unethical writer living in Edenton, who writes chiefly for Virginia papers," and that this same writer had told a reporter for the *Christian Science Monitor* that the whole "Lost Colony episode was soon to be exploded." He never identified the writer.

Crittenden couldn't decide whether the Dare Stone was real or fake. Regardlesss, he didn't like the way the story seemed to be getting out of his hands, or that this possibly important piece of North Carolina history remained in another state. Crittenden began to take heat from North Carolina citizens, angry that the director of the Historical Commission had let such a valuable state artifact slip through his fingers. Many felt that North Carolina universities were more than capable of doing the research necessary on the Stone. Crittenden tried to deflect the blame. He could not have prevented the Dare Stone from going to Brenau as no one knew it had existed and no one knew that Hammond had found it. Had it not been for Hammond's curiosity while in Atlanta, the Dare Stone could have just as easily have wound up in California. No, Crittenden did not like it. But he, and all North Carolinians, would just have to wait for more information.

Like Crittenden, Pearce and his Emory colleagues were not pleased with all the publicity leaking out about the Dare Stone. They had hoped to be left undisturbed and given plenty of time to make a thorough, unbiased examination. But the rumor that Virginia Dare's grave had been found was picking up steam. People were clamoring for more information, and all the publicity finally forced Emory to make an official statement. On January 30, 1938, Emory University issued a press release that told the story of the Dare Stone, omitting Hammond's name, at his request. The release provided details about the Stone, told how it was found, quoted the Stone's inscription, and gave a brief description of the Lost Colony tale.

Newspapers around the country picked up the story that Raleigh's Lost Colony had been found. "'Lost Colony' Stone at Emory," the *Atlanta Constitution* crowed. "Inscription May Solve Virginia Dare Mystery," the *Raleigh News & Observer* said calmly. Pearce was swamped with interview requests and had to decline a chance to appear in New York on the "We, the People" radio program. At the same time, the professors tried to quell the increasing public interest in the Stone. They especially wanted to play down the belief that they had found Virginia Dare's tombstone. They urged patience. "We intend to publish complete data on the investigation in historical publications before any popular interpretation is made," Pearce said.

For the next several months, the Emory team continued their investigation amid the clamor. Finally, on April 19, 1938, five months after Hammond showed up, Professors James Lester and J. Harris Purks announced the team's findings at the Emory University Faculty Club. Pearce was supposed to be there to give his take, but he had been called out of town. The responsibility for the report was left with the two physical scientists.

They described the stone as a moderately-sized flat piece of dark vein quartzite, almost fourteen inches long, about ten inches wide, and weighing twenty-one pounds. It appeared to be ballast stone from England; piles of similar ballast stones were found not far away from where Hammond discovered the Dare Stone. There were seventeen lines of apparently Elizabethan English that had been carved, it appeared, by a metal chisel. While Lester and Purks could describe the Stone and give its weight and height, could decipher the inscriptions and assert they were suited to Elizabethan times, could tell of their attempts to replicate the words, but in the end they could not say whether or not the Dare Stone was authentic.

A month later, in May 1938, the prestigious *Journal of Southern History* published the Emory team's findings in an article written by Pearce, titled "New Light on the Roanoke Colony: A Preliminary Examination of a Stone Found in Chowan County, North Carolina." Echoing Lester, Pearce used the article to provide his historical analysis of the Stone. And as he saw it, the Stone was the real McCoy. He explained how the Stone was found again leaving out the finder's name at Hammond's request, and gave the deciphered inscription and a short history of the Lost Colony.

In point after point, Pearce arrayed his historical evidence to show how the Dare Stone *could* actually be a last message from Eleanor Dare and the Lost Colonists. He cited writings by Captain John Smith, William Strachey of the Virginia Company, and others associated with the Jamestown colony, founded twenty years after the Lost Colony disappeared. Jamestown officials had sent out search parties for the Lost Colonists. They heard from Indians that there had indeed been an Indian attack and many colonists had been killed on the Chowan River—but there had also been English survivors.

Then Pearce analyzed the description in its historical context. Interpreting the events of Governor John White's 1590 search mission, Pearce pointed out that White had been seen by Indians when he returned to Roanoke Island and this corresponded with "salvage with message of shipp unto us." Pearce surmised it was White's discovery of his ransacked storage chests on Roanoke that caused the Indians to flee: fearing severe English reprisals—"affrite of revenge"—they "rann al awaye." When White was forced to abandon the search after only one day, Pearce concluded, Eleanor could not imagine that her father would desert her and so wrote of the ship "Wee bleeve yt nott yov." Though Pearce's evidence could not authenticate the Stone, the story it told certainly seemed credible.

That was enough for most Americans. If the Dare Stone could not be declared a definite fake, then it must be real. For many, the mystery of the Lost Colony had been solved. Virginia Dare and most of the colonists had been killed by Indians on the Chowan River. That was that, the story told and done. Or at least some of it, for the Stone tantalizingly said Eleanor and six other colonists had survived. For Pearce, the key to the entire riddle was the Second Stone with the list of those killed in the raid. But where was it?

*   *   *

The arrival of summer brought warm ocean currents closer, again, to the green islands. Fish were near and pentiful; berries began to ripen; hunting was easy in the long days. Men hunted and fished while women tended fields of corn. Cozy longhouses covered in straw mats kept large families warm in winter, but now with summer here, the mats could be taken down to allow the fresh ocean breezes to cool the homes and people. Wingina's people on Roanoke flourished, his power assured by the wisdom of his leadership.

But that summer also brought the English back to their shores. In July of the year the English knew as A.D. 1585, Raleigh's man, Colonel Ralph Lane, arrived on Roanoke. With him returned Manteo and Wanchese, the two Algonquian ambassadors who had gone to England with Amadas and Barlowe the previous year. But Lane had been charged with a different mission than had Amdas and Barlowe. He

A cutaway of an Iroquois longhouse typical of the kind that were used by eastern woodland tribes in the United States, including those in the South.

was not simply to trade goods and exchange welcomes, but to establish a privateering base on the island. A contingent of over a hundred veteran soldiers was to build a fort, defend England's claim, and locate anything valuable. English ships would use their outpost as a base to strike at Spanish possessions in the Caribbean. Wingina's Algonquians, whether they knew it or not, were now subjects of Queen Elizabeth and expected to give all obedience and assistance to Lane, the Queen's governor in Virginia.

A tough, argumentative man, Colonel Lane quickly alienated the Algonquian Indians of the region. Lane and his veterans of the Irish wars took a hard line with the Roanoke Indians, just as they had with the Irish. They would brook no insult or opposition from people they considered savages. For almost a year Lane and his men swaggered up and down the land, demanding food, attacking villages, taking hostages, and leaving disease, death, and destruction in their wake.

Wingina finally had his fill of Lane's insults. He became firmly anti-English and even changed his name to Pemisapan as an expression of his change of heart. The wiroans now withdrew his people from Roanoke Island in hopes the English would starve or leave. Lane took their abandonment as an act of war. On June 1, 1586, Lane's men made a surprise attack, shot down Pemisapan, beheaded him, and stuck his head on a pike as a warning to all who would not accept English rule. For the Roanokes, it was a declaration of war.

John White, the artist and scientist among the group, had witnessed Lane's attack. It had been a mistake of magnificent proportions. If the Roanokes and their allies were angry before, the murder of Pemisapan made them absolutely hostile to the English invaders. They withdrew even further, to the point that the headstrong Lane realized that the Roanoke colony had become untenable.

Lane's Englishmen were saved by the lucky arrival of Sir Francis Drake and his fleet. Drake had been terrorizing Spain's Caribbean colonies and had just come from raiding St. Augustine, Florida. With little food, the long-awaited supply ship nowhere to be seen, and no help available from the Indians, Lane and his men abandoned Roanoke and sailed home with Drake. Some saw Lane's departure as a humbling retreat. The English had been "chased from thence by a mighty army," wrote Richard Hakluyt, one of England's chief proponents for peaceful colonization, "for the hand of God came upon them for the cruelty and outrages committed by some of them against the native inhabitants of the country."

Lane had been gone only a few days when the supply ship from the mother country weighed anchor off Roanoke. Finding Lane and his men absent, the commander put fifteen of his own men ashore to maintain an English presence on Roanoke until White's new colony could return next year.

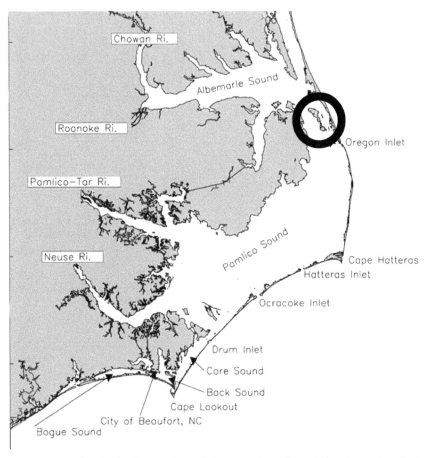

A map showing both Albemarle and Pamlico Sounds and the rivers that feed into it. Roanoke Island is circled. Image courtesy of NOAA.

CHAPTER 4

Searching for the Second Stone

The Dare Stone seemed to write an ending to the story of the Lost Colony. If its inscription was taken as true, as the searches made by John White in 1590 and those made by Captain John Smith and other Jamestown folk in the early 1600s also indicated, it appeared that some of the colonists left behind on Roanoke Island in 1587, including Eleanor, Ananias, and Virginia Dare, had gone west, up the Albemarle Sound about fifty miles, to the area where the Chowan River flows to meet the sound.

There they settled among the friendly Choanoac Indians. Over the next four years, according to Hammond's Dare Stone, about half of them died of sickness. Then in 1591, the remaining twenty-four colonists were suddenly attacked by unidentified Indians who became frightened when a ship appeared off the coast. Fearing English reprisals for some unnamed insult, they turned on the remaining colonists. All were killed except for seven who somehow escaped the slaughter. It all sounded so believable.

Of course the Stone gave no indication of what the colonists had been doing during those four years. Or how and why those seven escaped and what became of them. As for the seventeen dead, among them Virginia Dare and her father, Ananias, they were buried on a nearby hill a few miles from a river, likewise unspecified. Eleanor supposedly had their names inscribed on a rock similar to the Dare Stone. But where was it?

For Pearce, finding that Second Stone, the one with the colonist's names, was the key. Once found, it would lead him to the graves of the Lost Colonists. Then with the Stones and the skeletons as evidence, Pearce would be the historian to write the full conclusion to the Lost Colony story. The great mystery would be fully solved, and fame and fortune would rain down on him.

By February 1938, now that the inscription had been deciphered and announced to the public, Hammond had no more real need for the Stone. He and his wife had returned to California, leaving his Dare Stone in the hands of the Emory team. Their correspondence from now on would be by mail to his general-delivery address. If anything, the Emory professors were more worried that Hammond would sell his story or the Stone itself to someone else, than Hammond was that the university might cheat him out of the Stone.

Possessing such an artifact meant nothing to Hammond, so he offered to sell it outright to Emory University. Rumor had it that the going price was one thousand dollars. That was a hefty sum in those Depression days but not an outrageous price for a university like Emory to pay for such an amazing piece of American history. That Hammond was willing to sell seemed like good business to some observers. Others deemed it proof that he was perpetrating a hoax.

Emory officials debated the Stone's authenticity and considered whether the university should purchase it or not. Dr. Thomas English, who had been on hand when Hammond first came in with the Stone, thought that while it could be a forgery, "yet there is no circumstance in connection with it that definitely speaks of fraud. Our research, so far as it has gone, seems on the other hand more and more to suggest its genuiness." English had consulted with esteemed historian and rare-books bibliographer Dr. Randolph Adams of the University of Michigan, who concluded that the Stone could easily be authentic. Professor Morris Tilley of Michigan's Department of English, an expert in the English Renaissance, weighed in: "If this is a forgery, it is done by someone who knew a good deal about Elizabethan English."

Others felt it was "probably a fraud." Emory alumnus R. C. Mizell of Atlanta, a leading administrator in the University of Georgia system, unequivocally advised Emory to have nothing to do with the Stone: "By giving publicity Emory is allowing itself to be used to further a fraud." He further advised that until the Stone's authenticity could be established "beyond a reasonable doubt," Emory should attach no value to the Stone. "Because the possibility that the inscription may be a rather skillfully prepared hoax," Mizell wrote, "Emory does not wish to be instrumental in giving publicity to it." Instead, he suggested that Emory donate the artifact to "any reputable Historical Society." In the end, words of caution prevailed, and Emory declined to purchase the Dare Stone.

His proposal rejected by Emory, Hammond now considered putting the Stone on exhibit and charging admission. He felt it would draw well in North Carolina and Virginia. But Professor Purks of Emory warned against such a plan, lest Crittenden and the North Carolina Historical Commission raise ownership issues in the Tarheel State. Hammond might well find himself without anything.

Apparently, as per their contract, Hammond turned next to the group of four Emory professors. Whether they came down with a case of cold feet, or found the price tag too high, or were persuaded against the deal by peer opinion, they declined to buy as well. Speaking for the professor consortium, Purks now released Hammond to find a buyer wherever he could.

Hammond did not have to look far. Stepping forward solo after the consortium declined its option, and with the promise of a rock-solid funding source, Professor Haywood Pearce Jr. jumped at the chance to acquire the Stone. And his backers were none other than his own father, Dr. Haywood Pearce Sr., and Brenau College, the institution of which the senior Pearce was sole proprietor and president.

Pearce's enthusiasm for the Stone and its tantalizing story was infectious. In the course of his researches and expeditions he had piqued the interest of his father and mother as well. The entire family had come to trust wholeheartedly the Stone's account of Raleigh's Lost Colony. Romancing the stone was about to become a family business.

In the late years of the nineteenth century, when it was still not uncommon for an educator to both lead a school or college and hold a financial interest in it, Dr. Haywood Pearce Sr. purchased half ownership in the Georgia Baptist Female Seminary in Gainesville, Georgia. Gainesville, the seat of Hall County located about fifty miles north of Atlanta, was famous as the gravesite of one of the Confederacy's greatest heroes, Gen. James Longstreet. In the later twentieth century, it would become one of the South's greatest poultry producers and would help lead Southern farmers away from their dependency on cotton. It was always a forward-looking city, serving as a transportation hub in the

Brenau College in Georgia, from a postcard of the 1930s.

foothills region as far back as North Georgia's 1828 gold rush days. It gained popularity as a mountain resort community in the 1840s. In 1878, as Atlanta and northern Georgia recovered from the ravages of war and Reconstruction, former Tift College president W. C. Wilkes established the Georgia Baptist Female Seminary for Young Ladies, though it had no formal affiliation with the denomination.

Pearce Sr. evidently saw great potential for the seminary. After seven years of co-administering the institution with A. W. VanHoose, in 1900 Pearce bought it outright and reinvented it as Brenau College. The name was a blend of the German word *brennen*, which means "to burn," and the Latin *aurum*, "gold." Pearce Sr. envisioned his college as the crucible where young women would be transformed into "refined gold," their characters shaped and intellects forged by a serious but genteel single-sex education.

Few details about the Pearces' finances are readily available. The thousand-dollar price tag apparently posed no barrier though Brenau officials later claimed the Pearces only paid Hammond half that amount.

With the newly acquired artifact now enshrined at Gainesville, the small women's college became Dare Stone headquarters. Young Pearce began spending more time there, teaching classes at Brenau on weekends. Morever, funding from the college coffers enabled further searches in North Carolina. As the Pearces saw it, once they found the Second Stone, Brenau would mount a permanent exhibition of the pair. President Pearce wrote to Kenneth Beebe of the American Schools Association for advice on how to exhibit the Stone. More important, he wanted to know if charging admission to see the artifact would be acceptable. Once the Second Stone came into their possession, then these two vital pieces of American history would put Brenau on the map. On a personal level, it would make the career of Pearce Jr. Once the Second Stone and the colonists' remains were found, Pearce would write up his findings. He'd publish an article or two in the major historical journals, cultivate an article about the Stones in a high-circulation popular magazine, and finally put the Lost Colony to rest. If all went well, he would ride the publicity wave to fame and fortune as the historian who solved the three-hundred-fifty-year-old mystery. Solving the puzzle would skyrocket him into the upper circles of academia in his field, mentioned in the same breath as historians H. H. Bancroft, Charles Beard, and Samuel Eliot Morison. The Dare Stone would pave the way for Pearce to secure his reputation.

Everything certainly seemed to be going his way. Interest in the Dare Stone was mounting, with newspapers across the country clamoring for more information. To satisfy everyone's curiosity, in March 1939, Brenau College published a Brenau *Bulletin* titled "The Dare Stone and the Lost Colony of Roanoke." A near-reprint of Pearce's 1938 *Journal of Southern History* article, it retold the story of how the Stone was found, again omitting Hammond's name. It provided the transcription of the deciphered inscription and related Pearce's theory that it had been carved by a stonecutter's tool. It also gave a short history of the Lost Colony, and, like the earlier essay, concluded that the inscribed words seemed to be authentic Elizabethan English whose possible mistakes could easily be attributed to ignorance on the part of Eleanor or the stonecutter.

While the the authorities of Brenau College took pains in the issue to "make no claims as to the authenticity of the stone," they did believe that "the stone is at least credible, that no evidence has yet come to light, during the year in which it has been under examination, which would throw doubt upon its genuineness. They realize, however, that the authenticity of the stone can only be fully established by the discovery of the corroborative evidence in the Chowan river area or elsewhere. They are seeking such evidence." Pearce did not address questions he had posed in his earlier article: Why had the colonists carved "Croatoan" on the palisades at the Roanoke fort if they were going to the Chowan? Why did Eleanor Dare not tell exactly where she was when she dictated the words on the Dare Stone? Who were the six other survivors?

The 1939 *Bulletin* sparked more public interest in the Stone and the Lost Colony. Brenau received numerous requests for copies. The Southern Railway System wanted some. So did a lot of folk in North Carolina: Warren H. Booker of the North Carolina Board of Health; H. H. McLean of the Washington County Schools; the assistant librarian for the Union County Schools; Fred Winslow, an attorney in Rocky Mount, among others, called for copies.

Despite the growing interest in this Dare Stone, the Pearces knew that the case rested on finding the Second Stone, the one with the names of the seventeen colonists killed in the Indian raid. Pearce admitted that this Stone could be anywhere, but they hoped it was still on the Chowan. "With the second stone in hand," the Pearces wrote, "competent scientists may be enlisted who can proceed with confidence toward the search for the remains of the first Americans, Raleigh's Lost Colony of Roanoke."

Soon Pearce, along with his father and mother, undertook a series of trips to the Edenton, North Carolina area. Now the Pearces deigned to meet with Crittenden of the North Carolina Historical Commission and told him of their plans to solve the Lost Colony mystery. They also contacted landowners in areas that looked promising to them. The Pearces met with Edenton officials and spoke before the Chamber of Commerce, the Rotary Club, and the Lions Club. They told the story of the Dare Stone, showed pictures, and informed their audiences that they were looking for a stone with writing on it. Further, they announced plans to make replicas of the Stone, presumably to spread the word with less risk to the original artifact—and to pay five hundred dollars cash to anyone who could produce the Second Stone.

Such a sum would buy a car in 1939. In southern states still reeling from a decade-long depression, it was an attractive incentive. The Pearces had made the $500 offer in the 1939 *Bulletin*, and now they made it again in North Carolina. Word of the reward ran in the Edenton paper. "I believe our best chance to find it and also to find the burial place of the lost colonists is to give the matter as wide publicity as possible," Pearce Sr. wrote. "I would expect to find the skeletons of the lost colonists in fairly good state of preservation, and I personally have little doubt that they are in Chowan county."

* * *

As soon as the boat ground ashore on Roanoke, John White and his colonists made for the fort at the north end of the island, hoping to reconnect with their fifteen countrymen. A year had passed since Lane's departure—and in this strange land of Virginia, a great deal could happen. White and his colonists intended only a brief stop to pick up the fifteen. They were, in reality, bound for Chesapeake Bay, further north.

Lane's experiences had convinced everyone that Roanoke was useless as a colony. The inlet was too shallow for larger ships. More important, Lane had poisoned the relations with the Indians. Roanoke was too dangerous, too ill-suited for English habitation, so Sir Walter Raleigh, the colony's sponsor, now made a difficult decision. Roanoke would be abandoned in favor of the Chesapeake Bay. The Indians there were friendlier, or at least not yet angry with the English. So the new group would pick up the fifteen soldiers left on Roanoke Island and all head north to the Chesapeake. But the men were nowhere to be found.

White could see that the fort had been abandoned for some

John White's unsettling discovery of a skeleton at the deserted Roanoke settlement.

while. The log palisade had fallen down, and the houses were overgrown with vines and weeds. Deer grazed on melons growing wild in a forgotten garden. Then someone spotted it. The broken skeleton of an English soldier lay unburied out in the middle of Lane's fort. Later they would learn what had happened to the dead man. Barely had the supply ship sent the fifteen men ashore than Wanchese, who seemed to have taken up the mantle of Roanoke leadership from the murdered Pemisapan, ordered his Roanoke warriors to attack. The skeleton man was clubbed down first; the remaining Englishmen were chased down to their little boat. One more Englishman was killed at the water's edge, but the rest managed to sail away. They were never seen again.

The skeleton, its skull smashed in by Indian war clubs, sent a chill through Eleanor and the colonists on this steamy summer day. It was proof positive of just how bad this island was. Like nervous cattle, the colonists moved back toward the beach, instinctively retreating toward the safety of the ships. But then the unthinkable happened. Captain Fernandez refused to the let colonists back aboard. The ruthless privateer would allow only the governor or one or two of his representatives to return. As for the rest, they should forget the Chesapeake—Roanoke Island was to be their home. It was late in the sailing season, Fernandez maintained, and rich Spanish prizes lay for the taking in the Caribbean. Hauling colonists wasn't profitable, and this was as far as he would go. His boats would stay for a month unloading baggage and supplies, but come late August, the ships would sail south. The colonists would remain here, to fend for themselves in an unfamiliar world.

CHAPTER 5

No Stone Unturned

The Pearces' reward certainly made folks take notice. Residents of northeastern North Carolina eagerly began to step forward with leads. Mrs. J. Lester Forehand wrote President Pearce and invited him to come visit her place when he came to Edenton. A large deposit of marl had been found on their farm on the Chowan River, she informed him, and it had been used by the Choanoac Indians who had once lived there. She'd found all sorts of Indian relics and skeletons on the property. Maybe his stone was there.

In March 1939 came news from Tyner, North Carolina, about ten miles north of Edenton and four miles east of the Chowan River, of a stone bearing an inscription. T. E. Chappell reported he'd found a stone that had a visible "W" on it and some other words that he couldn't make out. Chappell's rock was reportedly found on top of a small hill, in an indentation in the ground, seemingly where the Dare Stone had said the Second Stone would be. Even more intriguing, the spot was surrounded by trees that seem much larger than those nearby, a result, Chappell surmised, of fertilizing by the decomposing bones of long-buried colonists.

As a rural letter carrier, Chappell had often passed the large stone, which weighed about sixty pounds. A few years earlier, when he had done some brickwork around his house, Chappell brought the stone to his property for use as a platform to break bricks. It was only after hearing of Pearce's talk that he recalled there were markings on the stone. Chappell immediately sent word to Gainesville and Pearce said he wanted to see it.

Oddly, as the *Elizabeth City Daily Advance* reported on March 29, 1939, the Pearces declined to come investigate the stone, for reasons only vaguely intimated: "It is believed they are somewhat skeptical concerning the authenticity of this recent find."

Nevertheless, when C. C. Crittenden of the North Carolina Historical Commission heard of Chappell's find, he jumped at the opportunity. He promptly wrote to one of Chappell's acquaintances, asking him to tell Chappell that the Historical Commission "would be glad to co-operate in every way possible in this manner." Further, Crittenden tried to dissuade Chappell from having anything to do with Pearce. "It would seem a shame for a historical relic as important as this one may be to go out of the State, particularly to Brenau College, where they have no graduate school and only very limited facilities for research," Crittenden complained. He felt Chappell's stone would be much better off at the University of North Carolina Chapel Hill or at Duke University in Durham. "Either of these institutions," he wrote, was "far better equipped to determine the authenticity of this stone than is any institution in the State of Georgia."

However tantalizing these possibilities might have been, they were quickly forgotten when a sixty-five-year old surveyor and his son from Columbia, North Carolina stepped forward with their curious find. Tom Shallington was a native and lifelong resident of Tyrrell County, one of North Carolina's least populous counties, which lay just west of Roanoke Island on the south bank of Albemarle Sound. A gregarious fellow, Shallington was a well-known local with a reputation for storytelling. In response to Pearce's offer of $500 cash for rocks with writing on them, the old man reported that the previous November he and his son Tom Jr. had pulled three large stones from an old, flooded cemetery on the east side of Alligator Creek, directly across from Fort Landing—about fifteen miles west of Roanoke and forty miles or so east of the Chowan River, where the Dare Stone was found. And at least one of the stones had words inscribed on it.

Hauling the stones from three-foot-deep water, Shallington had taken the three stones back to his home in Columbia. Only the largest, a two-foot long stone weighing a hundred pounds, had legible words on it. Unlike the Dare Stone's chiseled words, those on Shallington's stone had been pecked into the rock and were hard to see, much less read. But when Shallington applied a little chalk to connect the dots, he was amazed to make out the inscription

VIRGINIA DARE

B. AUG 1587

D. 1597

Here was another Virginia Dare tombstone! Newspapers in the area played it up big. They described the Tyrell County surveyor as a genial, honest man, well-known and well-liked by all. Many thought it was quite plausible for the Lost Colonists to have found themselves on the banks of Alligator Creek, the first high ground west of Roanoke. The Lost Colonists might well have sought refuge there from angry Indians. Connecting this clue with Pearce's Dare Stone, they held that from Alligator Creek the colonists could have easily sailed up the Albemarle to meet their fate on the Chowan River.

But the newspapers confused matters with a sloppy mistake. The *Elizabeth City Daily Advance,* which published the first major story on Shallington's find in late March 1939, misreported Dare's birthdate as "August 17, 1587," in obvious contradiction to the photograph it ran alongside. The mistranscription—as well as the error that any North Carolinian who knew Virginia Dare's August 18 birthday could have spotted—was picked up in paper after paper. More troubling was that none of the stories questioned the factual discrepancy between the two stones. While the original Dare Stone said Virginia Dare had been killed in 1591 near the Chowan River, at about age four, Shallington's stone recorded a ten-year-old Virginia dying in 1597.

This time North Carolina officials were ready. Crittenden and other North Carolinians urged Shallington to let the Historical Commission analyze his stone and its inscription. But Shallington hesitated to let the artifact out of his hands. "I know that the old man thinks there is a big piece of money in 'that thar rock,'" wrote W. O. Saunders, the controversial former newspaperman from Elizabeth City and the moving force behind the creation of Paul Green's *Lost Colony* pageant, who also was an acquaintance of Shallington.

Still, officials in North Carolina put pressure on Shallington. If he wouldn't allow the stones to be investigated, then they wanted him and his son to provide a sworn, notarized statement of the time, place, and circumstances of their discovery and removal of the stones. They also wanted Shallington to promise not to disturb the location further, but let authorized researchers take a look first. Tom and his son complied, providing the requested affidavits.

Eventually Crittenden himself traveled from Raleigh over to Columbia and got a look at Shallington and his inscribed stone. He again urged the old man to let the stone be taken to Raleigh for examination. Again the old man balked. Crittenden warned him that if the stone stayed in Columbia, it would never be authenticated. Finally, with a receipt from Crittenden and a promise they would be returned to him, Shallington allowed two stones to be hauled to Raleigh.

Prof. William P. Cumming.

There the Shallington Stones were immediately handed over to Harry T. Davis of the North Carolina State Museum for a quick look. Davis reported back that the stones were quartzite and had been exposed to weather for a long time. In examining the "shallow fracture marks" on the face of the stone, however, he determined they "might well have been made by [the] impact of a hammer blow transmitted to this hard rock by means of a chisel." While such a technique was certainly within the means of a member of Lost Colony, Davis believed the inscription to be recent. "These last markings have been made within the last few years. This opinion is based largely on the relatively unweathered condition of these marks and their position relative to older markings referred to as being natural."

With Davis's report in hand, the next day, May 17, 1939, Crittenden convened a panel in Chapel Hill to "consider the authenticity of the two old stones . . . taken from the bed of the Alligator River by Mr. Thomas B. Shallington of Columbia, N.C. . . . one of them purport[ing] to be the tombstone of Virginia Dare." The illustrious panel represented a cross-section of North Carolina humanities and sciences. In addition to Crittenden there were Prof. F. W. Clonts of the Social Science Department at Wake Forest College; Prof. John D. Barnhardt of the Social Sciences Department at North Carolina State College; Dr. A. R. Newsome; Dr. Wallace E. Caldwell, Dr. Hugh Talmadge Lefler, and Dr. Cecil Johnson, all of the Department of History at the University of North Carolina; Dr. W. P. Cumming of the Department of English at Davidson College; Dr. J. B. Bullitt, a lay archaeologist at the School of Medicine at the University of North Carolina; Joffre Coe, who would go on to become one of North Carolina's most prominent archaeologists; Dr. G. A. Harrer of the Department of Classics, Dr. R. B. Sharper of Department of English, and Dr. Guy B. Johnson of the Department of Sociology, all from the University of North Carolina; Dr. W. A. Mabry of the Department of History at Duke University.

The panel noted that the letters inscribed on the stone were modern Roman capitals and the numbers Arabic in the modern form, all made by pecking at the stone It took little deliberation, evidently, for the panel to report, "It seems to us evident that the inscription has been made very recently." The inscription showed no wear and under a microscope one could see "many fine, sharp grains projecting from the pecked surface." Some of the grains could even be rubbed off with a finger. Their findings were damning and direct: "Every mark seems as fresh as if made yesterday."

The next day, Dr. Jasper L. Stuckey, a geology professor at North Carolina State College, who had not been on the panel, gave a report of his separate investigation. Like Davis, Stuckey identified the stone as quartzite, noting also that this particular stone, native to the British Isles most likely made it to American shores as ballast stone left behind when sailing ships replaced ballast with homeward-bound cargo. So while the Lost Colonists might well have used ballast stone to carve messages, Stuckey did not believe that enough such stone "had accumulated to any great extent on the North Carolina coast by 1597, and especially in the locality where these so-called Virginia Dare Stones are reported to have been found." Echoing the panel's opinion, Stuckey found the condition of the inscription doubtful: "Somebody has gone over the rock with a sharp tool and outlined anew the letters as there are numerous freshly chipped points along the lines of the letters." Stuckey, too, did not find it plausible that the inscription was "put on the stone in 1597."

With all the investigative reports in hand, at the end of the month Crittenden announced the North Carolina Historical Commission's verdict on the Shallington stones. They were ballast stones that bore natural cracks and wear. However, there was no doubt that the inscription had only recently been pecked into the rock. The inscription itself showed no weathered discoloration, and loose grains of stone, which should have would have washed away long ago, were still present in the pecked letters. "I believe we can say, therefore, that this very interesting inscription is a mere hoax," wrote Crittenden, "so that the whereabouts of the grave of Virginia Dare (if indeed there is a grave) remains as much a mystery as ever." Crittenden ordered the two stones returned to the old man.

Once the report was made public, Shallington's two months of fame came to an end. North Carolinians turned on him as a crook. William Crouch, regional director of the Federal Writer's Project, expressed hope there could be "some verbal tarring and feathering of such persons." He bemoaned such hoaxes and the harm they could do to authentic finds in the mind of a skeptical public. Shallington's reputation for honesty came under attack. Even W. O. Saunders, who had been friendly with Shallington, now turned on him. Saunders, never one to spare a citizen's feelings in print, concluded "that the old man, contrary to his local reputation for veracity, is a clumsy old liar. We have been the victims of a hoax that ought to be exposed." Saunders said he was going to send a few friends over to Columbia "to worm out" of Shallington an admission of his deception.

Though the old man stuck by his story, he was of no more interest. When confronted with the Historical Commission's opinion, he ignored the implications of forgery, and instead pointed to the fact that the rock had come from Britain. "That is just what I wanted to know. The Lost Colony people had them on their boats for ballast. . . . Now I want you to return the stone. . . I am not going to give it up." The Commission complied and Shallington got his rock back, but not his reputation.

Whether Shallington himself may have been the victim of a forgery is not known. He certainly did not claim the $500 reward offered by the Pearces — who, spared the trouble of investigating themselves, may never have seen the Shallington stones. Lost in the hubbub was Chappell's stone found near Tyner. If the Pearces in one of their many trips to the Chowan River area talked with Chappell, examined his stone, and possibly discounted it, there is nothing about it in the Brenau archives. Neither did Crittenden seem to have taken any interest. Did Chappell's find become confused in people's minds with Shallington's

Dr. Haywood Pearce Sr., president of Brenau College, shows off the Chowan River Dare Stone with two unnamed co-eds. Brenau University Archives.

hoax, and likewise dismissed with it? The sixty-pound rock may still sit on the property of a Chowan County resident, waiting for a closer look.

With Shallington's stone discredited and Chappell's overlooked, Brenau College's Dare Stone only gained more credibility. Impossible to definitively write off as a hoax, it garnered an aura of authenticity that in turn only generated more publicity. While the original Dare Stone was placed on display at Brenau, the Pearces announced that they had made two replicas of it. One was to be shown at the 1939 World's Fair in New York, in the Georgia Building, where it indeed proved a popular attraction, seen by thousands of visitors.

The other replica, President Pearce decided, should go to an appropriate place in North Carolina. Edenton Mayor J. H. McMullan felt his town should be the home for one of the copies. It would fit perfectly in the town's Cupola House museum. The Pearces weren't so sure, but sent him twenty copies of the 1939 *Bulletin* instead. The museum at Fort Raleigh on Roanoke Island asked for one. Even the British government showed an interest in getting one for the British Museum, after English diplomat Sir Louis Beale saw it at the World's Fair.

But no site in North Carolina would ever receive a replica of the Dare Stone, because suddenly and without warning the trail of the Lost Colonists led away from North Carolina. The Pearces had been none too keen on North Carolina in the first place. They were Georgians in possession of a North Carolina historical artifact. They were actively searching for the Second Dare Stone in the Old North State, with the idea of taking any find back to Georgia. They certainly could not mistake Crittenden's antagonism toward them. Nor had North Carolina newspapers gone overboard in their support of the Pearces' enadeavors. As President Pearce wrote, "Considerable skepticism has been expressed and some ridicule from some sources in North Carolina."

But during the summer of 1939, soon after business of the Shallington stones had drawn to a close in North Carolina, an amazing revelation was made further south. When the staff of the Fort Raleigh museum on Roanoke Island again requested a replica of the Dare Stone, President Pearce could smugly write back in July, "We now have the grave stone which was placed on the graves of the seventeen massacred colonists. It contains the names of Ananias and Virginia Dare and fifteen others."

The Second Stone had been found!

And the eagerly sought relic had turned up not in the state of Virginia Dare's birth, where searchers had heretofore focused their efforts, but — as President Pearce informed North Carolina — "more than 300 miles from Roanoke Island." Now these two original Dare Stones were on display at Brenau, while replicas had been made and were "on exhibit [at the World's Fair] in the Georgia building." Pearce explained, "I decided to do this because the first stone was found in North Carolina, the second in South Carolina within fifty miles of the

Georgia line, and I have some reasons to believe that the seven members of the colony finally reached a well known Cherokee village in north Georgia."

Suddenly North Carolina's claim to the Lost Colony was thrown into doubt. From what the new evidence showed, the famous Lost Colonists might now belong to South Carolina, maybe even Georgia. And the change in fortune could all be credited to the sharp eyes of Bill Eberhardt, a stonecutter from Fulton County, Georgia.

*　*　*

White argued, threatened, cajoled, begged, pleaded. Certainly he explained that Fernandez was effectively sentencing to death these subjects of Queen Elizabeth. Chesapeake Bay was their only hope. Just about six or seven miles long and a mile or two wide, Roanoke Island could accommodate several farms, probably enough to feed the colonists, but by then it was too late in the season to plant crops. Supplies brought with them would not last long, nor would what little the colonists could glean from the abandoned Indian cornfields. The Roanokes had destroyed their own fishing weirs to prevent them from being used by the English and the settlers didn't know how to rebuild them. And without fish or corn, there was just not enough wild game, or enough nuts and berries on the small island to feed that many colonists through the winter. Besides, most of these English families had no knowledge of how to survive in the wild. The Indians certainly would not provide the vital support they needed. Just the opposite, they would see them as targets of opportunity.

Fernandez could not be budged. He would take two or three back aboard, either the governor or whomever he designated, but that was all. The rest would remain on Roanoke.

White let himself be browbeaten. The governor didn't have that iron in him that commanders like Lane and Fernandez had. He was a pensive man, a painter of pictures. He could faithfully capture the likeness, down to each bead and muscle, of Indian men, women, and children going about their daily lives along this foreign coast. But he could not capture the will of men.

Unable to change Fernandez's mind, the colonists accepted their fate and began repairing the fort and houses. Facing a tough winter, they would make do as best they could until help arrived from England. But there was no doubt they were in a dangerous situation. The only bright spot for White and colonists was Manteo, their loyal Indian guide and helpmate. Manteo of Croatoan and Wanchese of Roanoke, the latter now orchestrating the attacks on the English colonists, had gone back to England with the very first English reconnaissance of Roanoke three years earlier in 1584. Back then, in their native England, White, along with scientist Thomas Hariot, helped teach English to the two Indians, all while pumping them for information about their country. They

learned something of the Indians' tongue and studied the Algonquian dictionary Hariot had begun compiling.

As for the two Alqonguian emissaries, their short time in England changed them in completely opposite ways. Whatever Manteo had experienced made him a firm supporter of the English. He would remain a loyal friend of the English, serving as an interpreter and intermediary, even becoming a member of the Church of England. He saved Lane and his men time and again from traps and ambushes, and White knew he would do the same for his beleaguered colonists. In thanks for his loyalty and with Raleigh's blessing, White named Manteo lord of the towns of Roanoke and Dasemunkepeuc.

White's illustration of a male Indian encountered by the Roanoke colonists.

It was just the contrary with Wanchese. Whatever he had seen in England had turned him solidly against the English. God knows there was enough bad to be seen in 1580s London. When he and Manteo returned to Roanoke with Lane in July 1585, no sooner had the expedition landed than Wanchese deserted the English. He knew just how dangerous and brutal they could be and now became an implacable foe to all things English.

To hear it from Lane, Wanchese had urged the wiroans *— likely his maternal uncle — to wipe out the Englishmen while he had the chance. But the* wiroans *Pemisapan was killed before he could carry out an attack, and the angry Wanchese may well have assumed the role of* wiroans. *Lane and his soldiers abandoned Roanoke before he could take revenge. White knew the returning English would be at risk.*

Sir Thomas Hariot.

And he had been right. Within days of the arrival of White's colonists, Wanchese loosed his warriors. One day George Howe set out crabbing, alone. His fellow colonists found Howe's body riddled with sixteen arrows, his head clubbed to a pulp. White had no choice but to order a counterattack on Wanchese's town of Dasemunkepeuc. But Wanchese and his people had evacuated the town ahead of the attack. Instead White's men accidentally attacked Manteo's Croatoans, who were taking corn from the deserted village. It was another bad sign, as the Croatoans were some of the few friends the English had in the area. Now they'd managed to antagonize them. Manteo worked hard to smooth things over.

Still there was hope. Amid all the turmoil, White's daughter Eleanor, wife of his valued assistant Ananias Dare, gave birth to a child on August 18, 1587, just weeks after their arrival on Roanoke. They named the baby girl Virginia, after this new land they were settling. Virginia Dare became the first English child born in North America.

About a week later, Margery Harvie delivered her child. Her baby's name is lost to history.

Dare Stone Number 2, Front. Brenau University Archives

CHAPTER 6

A Diary in Stone

T all and lanky, porkpie hat on his head, denim overalls up to his chest, cigarette dangling from the corner of his mouth, Bill Eberhardt fit the stereotype of a rural Georgian during the Depression. Eberhardt claimed to be a stonecutter by trade, but he didn't really have a job, or at least not a regular one. From the Atlanta area, Eberhardt spent most of his time on the Chattahoochee River in north Georgia tossing out a line for catfish or just wandering the banks. A bachelor in his mid-thirties, he lived alone in a dirty shack and pretty much just got by. Many country folks did the same. Then Eberhardt got word that the Pearces over in Gainesville had a standing reward of $500 for rocks that had writing on them which related to the Lost Colony of Roanoke.

So one day in May 1939, Eberhardt drove up to Brenau College and showed the Pearces a stone he said he'd found on a South Carolina hill near the Saluda River south of Greenville. The two Pearces were unimpressed, probably even dismissive. If the original Dare Stone indicated that a second stone was nearby, then they were convinced that it had to be there — and there meant North Carolina. That's where they had concentrated their search for the Second Stone and where they'd expected to find it.

The words inscribed on Eberhardt's stone looked nothing like those on the Chowan River Dare Stone, which were sharp and clear though pushed together, with the appearance of having been made in haste by a chisel. The words on Eberhardt's stone were light and shallow, very hard to read, and formed of large letters made of loops and near-perfect circles. It was obvious they had not been carved by the same hand. Though the Pearces could see the date "1589," they couldn't make out the rest of the inscription. As this date predated the Chowan Stone, the Pearces pretty much gave Eberhardt the brushoff. He'd probably found an old Spanish tombstone, they told him.

Bill Eberhardt wasn't going to be turned away that easily. A couple of weeks later he returned to Brenau, bringing the Pearces two more stones from the hill in South Carolina. By this time, the Pearces were tired of Eberhardt and told him to leave the stones and they'd try to decipher the writing when they could get around to it. Again they could read the number "1589" on both stones, but not much more. The writing on these two stones resembled that on Eberhardt's first stone but showed no similarity to that on the Chowan Stone.

Eberhardt must have sensed he was being dismissed, and he quickly explained that he'd found even more rocks with writing on them on that South Carolina hill. The Pearces showed Eberhardt the Chowan River Dare Stone, described what they were looking for, and explained that they believed the Second Stone would be found in North Carolina. The Second Stone would also contain the names of the seventeen Lost Colonists killed by the Indians. After all, this is what the Chowan River Stone said. Two of those names should be Ananias and Virginia Dare, with a date of 1591.

So about a week later, Eberhardt returned to Gainesville with a long, narrow, flat stone that had a sort of scimitar curve to it. It was heavy and brown and bore many words in the same style as Eberhartdt's previous rocks. Somehow Eberhardt prevailed upon the Pearces to give this rock a closer look. Maybe he directed them to the date "1591" and suggested they read the seventeen English names on it. Now Eberhardt had their attention. This was what they had been expecting to find.

The inscriptions were shallow and hard to read, and they determined the best way to make them stand out was to fill the depressions with flour. As they did, an amazing find came to light. Inscribed on both sides of the stone and on one edge seemed to be the gravestone of Virginia Dare and the names of the sixteen other Lost Colonists the earlier Chowan Dare Stone had said existed.

The back and side of Dare Stone Number 2. Brenau University Archives

(Front)	(Back)	(Edge)
Heyr	Syndor	Father wee goe sw
Laeth	Boane	
Ananias &	Wigan	
Virginia	Birge	
Father	Polle	
Salvage	Carewe	
Mvrther	Bowman	
Al save	Sprague	
Seaven	Tuckers	
Names	Bolitoe	
Written	Smythe	
Heyr mai	Sakeres	
God hab	Holborn	
Mercye	Winget	
Eleanor	Stoate	
Dare 1591		

The 1591 date checked out. There was the mention of the death of Ananias Dare and possibly that of Virginia. There were the fifteen names of the other murdered Lost Colonists. And it was signed with the full name of Eleanor Dare, one of the survivors and author of the Chowan Dare Stone. The Pearces held in their hands what they had spent all that time and hundreds of dollars looking for: the long-sought Second Stone.

The family could not have been more excited. They persuaded Eberhardt to take them to the hill in South Carolina. Eberhardt agreed, but he admitted that he had already gathered up the stones from the site. That did not deter the Pearces, who explained they were also looking for the grave of the Lost Colonists. And they expected to find that where the Second Stone was located. So Eberhardt took them to the hill on the Saluda River, near the town of Pelzer, South Carolina. Along the way, he told them how he discovered the thirteen stones.

Eberhardt had a checkered past, not too unusual for a Southern man back in those days. He had bummed around a lot and did a variety of jobs that took him across the South. Some of those jobs were connected with moonshining. The Pearces would learn later that

Eberhardt's activities also involved the sale of fake Indian artifacts. But as Eberhardt explained it, back in 1931 he was driving along the road that cut across the base of the hill and had car trouble. Needing a nice flat stone to prop up his car, he looked around and discovered thirteen "soap stones" at the base of the hill. Then he noticed the writing and the early dates. He couldn't really make out the writing, but figured them for lucky stones. He threw one in the back of his truck and took it home to Atlanta as his "good-luck stone." He hadn't been back to the site since — until he learned about the Pearces' quest

Later, when he heard the Pearces were offering $500 for rocks with words carved in them, Eberhardt brought them his good-luck stone, the one he showed the Pearces in May. When they didn't appear interested, he went back to South Carolina. The good luck must have been holding, as Eberhardt managed to find the same spot from eight years earlier. Yes, the stones were still right where he'd remembered. He gathered up the remaining twelve and took them home to Atlanta.

Now the Pearces gazed at the hill where the stones had once lay. They walked its crest and imagined the bones of the Lost Colonists just inches beneath their feet. They had to have it. Within days, the Pearces had located the owner of the hill, a farmer named Charles Bennett, whose family had owned the land for generations. Bennett agreed to sell, and the Pearces paid him $800 for the parcel. They planned on coming back almost immediately to begin excavating for the graves of Virginia and Ananias Dare. Naturally, the Pearces had questions. Why did Eberhardt find all the stones together at the bottom of the hill? Shouldn't they have been on top, or strewn across the countryside? But the Pearces chalked it up to erosion, or possibly the removal of the stones by slaves or farmers during antebellum times.

At some point, Eberhardt discreetly reminded the Pearces of the $500 reward they'd been offering for the Second Stone. The Pearces were now forced to make a decision. They had already spent about $500 on searches and excavations in North Carolina and now had just put up $800 for a few acres of South Carolina real estate. Excavating was going to cost more. They had advertised a $500 reward for the second Dare Stone and Bill Eberhardt had apparently delivered. They were now going to have to accept the South Carolina stones as potentially authentic Lost Colony relics and pay Eberhardt his reward — or reject them as fraudulent and explain why they thought so. Of course, by denying Eberhardt's claim they would lose Eberhardt, his stones, and any others he still had. And that was part of what egged the Pearces on. Clues on Eberhardt's Second Stone indicated that more stones might be out there: "father wee goe sw." If there were these thirteen, then wasn't it quite possible there were even more to the southwest?

Still, the Pearces hesitated. The word "hoax" must have ricocheted in their heads. They had to recall Tom Shallington, who was at that very moment trying to pass off a Virginia Dare tombstone. They managed to stall Eberhardt long enough to have him checked out by a private investigation service. But the gumshoes couldn't find anything — short of the circumstantial evidence of Eberhardt's sometime occupation as a stonecutter — that would make them think Eberhardt was in on a hoax. Eberhardt seemed to be what he appeared: just a rural Georgian in his mid-thirties with about three years of schooling. The Pearces didn't believe he had the historical knowledge that would allow him to fake something like this. And they couldn't find that he knew anyone who did. Surely a stonecutter might just happen to have an eye for rocks.

The Pearces had Eberhardt's stones investigated as well. The weathering and patinas did not rule out the stones' possible authenticity. Just to be safe, and serve as one last check on Eberhardt's honesty, the Pearces offered a deal. They would pay Eberhardt the $500 cash reward if he wanted. Or they would give him $100 in cash and a half interest in whatever they found on the site — a possible fortune if the remains of the Lost Colonists were discovered there, or nothing if not. The Pearces also hinted that there might be other carved stones out there and they would pay for them. Much to the Pearces' relief, Eberhardt went for the $100 cash and the half share of the hill. Not only were they able to minimize their cash outlay, they felt they could now be more certain of Eberhardt's good faith. Though the Pearces would not find out until much later, once the Dare Stone publicity got big, Eberhardt secretly sold off his interest in whatever came out of the hill. No record on how much he got for it. Nevertheless, since the Pearces thought there were more stones out there, they believed Eberhardt would find them for them. And they figured Eberhardt understood there was more money to be made than a mere $500. But now he had a strong interest in helping with the venture.

So by mid-summer 1939, Brenau College owned fourteen Dare Stones. The baker's dozen of new stones were composed of granite and sandstone, weighing from 40 to 154 pounds, all displaying the distinctive circular pattern of writing. The Pearces assigned identifying numbers to all fourteen. Stone Number 1 was the original Chowan River Stone found by Hammond in 1937, the one that had sparked all the interest. The fifth Dare Stone found, and the fourth given by Eberhardt to the Pearces, which bore the names of all seventeen Lost Colonists killed by the Indians, was labeled Stone Number 2 by the Pearces.

However, Stone Number 2 exhibited some odd features. Of the names of the seventeen dead — Ananias Dare, Virginia Dare, Birge, Polle, Carewe, Bowman, Sprague, Tuckers, Bolitoe, Smythe, Sakeres, Holborn, Winget, and Stoate — only Ananias and Virginia were known to be among the English colonists who had come to Roanoke in 1587. The other fifteen names did not appear on the official colonial roster. Some names bore similarities to the historical document. While a Thomas Smith appeared on the roster, there was no one with the spelling Smythe. The colony's roster employed the spelling "Elyoner" Dare, while the stone bore "Eleanor." Of course, wide variations in spelling were common in Elizabethan England, for common words as well as proper names. Even Sir Walter Raleigh spelled his name many different ways, often as "Ralegh".

Stone Number 3, probably Eberhardt's "good-luck stone" and the first presented to the Pearces, read: (Front) *5 lae hyre mrd bie Inde 1589* (Back) *cy vane lae 200 se*.

Stone Number 4, whose inscription was almost identical to that of Stone Number 3, was probably one of the two Eberhardt brought on his second visit to Brenau. It reads: (Front) *7 lae hyre mrd bye Ind 1589* (Back) *cy vane lyh e 200 e se*. The slightly varying inscriptions indicated that five and seven Lost Colonists respectively "lie here murdered by Indians, 1589." The Pearces took the cryptic words on the backs of these stones to be directional information. An arc 200 miles to the southeast, or east-southeast, of the hill would encompass a swath from St, Augustine, Florida, to the Savannah River in Georgia.

Stone Number 5: (Front) *hyre lae Jvan Moleye Mulgrave ane childe 1589* (Edge) *Mrde Bye Inde loke 1 myle*. "Here lies Juan Moleye Mulgrave." The meaning is ambiguous: Mulgrave, a child, or Mulgrave and child, were "murdered by Indians" in 1589. The stones' author instructs the reader to "look one mile" away from where he has found this stone to locate the grave, but no direction is provided. There is no Moleye or Mulgrave listed on the roster of the Lost Colonists.

Stone Number 6: (Front) *Heyr laeth Nolan Ogle & wife* (Upper Edge) *1590* (Side) *mvrthed by salvage*. It was a simple tombstone: "Here lie Nolan Ogle and wife," both "murdered by a savage" in 1590. No Ogles are listed on the roster of colonists.

Stone Number 7: (Front) *Father looke tow barke of tree certan signe amang tham Eleanor Dare 1591*. This stone resumes the direct address "Father" used in stones 1 and 2. If Eleanor was giving instructions to her father, whom she expected to be looking for her, she was not only leaving messages cut into rocks for him, but also clues carved on trees to help him track them. "Father, look to the bark of trees for certain signs left among them. 1591."

Stone Number 8: (Front) *Salvage mvrther John Sampson William Sole Peter little John Farre Taylor Myllet haris 1591* (Back) *Henry Mylton John Borden Toppon Darige Johnson Tydway 1591*. This appears to be a memorial to several Englishmen, possibly twelve in all: John Sampson, William Sole, Peter Little, John Farre, Taylor Millet, Harris, Henry Milton, John Borden, Toppon, Darige, Johnson, and Tydway. All had been "murdered" by Indians in 1591. The date was given twice, once on each side. All of these names, including those given only as surnames, do appear on the Lost Colony roster. John Sampson was one the "assistants" and a colony official; the boy listed on the roster, also named John Sampson, was likely the assistant's son. While there was no Taylor Myllet on the roster, there was a Michael Myllet. There are two Thomas Harrises, as well as a Thomas Topan, a Richard Darige, two Johnsons – Henry and Nicholas – and a John Tydway.

Stone Number 9: (Front) *Heyr laeth lewes Wotton 1591* (Back) *salvage mvrther Henry Rufoote Rogers*. While Lewis Wotton and Henry Rufoote were both listed on the Lost Colony roster, there was no one with the last name of Roger or Rogers. There were, however, two men with the first name of Roger: Roger Baily and Roger Prat, both Assistants and colonial officials. This name might also be connected with Rufoote, the inscription memorializing two, rather than three, men murdered by Indians in 1591.

Stone Number 10: (Front) *Heyr laeth Richard Kemme Jame Hynd*. On this tombstone for two men cited on the roster, Richard Kemme and James Hynde, no date is provided.

Stone Number 11: (Front) *Heyr laeth Daniel Bagby hee Mvrther bye Salvage 1591* (Back) *Fovre lae Heyr They Die of moche* *miserie.* In addition to Daniel Bagby, killed by Indians in 1591, this stone memorializes four others whose names were not recorded but who "died in much misery" — possibly by torture, a common practice for captives taken by Southeastern Indians. There is no Daniel Bagby listed on the roster.

Stone Number 12: (Front) *Heyr Salvage mvrther Samuel ToThill wife & cherl 1591.* It is not clear whether this cryptic inscription was meant as a tombstone or an event marker for 1591, Was Samuel ToThill and his wife and child killed here, or was it ToThill's wife and child only? Does "cherl" mean "child?" As always, they were "murdered by savages." The name ToThill does not appear on the colonial roster.

Stone Number 13: (Front) *Heyr laeth Dyonis Harvie wife & dowter* (Back) *Will Dye spend love 1591* (Edge) *Mvrthed by salvage.* The burial stone for Dyonis Harvie, his wife, and daughter indicates they were "murdered by savages in 1591." All three of these people are on the roster, Dyonis serving as one of the colony's assistants. Along with him was his wife, Margery, who was pregnant on the journey and gave birth to a child soon after Virginia Dare was born. The stone would also appear to be the grave of a Will Dye, but there is no one by that name on the roster. John Spendlove, listed on the roster, was also apparently buried here.

Stone Number 14: (Front) *Father wee go sw with fovre goodlie men the yr shew moche mercye theyr ar god sovldiovrs theyr saide theyr browt vs tow yov Eleanor 1591.* (On Edge) *with moche labovr wee pvtt certan names heyr.* Eleanor was leaving more clues for her father, whom she believed was actively looking for her. In a turn of their sad fortunes, the Lost Colonists appear to have obtained welcome assistance from the Indians, to whom Eleanor asks her father to be kind. But death still stalked the Colonists as more names were carved on stones. "We go southwest with four goodly men. They showed us much mercy. They are good soldiers. They said they brought [will bring?] us to you. With much labor, we put certain names here. Eleanor 1591."

These thirteen stones, if accurate, imparted a great deal of information. Eleven tombstones account for about fifty-nine colonists. Of the forty-two names written on the stones, only twenty-two, including Eleanor Dare, were actually listed on the Colony roster. Two of the stones provided instructions from Eleanor to her father, telling him to look for clues on trees, and that they were going southwest. A few of the tombstones also bore directional messages.

Taken together, the South Carolina stones told a horrific story. Apparently once the Lost Colonists had left Roanoke Island, for whatever reason they began moving southwest into present-day South Carolina. As early as 1589, maybe earlier, the Colonists had come under attack from Indians and suffered heavy losses, as the tally of tombstones and the oft-repeated "murdered by savages" attest. Eleanor never gave up the hope that her father was searching for her and left clues carved on trees and in the stones for him find and follow. At some point, the surviving Colonists were befriended by Indians who helped them continue southwest. Her father should be kind and generous to these Indians who would lead him to her.

While the cache of stones found by Eberhardt in South Carolina certainly excited the two Pearces, surely they also gave pause. These South Carolina Stones, made by such a different hand, contradicted the original Chowan River Stone. And what were they to make of the long list of names not known to the historical record? Further, the Chowan River Stone told of colonists suffering from sickness and dying from disease, a circumstance not mentioned in any of the South Carolina Stones. But most puzzling of all, if Virginia, Ananias, and Eleanor Dare were living near the Chowan River in 1591, then what had they been doing in South Carolina in 1589? The Chowan was not southwest of where the South Carolina Stones were found, but far northeast, back in the colonists's original region. And what could account for two apparently contradictory tombstones of Ananias and Virginia in these two widely divergent locations?

Nevertheless, the Pearces brushed aside such questions for the moment. They decided to excavate the top of their newly purchased hill. If they discovered the graves of the seventeen then their case would be proved and somehow the questions would sort themselves out. In the meantime, Eleanor's clue that the group were heading southwest intrigued Prof. Pearce. If Eleanor was moving southwest and leaving rock clues along the way, that would take her into Georgia, possibly along the Chattahoochee River, which rises in the Appalachian foothills just west of Greenville, South Carolina, runs southwest through Gainesville, and skirts the northern edge of Atlanta before forming part of Georgia's boundary with Alabama. So now Pearce asked Eberhardt if he would look for more stones along the rivers of northern Georgia. Eberhardt agreed, for a price: for every carved stone he found, the Pearces would pay anywhere from ten to twenty-five dollars, maybe more, depending on the stone.

So while Eberhardt turned over rocks along the banks of the Chattahoochee, the Pearces took shovels to the hilltop in South Carolina. They spent several weeks of hot digging in July 1939, but found nothing. No bodies, no artifacts, no stones, nothing. As President Pearce complained to Dice Anderson, president of Wesleyan College in Macon, Georgia, "The soil there is red clay and parties who have had experience in this area report that nothing is left after fifty to seventy-five years." So again, no evidence was the best evidence, and the Stones could not be disproved. "All the evidence which we have thus far," President Pearce mused, "points to the fact that the stones at least are genuine." Still, finding no evidence to back up the messages they bore must have been disheartening.

About this same time, word of Eberhardt's find was beginning to spread. So on July 25, 1939, Brenau College officially announced the discovery of the South Carolina Stones. The *Atlanta Constitution* ran a front-page story headlined "Find 13 More 'Lost Colony' Grave Stones: Brenau Reveals 'Virginia Dare' Discovery That May Change History." A picture on page four showed the thirteen Eberhardt stones laid out on the floor, their inscriptions made visible with the help of flour. The two Pearces, father and son, their faces turned down from the camera, kneel over them. Pearce Jr. rarely seemed to look directly at a camera. The newspaper article related the story of the Lost Colony, then described how Bill Eberhardt had found the stones and how the Pearces had come to be involved. "If the authenticity of these stones is established," the *Constitution* posed, "some commonly accepted facts in American history must be discarded. The Roanoke colony did not perish in North Carolina or Virginia but in South Carolina; Englishmen were first in South Carolina as early as 1589 instead of much later as has been previously believed."

Papers nationwide picked up the news. Throughout the summer the Pearces were inundated with calls for more information on the Stones and proposals on how to publicize their historical treasures. Laura Kingsbery, a former southerner now living in Los Angeles, explored the possibility of creating a screenplay about the Dare Stones. She saw this as a six- or eight-reel picture which would weave together

Stone finder William "Bill" Eberhardt (left, kneeling) and Dr. Haywood Pearce Jr. of Brenau College (right, standing) in the field.

the story of the colony and its migration southwest. "Your part would be to furnish all the information you have on the subject," she wrote, "mine, to work this material into a screen story of universal appeal that would be acceptable to the producer and the public." If the two Pearces would provide her with information on the Stones, she would give them jointly thirty-five percent of the sale of the script. She volunteered references if they wanted them.

While President Pearce was interested in the movie deal, he did not yet have enough information on the South Carolina Stones, or ironclad proof of their authenticity. The Pearces had other ideas in any case. First, they planned to hold a large scientific conference at Brenau the first week of September, during which scientists, historians, archaeologists, and other scholars would get a chance to inspect the stones and judge for themselves their validity. Then, Pearce Jr., the historian, would draft an article about the Stones for a popular magazine. But even better, the Pearces hoped to create an outdoor drama similar to Paul Green's *The Lost Colony*. Though the Pearces wanted to give Green a run for his money, they felt theirs would function as a sequel to his Roanoke Island story.

The idea for a new South Carolina-oriented outdoor drama may have come from Martha Mathis, a fifty-two-year-old teacher living on Roanoke Island. Mathis had worked on Green's 1937 *Lost Colony* production at Manteo, North Carolina, and the two seemed to have had a cordial relationship; she would later ask Green for a letter of recommendation. Now Mathis proposed to President Pearce that Brenau hire her. She said that she had always been interested in early American history, hence her choice to live on Roanoke. But having heard of the Brenau Stones, she wanted a job there so she could satisfy her craving for colonial history. President Pearce turned her down. Mathis wrote again to clarify: she would be willing to teach freshman English and had the credentials to do it. Even better, she "wrote and produced America's Cradle Song, a pageant of the Lost Colony, the year before Mr. Green's production. Mr. Green had the privilege of using my material in helping him to write his pageant along with his other researches, and has given me full credit for it."

The Pearces must have had their hands full responding to the flood of correspondence from all fronts. Freelance writer Russell McFarland had planned on writing an article on the Chowan River Stone, but now that he'd heard of the South Carolina Stones, he inquired for more information. He also wanted pictures of the hill and the burial place of the bodies and other details, such as the route taken by the colonists. Pearce replied that he was already writing an article on the Stones, but would be glad to send McFarland a copy of the 1939 Brenau *Bulletin* and the July 25 press release about the South Carolina Stones. Pearce admitted they had no picture of the "burial mound" and as for the route the Lost Colonists took to South Carolina, "if you will take a map of the southeastern coastal region and lay a ruler southwestward from the region of the North Carolina coastal island to a point thirteen miles south of Greenville, South Carolina, you will have the probable trail of the refugees, so far as it is revealed by the stones."

Others wanted to help. Dr. G. R. Brigham, director of Brenau's own journalism department, offered an etymology of some of the names found on South Carolina Stone Number 2. "Sydnor – A well-known name in Virginia, as Henry Syndor Harrison, the author. Boane – probably pronounced Bone (I have seen Doane, so spelled and pronounced). Wican – probably same as Wiggin. Birce – sometimes Berse, or Berce, or Peirce (pr. purse). Carewe – A common name in England. Holborn – " " " " in England. Holborn – " " " " Scotland. Bowman – " " " " England, dating back to archery days. Spagne – probably a Spaniard, perhaps in disguise, or so-called, as we say 'Frenchy' or 'Dago.' Sakeres – might be Zacherys – the name Sacheverell is an author in England today. Bolitoe – probably an English name – William Bolitho, the English journalist, is living and writing today. Winget – probably Wingate."

Mary Sue Paris of the Nashville, Tennessee area wondered if the Smythe mentioned on Stone Number 2 might be related to Reverend Thomas Smythe, first pastor of the old Presbyterian Church in Charleston, South Carolina.

Some remembered seeing other rocks with writing on them. Up near Inman, South Carolina, about fifty miles north-northeast of where Eberhardt found his thirteen stones, a stone was found on the Bryson Hammett farm in 1935 that had a clearly visible date of 1587 on it and an arrow pointing toward the southwest. Many thought this was a Dare Stone and hoped to have the Pearces look at it. Others weren't so sure, as the 1587 date worried them. They felt that if Eleanor Dare and Margery Harvie gave birth in August 1587, it would be difficult for the colonists, with at least two newborn babies, to have arrived in South Carolina during that year. Still, it was something to consider.

W. Lindsay Wilson of Greenville, South Carolina, wrote Pearce that about fifteen years earlier he had found a stone with writing on it on a farm hilltop about fifteen miles from Greenville. If he remembered correctly, it said something like "18 others lye buried here." Wilson believed he had stumbled upon the grave of some English soldiers killed in the mid-1700s by Cherokee Indians and hadn't done any excavation as he did not want to disturb soldier's graves. It wasn't until he saw the newspapers about the South Carolina Stones that he wondered about a connection to the Lost Colony. He offered to meet Pearce in Greenville and do a search of northern South Carolina counties for more stones. Pearce was certainly interested. He invited Wilson to attend the big conference at Brenau planned for September 5-7.

In North Carolina, C. C. Crittenden had also received his invitation to the conference. Regardless of his opinions of the Pearces and their ways, there was no way he was going to miss this. He was still upset that the Brenau men, despite his endeavors, had "never taken kindly to the suggestion that the stones be made available for study here in North Carolina." Still, he wrote, "Just from what I have picked up from this distance, I believe that there is a fair chance that the stones are authentic."

Then, in early September 1939, days before the conference at Brenau was to begin, the Pearces telegraphed all those invited that the conference would have to be delayed a year. "New developments bearing on the 'Dare Stones' have occurred which may or may not throw considerable more light on the fates and movement of the colony," they explained. "At the present time we cannot present this new evidence." The conference would instead be rescheduled for October 1940.

The new evidence was the discovery of several more stones that effectively moved the Lost Colonists out of South Carolina and firmly into Georgia. One Isaac Turner of Atlanta wrote to Pearce that in March he had been hunting up on the Chattahoochee River in Hall County, where he had discovered a stone with writing on it, which he took home with him. In July when he saw the newspaper articles detailing the South Carolina Stones, he made the connection between the two. Turner brought his stone to the Pearces and they apparently purchased it from him for an undisclosed amount. The inscription on the stone was in the same style of carving as found on the other thirteen South Carolina Stones and appeared to have been carved by the same hand.

Dare Stone Number 15, Front (left), and the back of the same stone (opposite page). Brenau University Archives.

Stone Number 15 read: (Front) *Father looke vp this river to great salvage lodgement wee pvtt moche clew bye waye* (Back) *Father the salvage shew moche mercye Eleanor Dare 1591.* Here was another set of instructions from Eleanor to her father. "Father, look up this river to great savage lodgement. We put much clues by the way." On the back, "Father, the savages show much mercy. Eleanor Dare 1591." It seemed the Lost Colonists were being led to a large Indian town somewhere in Georgia. Eleanor was leaving clues for John White to track them. He would find them on the Chattahoochee and he should be kind to these Indians who had helped them.

The Pearces had to be elated. Not so much because another stone was found, though that was great news, but that it had been found in Georgia. As the Pearces had predicted, the Lost Colony survivors, among them Eleanor Dare, had seemingly trudged out of South Carolina under Indian attack. But with the help of friendly Indians, they had come at last to the region that would become the state of Georgia, stopping at least for a time at a site only six miles north of Gainesville itself. The Lost Colonists, it seemed, had landed at the Pearces' front door. Father

and son now believed that if one Dare Stone had been found in Hall County, then there might be more. They showed the new Stone to Eberhardt and urged him to redouble his efforts along the Chattahoochee and other rivers in that part of the state. The stone hauler wouldn't let them down.

Bill Eberhardt had to be the luckiest rock hunter in the South. The inscriptions on these stones were shallow, faded and very hard to see. They could easily be overlooked as they apparently had been for the past three hundred fifty years. Filling the inscriptions with flour made them easier to read. In the field, it took a talented eye not just to find the right rock, but to spot the inscription on it as well. But Eberhardt, like Louis Hammond, was lucky that way.

In late August 1939 Eberhardt returned to Brenau with an impressive haul: nine more Dare Stones he'd found in Habersham County, Georgia, about twenty miles northeast of Gainesville. The Pearces had urged Eberhardt that if he found any more stones, he should leave them in place and alert them. Eberhardt ignored them and brought the stones all in one batch — for which he was nonetheless paid according to their agreement

In these nine Habersham County Stones, Eleanor continued the story of the Lost Colonists for the next few years. She also left instructions for her father. Again, since Eberhardt delivered the nine stones at one time, no effort was made to determine which one he found first or second or where. So the Pearces probably numbered and arranged them in chronological order and they were added sequentially to the Chowan River, South Carolina, and Turner Stones.

Stone Number 16 read: (Front) *Father look 5 dae tow backe trale burie al vppon* (Edge) *Hil neere river* (Back) *Eleanor Dare 1591.* This is both an instruction for her father and apparently the mention of more dead. "Father, look five days back up this trail where we buried some of the dead upon a hill near a river. Eleanor Dare, 1591." But it does raise a question. If there were only seven survivors who escaped the South Carolina attacks and began moving southwest — Eleanor and six others — then these dead in Georgia pose a mystery as to who they were. They were not any of the seven survivors.

Stone Number 17: (Front) *Father shew moche mercye tow salvage weste of hil whe* (On Side Edge) *re Ananias* (On Top Edge) *& Virginia slayne* (Back) *Eleanor Dare 1591.* A request for her father. "Father, show much mercy to the savages west of the hill where Ananias and Virginia were slain. Eleanor Dare 1591." But if Ananias and Virginia were killed on the Saluda River in South Carolina or the Chowan River in North Carolina, then why was this stone found far to the south in Georgia?

Stone Number 18: (Front) *Father thee accurse salvage of the easte they hab slayne* (Back) *Al save seaven Revenge Eleanor Dare 1591* (Edge) *Ananias mye dowter.* A strange stone as it seems to apply to events back on the Saluda or Chowan Rivers. It repeats information provided in earlier stones. "Father, the accursed savages of the east, they have slain all save seven. Revenge. Ananias and my daughter [also slain]. Eleanor Dare, 1591." The word "Revenge" is rather cryptic. Did she mean it was revenge over some wrong that caused the Indians to attack the colony? Or was it the Indians' fear of revenge from the English, as the Chowan Stone implied, that caused them to attack the Colonists? Or was she calling on her father to take revenge on these Indians that had killed Ananias and Virginia? And who were the Indians of the East?

Stone Number 19: (Front) *Father day by day some amang vs endeavourer tow Reconn* (Back) *oittre For signe of yov Eleanor Dare 1591.* Eleanor seems to be encouraging her father to keep looking for her. And the Colonists are still looking for him. "Father, day by day some among us endeavor to reconnoiter for a sign of you. Eleanor Dare, 1591."

Stone Number 20: *(Front) Father wee goe tow great Hontaoase lodgement ther king (Back) shew moche mercye Eleanor Dare 1591.* Finally, a place name, the first given in all the Stones, as Eleanor leaves more clues for her father. "Father, we go to the great Hontaoase lodgement. Their king showed us much mercy. Eleanor Dare, 1591." For some, Hontaoase sounded very similar to the old Cherokee Indian town of Hiawassee in the mountains above the Chattahoochee River in Towns County, Georgia, about seventy miles north of Gainesville. There is also a Hiawassee in western North Carolina and a Hiwassee River runs north out of Georgia into North Carolina and eastern Tennessee. Eleanor implied that these Cherokees, if that was accurate, had shown them "much mercy."

Stone Number 21: *(Front) Father it Has bene 5 yeeres sithence yov hab (Back) departe maie God brynge yov hither Eleanor Dare 1592.* This takes them to a new year, 1592. It is a plea from a lost daughter to her father whom she has not seen since August 1587. "Father it has been five years since you have departed. May God bring you hither. Eleanor Dare 1592." One can hear her desperation.

Stone Number 22: *(Front) Father wee bene hyr 5 yeeres in primaeval (Edge) splendour (Back) Eleanor Dare 1592.* A very strange message and why would Eleanor even have the stonecutter spend time carving it? "Father, we have been here five years in primeval splendor. Eleanor Dare. 1592." Primeval splendor!? Strange words from a woman whose people had been under almost constant Indian attack for the past five years. Was she admiring the country? Expressing beauty? Was she enamored with their now seemingly safe position at Hontaoase? And was "primaeval splendour" a phrase an English woman would use in the late sixteenth century?

Stone Number 23: *(Front) Father seaven survive Hither (Back) Eleanor Dare 1592.* Another short comment. "Father, seven survive here. Eleanor Dare, 1592." Where did they survive? Where was "here?" Was it the Hontaoase Indian town or someplace nearby?

Stone Number 24: *(Front) Father seaven survieve (Edge) Hither Eleanor Dare (Edge) 1593.* A virtual repeat of Stone Number 23, but with a different date. "Father, seven survive here. Eleanor Dare, 1593." Eleanor is marking the passage of another year. The stones are both her personal journal and her message to her father that of the 117 men, women, and children dropped off on Roanoke in 1587, only seven survive in this new year.

The story the ten newly found Georgia stones told was a continuation of attack, death, and misery experienced by the Lost Colonists since they left North Carolina. Apparently the few surviving colonists passed out of South Carolina, leaving thirteen or more stones telling of their time there, and then continued their march southwest. As they moved into Georgia, they left more dead along the trail and more stones telling the death of Ananias and Virginia Dare. However, some friendly Indians had come to their aid and led them to the Indian town of Hontaoase in the mountains of northern Georgia. By 1593, only seven of the colonists survived, though they still imagined John White was actively tracking them.

The stones and inscriptions found in the Georgia Stones were almost exactly like those found in South Carolina, but nothing at all like the Chowan River Stone. Of the ten Georgia Stones, none were tombstones marking the death of a Colonist. In fact, none of the ten even mentioned a name other than Ananias, Virginia, and Eleanor Dare. Only Stone Number 16 spoke of a burial when Eleanor told her father to look five days back up the trail for some buried on a hill near a river. Rather, all ten stones were either clues instructing her father where the colonists were going, such as to Hontaoase town, or they were almost personal messages to him, telling him the state of the colonists, that seven still lived, they still missed him and looked for him, and they were living in "primaeval splendour."

So as 1939 and the decade of the Great Depression drew to a close, tiny Brenau College had a historical treasure trove on its hands. As a historian with a career to make, Haywood Pearce Jr. couldn't have been happier with his institution's sudden fame. But at the same time, as a scholar he could still not reconcile the conflicting names and threads of stories. And what was he to make of such unusual and suspect phrases like "reconnoittre" and "primaeval splendour," which did not ring true even in the flexible lexicon of Elizabethan English?

In his 1938 article in the *Journal of Southern History* and in Brenau's 1939 *Bulletin*, Pearce had gone to great lengths to show how the Chowan River Stone meshed with accepted history. He had described the colonists' plans to go fifty miles inland, which would put them on the Chowan River. He had quoted Captain John Smith and William Strachey, both of Jamestown, who later reported hearing stories of an attack on the colonists in the Chowan River area from which only seven had survived, including a young woman. Pearce had in fact done such a good job marshalling his evidence that he had convinced most people that the Chowan River Stone was the last testament of Eleanor Dare. Now, since the other twenty-three stones told a different story, Pearce was going to have to recant all that he had professed before.

The young historian was up to the task. On January 1, 1940, Brenau University published its second *Bulletin* on the subject, simply titled "The Dare Stones." The January 1940 *Bulletin* provided front and rear photographs of Stone Number 1, the Chowan Stone, discovered in North Carolina in 1937; Stone Number 2, the Virginia Dare tombstone, discovered on the Saluda River in South Carolina by Bill Eberhardt; and Stone Number 15, discovered by Isaac Turner in Hall County, Georgia, in March 1939. Along with the photographs, the *Bulletin* also provided a verbatim transcription of all twenty-four stones. Besides the photos and text, the Pearces also put forth what they saw as a new history of the Lost Colony. "The colony left 'Croatan' soon after their removal from Roanoke Island and traveled southwest through North Carolina and South Carolina," the *Bulletin* reported.

This brass ring bearing William Strachey's coat of arms was found during excavations at Jamestown.

The Pearces theorized that it was lack of food and Indian hostility that drove the Colonists out of Croatoan and into South Carolina. But there on the Saluda River the Colonists were attacked, and fifty-four of the Colonists either died or were killed by Indians, including Ananias and Virginia Dare. The remaining seven began marching southwest. "As our record only accounts for sixty-one members and there were originally 110 members, manifestly 49 were lost or killed on Roanoke or in the journey from Roanoke to Greenville County." As the Pearces saw it, the surviving few Colonists arrived on the Chattahoochee River in Georgia sometime in 1591 and stayed until 1593. There they were protected by "the King (presumably of the Cherokee nation or their predecessors) who showed them 'moche mercye.'" The Pearces also announced that further searches were then being made for more stones along the Chattahoochee River and in the Nacoochee Valley of northern Georgia.

But how to account for the disparity between the story the first Chowan River Stone told, that Virginia and Ananias had been killed near the Chowan River in 1591, and that of the South Carolina Stones which said they died there on the Saluda River? Pearce had it all worked out. He accepted that it was on the Saluda River in South Carolina where Virginia Dare, her father Ananias, and a host of other Lost Colonists had met their deaths. "It would therefore appear that the stone found on the banks of the Chowan River in North Carolina must have been carved by Eleanor Dare on the banks of the Saluda River, S.C., and the most tenable theory seems to be that Eleanor sent this stone by a friendly Indian to North Carolina in the hope that it might be delivered to her father whom she constantly expected to return to his colony." No mention was made about the obvious difference in the appearance of the inscription between the Chowan Stone and the Saluda River Stones.

And what of the names on the Saluda River Stones that did not appear on the roster of the Lost Colony? "'It may be,' Dr. Pearce suggested, 'that Governor White made errors in his list. Or it is possible that some of the colonists were not in good standing at home and gave assumed names. Then, too, Eleanor Dare, to whom the lettering of the stone is attributed, used phonetic spelling, increasing the possibilities for discrepancies. This point is going to be one of considerable discussion among historians.'"

There was one other bit of news about the Lost Colony in the January 1940 Brenau *Bulletin*. Maude Fiske LaFleur, a faculty member in Brenau's School of Speech, had written a "romantic drama" about the Lost Colony. It was to be presented in May 1940 as part of the college's commencement exercises. Students and Gainesville community actors would play the roles, and there was hope that North Carolina Cherokees might participate. "The drama includes scenes from the Court of Queen Elizabeth in England when permission was granted to Raleigh to send the colony under the leadership of John White and also scenes on Roanoke Island, the perilous journey across the Carolinas, the massacre near Greenville and finally the more peaceful but still stirring scenes on the banks of the Chattahoochee."

Pearce and others at Brenau College were already revising history, well before the new Dare Stones could be examined by authorities and determined to be authentic or not. Nevertheless, Pearce had Eleanor and the surviving Lost Colonists marching out of North Carolina and into Georgia. And it was Georgia that would now control the story of the Lost Colonists, with North and South Carolina only bit players.

* * *

By late August 1587, with the baggage and supplies unloaded and the colonists settling in, Fernandez prepared to sail for the Caribbean. Despite the birth of the children and the help of Manteo, the colonists understood their difficult position. They knew George Howe would not be the last one killed by Wanchese and his Roanokes. So White and his colonists concocted a plan. First, someone would have to return to England for help and supplies. The Colonists selected Governor White to make the trip, though he was reluctant to leave his people in such a perilous situation. But he was the logical choice. He had Raleigh's ear and had been a member of all three earlier expeditions. He knew the land, understood their predicament, could explain it more fully, so had a better chance of obtaining help. White reluctantly agreed to sail home. Most expected him back before a year was up.

Everyone realized that the colony could not remain on Roanoke. At their back was the ocean, leaving them vulnerable to the Spanish in Florida, who would love to get their hands on these Protestant English. Wanchese and his warriors would pick them off one by one, unless starvation or the Spanish got them first. Other than the Croatoans, the only friends they had in the area were Menatonon and his Choanoac Indians to the west along the Chowan River. Menatonon had made peace with Lane the year before. And the old wiroans *had lived up to his word, refusing to support Pemisapan's plans to rid his land of the Lane and his soldiers.*

With that assurance in mind, the colonists determined that once White left, they would go to Menatonon on the Chowan River, where they would find plenty of good land for farming and protection from the Roanokes. So they planned on relocating "50 miles further up into the maine." This would put them in Choanoac territory, near what would eventually become Edenton, North Carolina.

The final part of the plan was devising a way for White to find them when he returned. When the time came for them to evacuate Roanoke, the colonists said they would leave clues for White by carving the name of their destination on a tree or post. If the colonists should be attacked and driven from Roanoke by force, then they would add a cross above the name.

Within days, John White was aboard ship and Simon Fernandez and his small fleet of three ships sailed south to capture Spanish ships in the Caribbean. As the wind drove the ship farther from his brave daughter, his trusted son-in-law, and his newborn granddaughter — among the hundred-odd other souls entrusted to his care — White consoled himself with the belief that he would soon be back on Roanoke and with assistance that would save his colony.

CHAPTER 7

Pearce Rewrites History

As 1940 dawned, the Pearces had to think that this would be their year. They were now big players in the Lost Colony story, having shifted the focus of North Carolina's beloved creation tale out of the Old North State and into Georgia. Brenau College in Gainesville owned and displayed the twenty-four Dare Stones, all together found by three different people: Louis Hammond, Bill Eberhardt, and Isaac Turner. Taken together, the Stones told a horrific story of almost constant Indian attacks and colonist deaths. And if the Stones were authentic — and the Pearces were always careful to say they could not vouch for their authenticity — then by 1593, the seven survivors of the Lost Colony were living in apparent safety at a Cherokee town in northern Georgia's Nacoochee Valley.

It was a pretty good story that neatly answered the ages-old question of what became of the Lost Colonists of Roanoke Island who disappeared in 1587. All the Pearces needed was archaeological evidence to verify the Stones. That should fall into place within the year. The Stones also needed the stamp of authenticity from the academic community. Haywood Pearce Jr. hoped that would transpire this autumn, with the big scientific conference to be held at Brenau. Top historians, archaeologists, and scientists from around the country would come to Gainesville, examine the Dare Stones, and if all went as he imagined, the Stones would be declared authentic.

Pearce was, however, disinclined to wait for the judgment of the academic community. Of course he always demurred when it came to the Stones' authenticity, but he really believed he had actual evidence of what became of the Lost Colony. And he was ready to begin rewriting its history even before his evidence had been proved. The new Pearce interpretation of what happened to the Lost Colony was best seen in Maude Fiske LaFleur's play, performed with full pomp and circumstance at Brenau's 1940 spring commencement exercises.

Writing as Maude Fiske, she titled it *This Heritage: A Play Concerning Eleanor Dare and those English Colonists who went with Her from Roanoke after Landing there in July 1587.* The curtain went up at Brenau's outdoor amphitheater on May 24, 1940, at 8:30 in the evening, presumably for that semester's graduating class and their families. It was a big production with about sixty cast members, including eight Eastern Band Cherokees from their Qualla Boundary Reservation in western North Carolina – Grey Eagle, Young Deer, Trail Boy, Black Crow, Thunder Boy, Medicine Man, Frog Boy, and Tall Tree. They would perform various Indian roles in the play, though Manteo and Wanchese were both played by white actors. Haywood Pearce III, son of the history professor, played the role of Ananias Dare. There was also a twenty-two-piece orchestra and scenes which ranged from the ocean to woodland hills and Queen Elizabeth's Court, with villages, forts, and throne rooms all thrown in.

Though there was the challenge of a mid-twentieth-century playwright trying to pen Elizabethan dialogue, the play itself was probably entertaining to watch. There was also language that would be deemed politically incorrect by today's sensibilities; for example, in her stage direction and background information, Fiske often referred to the Indians as savages. Nevertheless, Fiske had a nice way of heightening the drama, tying up loose ends, and pulling the audience along.

The main character was Eleanor Dare. In the play, Eleanor's character loves just about everything. She loves her husband, Ananias, and there is a touching banter between the two that runs throughout the play about Eleanor's blue eyes. When Ananias is tortured to death by the Indians, it is her "blue eyes" that form some of his last words. Eleanor also loves her daughter, Virginia, and is overcome with despair when the Indians kill Virginia and Eleanor hears her daughter's tortured last words: "Mummy, why don't you come? He hurts me. You ought to come! (It ends in a shuddering scream.)" She also loves her fellow colonists and has Stones carved so their burial places will not be forgotten. She loves her father, John White, and through the Stones begs for him to find her. She loves England, but she also loves this wild new country, despite her troubles in it.

Another important character was Manteo, the Croatoan Indian who went to England with an earlier expedition and returned in the company of the colonists in 1587. Fiske portrayed him as a complex man, both sinister and helpful. He despises the colonists for their refusal to accept their new world on its own terms. Most of the colonists' problems, as Manteo saw it, are of their own making, including their refusal to take his advice seriously. Nevertheless, it falls to him to pull them out of the fire. It is Manteo who warns the abandoned colonists of an impending Indian attack. He suggests they go to his home island of Croatoan, where they will be safe. Once they arrive there, he warns them not to leave, as they are surrounded by enemy Indians.

After about a year on Croatoan, Fiske has the Colonists make a fatal separation, creating the contingent of twenty-four unfortunate men and women that were mentioned on the original Chowan Stone. One of the Colonists has been badly burned and needs medical attention. They remember a medicine chest Governor John White left buried on Roanoke with his other possessions. Disregarding Manteo's instructions, two dozen, including Eleanor, Ananias, and Virginia, thinking of it as a pleasant outing, take a small boat back to Roanoke where they dig up the chest. However, as the party sails back to Croatoan, the boat wrecks and the twenty-four find themselves stranded on the mainland, within the clutches of unfriendly Indians.

Seemingly just in time, Manteo appears among them. He berates them. "You were told stay at Croatoan. Because you would not, some die already. Many more will — since like young dogs you English have to play." Instead of taking them back to Croatoan Island, Manteo takes them southwest. "To a hilltop I will take you. Suns to the westward, it is. Nearer our own great lodgment which lies in a fertile valley. There our crafts and arts do flourish. Yes, and we are better governed. There they'd have obeyed my orders. East is one camp; west, another, and the hilltop lies between them. There you Englishmen may settle." So the twenty-four now truly lost Lost Colonists follow Manteo southwest to a hilltop a few miles south of what will become Greenville, South Carolina. There they are reunited with those Colonists who had remained on Croatoan but who have also been removed to the hilltop. The play, and probably

Gov. John White and his men inspect the word "CROATOAN" carved into a
tree at the abandoned fort where he last saw his daughter.

Pearce himself, was rather sketchy on how the two parties may have
reunited.

In the play, the Colonists spend a tough four years in South
Carolina. They are at the mercy of the Indians and are somewhat
terrorized by them. Several Colonists were killed during this time,
including children, often for mere slights. As One Woman tells Eleanor
in the play, "The Mulgraves and their child were killed because the little
one stuck out her tongue at the head medicine man." A First Man asks,
"Why do they hate our little children?" A Second Woman wails that
"Two years ago, and its not stopped since, the killing — little by little,
one after another, they pick us off. Our poor few are always fewer." It is
during their time in South Carolina that Eleanor orders "Henry," the
stonecutter, to make tombstones for their dead. "When we die we want a
monument. Die natural — or — murdered. We should all be mentioned,
and will be while I keep the chisel."

Then in 1591, while Manteo is away, an Indian messenger
arrives at the South Carolina camp and tells the Colonists that a ship has
come to Roanoke. A white man went to the island and saw all the goods
dug up and scattered about. He spotted the message carved into the tree
that they were going to Croatoan. The Colonists are excited and Eleanor
prevails upon the Indian to take a message back to her father, whom she
feels must now be on Croatoan Island looking for them. However, the

Indian is killed by the Medicine Man, presumably the same one that killed the Mulgrave family. The Medicine Man and his people now tie up the twenty-four Colonists. "Sails to the east — mean more you devils come. They shall not find you; we shall kill you." And so at a signal, the Indians begin the torture and killing of the twenty-four, which was recorded on the Chowan River Stone and the Eberhardt Second Stone as well. Ananias is killed, his last sight being Eleanor's blue eyes. Virginia is killed calling for her mother. Seventeen are killed before Manteo and the Cherokee "King" appear and stop the slaughter. Only seven Colonists remain alive, including Eleanor. They are untied and led southwest to the safety of a Cherokee village in northern Georgia.

There they are considered "honored prisoners" by the Indians and allowed to live peacefully for the next few years, when the story of the Stones comes to an end. "Twas the King that saved us, those who now survive," Eleanor says. "I said carve no more, but carve this once again. 'Father, seven survive hither.' Carve it again. It is another year. Tis 1593. Say that the King is very kind, and seven survive." In a final soliloquy, Fiske has Eleanor making a tenuous peace with herself and her New World. "This is my heritage. How long, O God, how long?"

While Brenau's archive holds no record of the audience's reaction, the play was probably received rather well. One wonders if Bill Eberhardt was invited to see it and what he thought. The Pearces, since it essentially told their interpretation of the Dare Stones, had to have been pleased. In fact, Fiske, in her acknowledgments, thanked President Pearce for his "personal interest" and Pearce Jr. for "his exposition on the Dares Stones and for the Elizabethan background."

But father and son probably saw in the play something much more than a production to be trotted out every May for the college commencement. The Pearces may have envisioned this not so much a sequel to Paul Green's symphonic drama, *The Lost Colony,* but as an alternate. Essentially, the Pearces intended to take the Lost Colony from North Carolina and bring it to the Atlanta area. Of course, the Pearces didn't think there was anything wrong with that. They were doing what historians do – searching out the truth. They had discovered evidence that now completed the story of what happened to the Lost Colony. It was just too bad for North Carolina if their beloved Lost Colonists left the Tar Heel State and made their way to metropolitan Atlanta. As the Pearces saw it, the story now belonged to Georgia.

There also had to be a bit of regional boosterism in it. These were the days of "Forward Atlanta," when the city was just beginning to establish itself as the economic and cultural capital of the Deep South. The home of Coca-Cola, in 1940 "Hotlanta" was the twenty-second largest city in America, with a metropolitan population of 820,000 and growing. And there was already a natural connection between the Dare Stones and Atlanta, as the first one had shown up at Emory University in 1937. And with Gainesville just about fifty miles to the northeast, the

Pearces were already strengthening ties with the city. In April 1940, the twenty-four Dare Stones went on display for several days at the city's famed downtown Biltmore Hotel. Pearce called them a "diary in stone."

The Atlanta Cyclorama (above) and a scene from its historical depiction of the Battle of Atlanta (below).

It was surely not lost on the Pearces that the city was then in the forefront of the nation's cinematic consciousness. The film adaptation of Atlantan Margaret Mitchell's novel *Gone with the Wind* had hit the big screen in December 1939 and it was a blockbuster. Set in Civil War Atlanta, the torrid on-screen romance between the scheming Scarlett O'Hara, played by Vivien Leigh, and Clark Gable's dashing Rhett Butler, was just about as hot as the incredible burning-of-Atlanta scene. The movie swept the 1939 Academy Awards, presented in February 1940 in Los Angeles.

Businesses were flocking to Atlanta, and so were visitors. A fledgling heritage tourism industry arose around the many Civil War battlefields about the city. The Cyclorama, boasting one of the largest and longest historical paintings in the world, gave visitors a 360-degree view of the Battle of Atlanta. Now the Dare Stones and the new Lost Colony play provided additional attractions. After a full day of shopping and exploring Atlanta, tourists could drive up the road to Gainesville and see what had really happened to the Lost Colony. And Atlanta was much easier to get to than Roanoke Island. If all went as planned, North Carolina was about to lose its claim to Virginia Dare and the Lost Colony.

For much of the spring and summer of 1940, the Pearces sat back at Brenau College and finalized plans for the big fall scientific symposium they hoped would authenticate the Dare Stones. The twenty-four Stones were on display at Brenau, where they could be "seen and studied by any interested persons without charge or obligation." President Pearce urged historians, geologists, and any other authority to inspect the stones. "Every facility will be afforded them, and criticism, whether favorable or adverse, is invited."

In the meantime, the Pearces conducted further field research, making a few trips to the Nacoochee Valley where the University of Georgia was undertaking archaeological excavation on an Indian mound there. Nothing turned up related to the Lost Colonists. At the same time, they publicized their interpretation of the Stones, even holding an essay contest on "The Background of English Colonization in America." About ten entries in all were received; first prize of a $600 scholarship to Brenau went to Dorothy Brewster of Meridian, Mississippi, for her submission titled "Walter Raleigh's Contribution to English Colonization in America."

It was also during this time that the Pearces, in an attempt to cover their bases, again contracted for background investigations of Eberhardt, Hammond, and Turner, the three men who had actually found the Stones. With the large number of Stones turning up, the Pearces and their friends were wise to be skeptical. Eventually, President Pearce admitted that "the former head of a very large organization with branches in all sections of the nation offered to have the three men who thus far had delivered the stones, investigated. We of course were glad to avail ourselves of this offer. After several months of careful investigation our friend's agents reported that they had been able to find no evidence of collusion."

In reality, the private eyes conducted only a cursory investigation, mainly interviewing Eberhardt and Turner and taking them at their word. No effort was made to actually tail the subjects or follow up on leads. No one really tried to locate Hammond.

For the Pearces, all seem well. They eagerly anticipated the gathering of scientists and historians in October. But there was one thing that still bothered them. While they had essentially unraveled the mystery of the Lost Colony and had assembled evidence of their trek to Georgia, the story was not fully complete. There were still seven Colonists to account for, including Eleanor Dare herself. According to her last stone, carved in 1593, the seven had been living with the Cherokee King at Hontaoase town in the Nacoochee Valley, northern Georgia. So what had happened to Eleanor and her six castaways? The story needed a final and complete ending.

* * *

Reaching England's familiar shores again in November 1587, John White now set about rescuing his colonists abandoned on Roanoke. Within days he met with Sir Walter Raleigh, explained the situation in Virginia and the trouble his colonists were facing. Raleigh readily agreed to send a relief expedition. He planned to send out immediately a speedy pinnace with supplies. That craft would soon be followed by Sir Richard Grenville, who had already been to Roanoke in 1585, with a larger fleet carrying more supplies and additional colonists. But before this expedition could be undertaken, international events interceded.

By 1587 King Philip II of Spain had grown tired of English privateers attacking his ships in the Caribbean. Spain had lost much treasure to English sea-dogs, and now he planned to do something about it. Spain set about assembling a huge armada of ships and soldiers with the intention of invading England the following summer. England got wind of King Philip's plan—and John White found himself returning home as England was gearing up for war with her continental nemesis. Already in October 1587 the Queen had issued an order forbidding any ships from leaving England until the threat of war was over.

Nevertheless, Raleigh felt confident that a mission to save the colonists abandoned in Virginia would meet with approval from the Queen and her Privy Council. He began assembling ships and supplies throughout the late winter and early spring of 1588. But toward the end of March 1588, as war seemed imminent and Grenville's fleet merely awaited a favorable wind, the Queen's Privy Council stepped in. Grenville's fleet was strictly prohibited from sailing. His ships would instead be transfered to the service of the Queen under the command of Sir Francis Drake.

Raleigh, Grenville, and White thought they still had a way to help the Roanoke colonists. According to the Privy Council's order,

Grenville and Raleigh could do what they wanted with any ships that Drake did not need. And Drake did not need all of Grenville's ships. So Raleigh selected two small craft to bring assistance to those on the other side of the Atlantic.

One of these was the Brave, a thirty-ton bark commanded by Captain Arthur Facy and on which John White would sail. The other was the Roe, a twenty-five-ton pinnace. Both ships carried supplies for the Roanoke colony as well as about fifteen or sixteen additional men and women bound for the colony.

The Brave and the Roe left Bideford on England's southwest coast on April 22, 1588. John White's bad luck followed him. Captain Facy proved to be not at all interested in rescuing the Roanoke colonists. Instead of making for Virginia, Facy immediately began attacking other ships, chasing them down, forcing them to heave to, and then looting what he could. To Facy's disgust, he gained little from these ventures. Nevertheless, over their first four days at sea, Facy's men had boarded and raided six ships. Over the following three days, from April 26 to 29, the Brave chased a 200-ton Dutch hulk, but other than a few exchanges of cannon fire, nothing came of it and both ships steered away from each other.

Sir Richard Grenville (above) and Sir Francis Drake (below).

By the first days of May 1588, with not much to show for their attacks, the Brave and the Roe now made for Madiera, an island off the coast of Portugal. The two English ships separated and the Brave was left alone. Then, on May 6, John White, Captain Facy, and the Brave became the prey. Two French ships from La Rochelle spied the Brave and gave

The great Spanish Armada, which threatened Elizabeth's throne and delayed Gov. White's return to Roanoke.

chase. The Brave, *living up to its name, fired broadside cannons at one of the French ships, but could not stop itself from being grappled and boarded. A desperate hand-to-hand fight took place which, White said, lasted for over an hour and a half. Many were killed on both sides; just about every person on the* Brave *was injured, most several times over. White himself was wounded in the head by a sword and again by a pike. He was also shot in the side of his buttocks. In the end, the* Brave *fell to the French, who looted her of just about everything. "They robbed us of all our victuals, powder, weapons and provision, saving a small quantity of biscuit to serve us scarce for England."*

Barely afloat and alive, the Brave *could only limp back to England. Rescuing the colonists at Roanoke was an impossibility. The sorry lot anchored at Bideford on May 23, 1588. Two weeks later, the* Roe *also returned to Bideford, "without performing our entended voyage for the relief of the planters in Virginia, which thereby were not a little distressed."*

On May 28, five days after White returned to England shot up and defeated, King Philip's great Spanish Armada sailed from Lisbon, bound for the English Channel. There would be no more attempts to rescue the Roanoke colonists that year, as England was fighting for its very survival. For the rest of the summer the faster English ships wreaked havoc on the lumbering Spanish galleons and merchantmen. Nature itself seemed on the English side as huge storms and raging seas forced the remnants of the Armada up and around the north of Britain and down the Irish coast. What Spanish ships weren't destroyed by the English were sunk or driven aground by the waves. Of the 130 ships and 26,000 Spanish soldiers and sailors who left Spain that May of 1588, only sixty-seven ships and 10,000 men returned home. It was a devastating defeat for Spain.

Though England was now safe, 1589 was another wasted year from John White's perspective. No ships were sent out to bring relief to the Roanoke colonists. It would not be until early 1590 that White could persuade Raleigh to send out another rescue expedition to Roanoke.

This time there would be no more colonists dispatched, just a few supplies and the hope the Roanoke colonists could be brought back to England.

In April, Governor John White sailed with Captain Abraham Cocke on the Hopewell, *bound for the Caribbean and then up to his charges on Roanoke Island. Captain Edward Spicer of the* Moonlight *caught up with the* Hopewell *in the Caribbean on July 2. For the rest of the month, the ships prowled the Caribbean, taking any available Spanish prizes. Then they began their true mission of going to Roanoke. July 28 found the ships off the Florida coast. By August 13, they*

White was aboard the Hopewell when it returned to Roanoke.

had anchored off Croatan Island. Then on the evening of August 15, the two ships lay off the barrier island to the east of Roanoke. It was then that White spied the column of smoke over Roanoke that he thought was a signal from the colonists.

It would not be until three days later, August 18 and the third birthday of his grand-daughter Virginia Dare, that White would actually set foot on Roanoke Island. And it was then he would discover all his colonists missing, their houses carefully taken down and removed, his own personal items dug up and scattered about, the clues directing him back to Croatan.

But weather would keep White from ever making it to Croatoan. White would never see his family or his colonists again, nor would any other Englishman. The colony was lost. Their fate would become one of the great mysteries of American history.

CHAPTER 8

Eleanor among the Indians

If the Pearces needed to know what happened to the seven survivors at Hontaoase, then Bill Eberhardt wasn't going to come up short. In August 1940 he showed up on the Brenau campus with three more stones. He said he had found them on the banks of the Chattahoochee in Fulton County about ten miles north of Atlanta, south of Gainesville and much further south than the Nacoochee Valley.

The Pearces were a little peeved at Eberhardt for once again removing the stones from their setting. Even worse, he had cleaned them with a wire brush. It was essential for professionals to get a look at the stones where they lay in their natural state. Nevertheless, Eberhardt was willing to take the Pearces to the place where he found the stones. "We were shown the places where three of them had lain. One of them, about 2-1/2 feet long, twelve inches wide and three inches thick had been standing fifteen inches deep in the ground," President Pearce wrote. "The stone fitted exactly into the hole which had been left. Several stones were found in the same vicinity, by the same man, but we were not shown the exact spots where they were found."

Nevertheless, despite their express instructions, when the Pearces arrived at the site, just four miles from Eberhardt's home, Eberhardt handed them four additional stones he'd recently found. He also led them to a cave on the banks of the Chattahoochee and showed the Pearces an inscription carved on an inside ledge:

Eleanor Dare
Heyre sithence 1593

Within days, the Pearces had deciphered the inscriptions, and what they read astounded them. As they announced in their August 18, 1940, press release, these eight new Dare Stones, "if authentic, record the removal of the colonists from north of Gainesville to a point within ten miles of Atlanta, and the final death and burial of Eleanor Dare, mother of Virginia Dare, on the Chattahoochee River, in 1599." But there was much more. One of the new Stones also stated that the Indian king who had rescued the seven colonists had taken Eleanor as his wife in 1593. And if that was not enough, Eleanor Dare had given birth to a daughter by him. So much for the ending of Maude Fiske's play and Eleanor carving no more.

The seven new Fulton County Stones, eight including the one in the cave, bore carved inscriptions only on one side, but the inscriptions were all the same style as those on the other twenty-three stones found either by Eberhardt and Turner. Again, the Pearces added them to the Stones they already had and numbered them sequentially.

Stone Number 25 read: *heyr laeth eleanor dare 1599 seaven heyr sithence 1593.* This was Eleanor's tombstone. "Here layeth Eleanor Dare, 1599." But the last bit of the inscription left a little more information: "seven here since 1593." But where was "heyr?" Did it mean they had been at the Indian king's village of Hontaoase since 1593, or living in the cave in present-day Fulton County since 1593? Of even more importance was that this was the first Stone definitely not carved or dictated by Eleanor Dare. The style of this Stone's inscription, similar to its predecessors, proved that the carver had to have lived on after Eleanor.

Stone Number 26: *Father shew moche mercye tow greate salvage lodgement Ther King hab mee tow wife sithence 1593 eleanor dare 1595.* This Stone made an astounding revelation: "Their King has me to wife since 1593. Eleanor Dare 1595." Eleanor Dare, widow of Ananias Dare, had been taken as a wife by the Indian king two years ago in 1593. Now part of an Indian family, she also asked her father to "show much mercy to the great savage lodgment," the Indian town.

Stone Number 27: *Father sithence c 1593 wee hab manye salvage looke for you eleanor dare 1598.* This stone, like so many before it, was merely a note to her father, advising him that people, in this case,

Indians, were searching for him. "Father, since c. 1593 we have many savages looking for you. Eleanor Dare, 1598."

Stone Number 28: *Father I beseeche yov hab mye dowter goe to englande Eleanor dare 1598*. Here was another shocker. "Father, I beseech you to have my daughter go to England, Eleanor Dare, 1598." We know Virginia Dare was killed in 1591. There were too many Stones that announced it or served as her tombstone. So Eleanor must have had another child, another daughter while she was the wife of the Indian king. But Eleanor doesn't want her daughter to remain among the Indians. She adds more pressure to her father, urging him to take her daughter back to England. While this may at first seem a testament to Eleanor's racial beliefs that she did not want her child reared among "savages," in reality it may well have been a part of Southeastern Indians' matrilineal kinship system. Children were born into their mother's clan and their descent and kinship was traced only through their mother's side of the family. A child was a citizen of the Cherokee people through its mother. But Eleanor was an outsider. She belonged to no Cherokee clan or lineage, so to the Cherokees, Eleanor's daughter, despite being the daughter of the Indian King, was not really a part of that nation. Eleanor may have understood this and knew her daughter might not be accepted there.

Stone Number 29: *Father hab mercye Eleanor dare 1595*. "Father, have mercy. Eleanor Dare, 1595." Another plea from a daughter. Was she asking for her father to show mercy to her by finding her, or was this another request for him to show mercy to her husband's Indian people?

Stone Number 30: *Father I hab moche svddiane sickene s Eleanor Dare 1599*. She is recording the illness that would probably take her life. "Father, I have much sudden sickness. Eleanor Dare 1599."

Stone Number 31: *Father hab salvage shew yov greate rocke by trale Eleanor Dare 1599*. Another set of instructions to her father. "Father, have the savages show you the great rock by the trail. Eleanor Dare, 1599." In this case, the "great rock" seemed to mean the cave on the Chattahoochee near Atlanta where one of Eleanor's inscriptions was found carved into the wall.

Eberhardt, it appeared, had landed the big prize with these seven stones and the cave inscription. Discovering that Eleanor Dare had married a Cherokee chief and had a daughter by him, and discovering her tombstone as well, that was big news, and the papers played it up.

Now Eberhardt began to get his share of publicity. The *Atlanta Constitution* ran a story on this "Farmer – Fisherman – Archeologist." The paper touted him as just a down-home Georgia country boy, an overalls archaeologist who just "may go down in history. He's the man who looks like a Georgia farmer and yet is causing as much excitement as did Lord Carnavan [*sic*] when he opened the tomb of King Tutankhamen." The paper was amazed that the mystery of the Lost Colony could be solved by such a simple man, who lived in an "unpainted, two-room cottage . . . [with] windows covered with tar paper and is littered with soiled clothes, empty tobacco sacks, and remnants of the night before's meal." Eberhardt even took the *Constitution* reporters to the cave and showed them Eleanor Dare's inscription that she had been living there since 1593.

Eberhardt's new stones closed Eleanor's story, but opened up another: what of her child and the six other surviving colonists? What became of them? So Eberhardt continued searching for stones, reasoning that if Eleanor had lived in the cave for the six years prior to her death, then there might be more stones scattered about that area. He began using the cave as his base of operations and scouted out from there.

Once again, Eberhardt's luck held. In September he discovered another thirteen Stones along the Chattahoochee River, only a few miles from his Atlanta home. As was his way, Eberhardt chose not to leave them in place, but delivered the Stones piecemeal to the Pearces throughout the month. Amazingly, except for one, Eberhardt seemed to find the Stones in dated order. As with all the Stones found by Eberhardt, these thirteen had inscriptions which all looked similar, showing that all the Stones except for the original Chowan River Stone had been carved seemingly by the same hand. All these were carved only on one side. As usual, the Pearces numbered them sequentially as they came in.

Stone Number 32 read: *I hab moche sickeness Eleanor Dare* [Stone broken here.] This was a stone fragment, so no date was available. Eleanor was again taking the time to dictate to the stone cutter that she was sick. "I have much sickness. Eleanor Dare."

Stone Number 33: *Father some amange vs pvtt manye message fo yov bye trale Eleanor Dare 1598*. This is another message to her father telling him to keep an eye out for more stones. "Father, some among us put many messages for you by the trail. Eleanor Dare, 1598."

Stone Number 34: (Fragment) *many yeere yov com heyr Eleanor Dare 1599*. This stone was also a fragment with only part of the message available. ". . .many years you come here, Eleanor Dare, 1599." This appears to be another message to her father, again stating the obvious that it had been many years since she has seen him and wants him to come to the cave for her.

Stone Number 35: *Father I hab dowter heyr al save salvage king angrie Eleanor Dare 1595*. This was a strange inscription. "Father, I have a daughter here. But all are angry except the savage King. Eleanor Dare, 1595." The message is for her father, again telling him that she has a daughter born here. However, all the Indians in the King's town are angry about something, though the King himself is not. The stone seems to imply that the Indian people were angry about the King having a daughter with Eleanor or at least him taking a refugee woman as a wife. Was this anger the reason the King sent Eleanor to live in a cave on the Chattahoochee?

Stone Number 36 was not an Eberhardt find. William Bruce, an Atlanta grocer, had been reading about Eberhardt's discoveries in the newspapers. He contacted the Pearces in Gainesville and told them that he'd found a stone with strange markings on it in Fulton County, just north of the Powers Ferry Bridge, not far from where he lived. The Pearces looked it over and saw the inscription looked the same as the stones Eberhardt had been finding. They deciphered the message, declared it to be a Dare Stone, and gave it number 36.

Bruce's **Stone Number 36** read: *Anye Englishman shew John White dowter bvrie vppon great hil 1599*. Not only was this Stone found by someone other than Eberhardt, this was the second Stone not to be dictated by Eleanor Dare, the first being Stone Number 25, Eleanor's tombstone. So the stone cutter must have inscribed this on his own. Rather than an address to John White, it asks that "any Englishmen, show John White that his daughter is buried upon the great hill, 1599." So Eleanor's death in 1599 was again mentioned and her father told that her body was buried on the "great hill." This great hill appears to be the same hill as that of her cave home.

Stone 37 was a joint discovery by Eberhardt and Isaac Turner. They found it on Ball's Creek, near the Chattahoochee River in Fulton County. Turner had already found Stone Number 15 back in March 1939 while hunting in Hall County, Georgia. He'd been paid by Pearce and since then had continued searching. He now recalled that as a boy near

Roswell, Georgia, he had hung around a mill owned by the Jett family. There had been a stone at the mill which had strange markings on it which no one could make out. It looked like it had "8's" on it, but everybody just considered the characters "Indian writing." Though the mill was long gone, Turner thought that the stone at the mill might be a Dare Stone. He took the Pearces and Bill Eberhardt out to the old mill site where they all scoured the area but couldn't find anything. But Turner and Eberhardt weren't about to give up. The next week the two men, Turner and Eberhardt without the Pearces, returned to the old mill site. Amazingly, they found Stone 37 in a nearby ditch, only fifty yards from where the mill once stood.

Stone Number 37, found by Turner and Eberhardt near Roswell in Fulton County, September 1940, read: *Any Englishman Shew John White Eleanor Dare & salvage kinge ha* (incomplete). "Any Englishman, show John White that Eleanor Dare and the savage king ha. . ." Have what? Have done what? The message ended there in mid-sentence, as if "the carver was apparently interrupted at this point for there is sufficient space on the stone to have completed the sentence," Pearce later wrote. "Was he killed or his work interrupted by some sudden Indian attack or other reason to leave the vicinity?"

Eberhardt was back on his own when he found the next few Stones in September 1940. These were near the cave on the Chattahoochee in Fulton County, just north of Atlanta.

Stone Number 38 reads: *heyr laeth william withers heedye of brief sicknesse 1599.* Other than Eleanor's, this was the first tombstone found in awhile and after Eleanor, the next of the seven Lost Colony survivors to die. "Here layeth William Withers, he die of a brief sickness, 1599." A William Wythers was listed as a boy on the 1587 colonists' roster, though no adult Wythers or Withers was listed. He may have been an orphan or a servant boy and so was attached to another family. Though he had survived the Indian attacks, now he was dead of an illness in the same year Eleanor died. Now only five Lost Colony survivors remained, not counting Eleanor's daughter.

Stone Number 39, found by Eberhardt in Fulton County, September 1940, read: *He aet Robe Lis 1599.* It appears that some of the letters were either not put into the inscription or were so light or weathered they could not be seen. The Pearces believed it should be translated as "Heyr laeth Robert Ellis, 1599." If so, then that made it another tombstone. There was a Robert Ellis listed as a boy on the 1587 roster, while there was an adult listed as Thomas Ellis. Possibly they were father and son. So it appeared that a second of the seven survivors had been a child, and now three were dead and accounted for.

Stone Number 40: *heyr laeth Henry Berry hee hab sickness growen vppon him 1601.* "Here lies Henry Berry. He had sickness growing upon him. 1601." This is the first of the stones to move into the seventeenth century, fourteen years after the colonists had been left at Roanoke and ten years after the great massacre of Ananias and Virginia Dare. Henry Berry was also listed on the 1587 roster. Four of the seven survivors had died.

Stone Number 41: *shew John White Thomas Elis Slaine heyr 1601.* Seemingly addressed to anyone who finds the Stone: "Show John White that Thomas Elis was slain here, 1601." A Thomas Ellis listed was on the 1587 roster. He was probably the father of Robert Ellis, whose death from sickness had been recorded on Stone Number 39. Only two of the seven survivors remained.

Stone Number 42: *Griffen Jones James Lasie Agnes Dare 1602.* A very intriguing stone that does not appear to be a tombstone, as it accounts for the two remaining survivors and an extra. The last two Lost Colonists left alive were Griffen Jones and James Lasie, both who were listed on the 1587 roster. One of these two men had to be the stone carver. We also now meet Agnes, the daughter of Eleanor Dare and the Indian king. Agnes appears to have been born in 1595, possibly in the cave on the Chattahoochee. She would be about seven years old in 1602.

Stone Number 43: *Heyr James Lassie dye 1602.* The last of the tombstones. "Here James Lasie died, 1602." This revelation left only Griffen Jones as the last survivor of the Lost Colonists. He all along had been the carver of all the Dare Stones, save the original Chowan Stone. It could only be Jones who could carve these last tombstones whose inscriptions are the same as those on all the other stones found outside of North Carolina. It also marks one of the great coincidences in history in that the one person who carved the stones and so kept a record of the Lost Colony would be the very last survivor. Who could imagine that after all the attacks, sickness, and accidents that the stone carver would outlive everyone to preserve a record to the very end?

Stone Number 44: *Griffen Jones & Agnes Dare heyr 1603.* This was the last stone chronologically. So here the story of the Lost Colony ended, with "Griffen Jones & Agnes Dare here, 1603." Exactly where is not known. Probably the cave on the Chattahoochee as Eberhardt found it in that vicinity. The Lost Colony was down to these two. All Colonists mentioned in the Stones had been accounted for with Griffen Jones, the stone carver, and Agnes Dare, the eight-year-old daughter of Eleanor and the Indian king, alone and waiting to be found by John White or any Englishman.

Over the next few weeks, a few more rocks arrived in Gainesville, which the Pearces declared as Dare Stones. They were numbered into the Brenau collection. Stone Number 45 was found by William Bruce, who had found Stone Number 36 near the Powers Ferry Bridge in Fulton County about fifteen miles north of Atlanta. Buoyed by finding his first stone, Bruce kept searching, and in September 1940 found a second Dare Stone near the bridge, in the same vicinity as his first.

Stone Number 45 read: *She oh Eleanor dye February dowter name Agnes heyr Grifen Jone 1599*. "Show John White that Eleanor Dare died in February. Her daughter's name is Agnes. Here is Griffen Jones, 1599." Another testament to Eleanor's death in 1599, but now we are told that it was in February. Chronologically, it would be the first time Eleanor's daughter's name – Agnes – was given. It would also seem to be a gravestone for Griffen Jones. But this cannot be as we have just seen, Jones's name appears on later stones and everything pointed to Griffen Jones as being the stonecutter who inscribed all the Stones save that on the Chowan River.

The next stone, Stone Number 46, was an amazing find. The strange circumstances of its discovery appeared to authenticate the Stones and absolve Eberhardt and all other finders of being in on a hoax. It certainly convinced Pearce that he was actually on the trail of the survivors of the Lost Colony. It would later convince more historical heavyweights than Pearce that the Stones were authentic.

After Eberhardt and Turner had found Stone Number 37 at the old Jett Mill near Roswell, Georgia, they had decided to go down and talk to Jett himself. Tom Jett and his family had once owned the mill near Roswell, but about fifteen years earlier, in the mid-1920s, the Jetts had left Roswell and moved to a farm south of Atlanta. When Turner and Eberhardt brought Stone Number 37 to him to see if he could identify it as the one that had been around his old mill, Jett immediately recognized it. But Jett really got the two rock hunters interested when he told Turner and Eberhardt there had been another stone there with strange carvings on it. His brother had found it near the river and brought it up to the homestead. Though they noticed the strange carvings on the stone, no one could read them, so they broke the stone in half and used one part as a support for a barn post. Jett led Turner and Eberhardt back to their old property near Roswell, which was now occupied by Jett's nephew, Henry Campbell. Campbell said he didn't know anything about any stones and besides, the old barn had been torn down years ago.

Discouraged, the three returned to the Jett farm south of Atlanta. While the trio were sitting around the table, Mrs. Jett came in and asked what they were talking about. The three told her the story of the Dare Stones and their search for them. Then Mrs. Jett remembered that when they had moved from the old mill fifteen years earlier, she had found a stone with strange carvings on it and had thrown it into her father's tool chest. He was a railroad man and kept a huge chest full of tools that he used for working on railroad cars. As far as she knew it was still in her father's chest in Jonesboro, Georgia, just south of Atlanta. They all drove over to Jonesboro, found Mrs. Jett's father's tool chest and, sure enough, there was the fragment of Dare Stone in almost perfect condition.

Now they just needed the other half of that Stone. It had held up a barn post, and though the barn was gone, the stone might still be lying around somewhere on the property. Turner went back to the old Jett place and met again with Henry Campbell. The two men spent a couple of hours down at the riverbank, where Campbell fished while Turner filled him in on the Dare Stones. After a while, Campbell remembered that last year while plowing his corn, he'd picked up a large rock along the road to use as weight on his cultivator. When he'd finished plowing, he threw the rock back into the weeds alongside the road. But he didn't notice any markings or anything on it. Turner excused himself, saying it was time to go, and walked back up to the house. But instead of leaving, he began searching the ditches alongside the road near the house. His luck was as good as Eberhardt's. He "found the half stone lying almost covered by grass and weeds."

Turner now raced back to the Jett farm to match the fragment with that one found by Mrs. Jett in her father's tool box in Jonesboro. The two pieces, found fifty miles and fifteen years apart, joined up perfectly to create **Stone Number 46**, which read: *Father wee dweelde in great rocke ppon river near heyr Eleanor Dare 1598.* This was another message from Eleanor to her father in the year before she died. "Father, we dwelt in great rock upon the river near here. Eleanor Dare,

1598." She was again telling him that she was living in the cave along the Chattahoochee and he should look there.

Stone Number 47 was actually found back in August 1940. It was the inscription carved on the rock ledge in the wall of the cave on the Chattahoochee, where Eleanor Dare had lived for several years before she died. **Stone Number 47** read: *Eleanor Dare Heyr sithence 1593.*

So by October 1940, just in time for the big scientific conference, Brenau boasted forty-seven Dare Stones. Five people had been involved in finding them. Louis Hammond of California had found the first one on the Chowan River in North Carolina in August 1937. Bill Eberhardt of Atlanta had found a total of forty-one stones, thirteen on the Saluda River in South Carolina; nine in Habersham County, Georgia north of Gainesville; and nineteen in Fulton County, a few miles north of Atlanta and centered around a cave on the Chattahoochee. Isaac Turner of Atlanta had found three stones: one on the Chattahoochee, north of Gainesville, and another on Ball's Creek at the old Jett place in Fulton County when Eberhardt had been with him. He was also involved in finding the broken Stone Number 46, with one part found by Turner on the Jett homeplace and the other in Mrs. Jett's father's tool chest in Jonesboro. William Bruce found two stones in Fulton County near the Powers Ferry Bridge over the Chattahoochee.

Depending on how one read them, the Stones accounted for between sixty-two and sixty-four colonists who died in North Carolina and South Carolina, though only fifty-one names were listed. Still, these numbers accounted for a little over half of the total number of Lost Colonists, set at 117. So there would have to be many more dead colonists who either received no tombstone or the stone was yet to be found. Six colonists were listed as having died in Georgia, including Eleanor Dare. The last survivor of the Lost Colonists was Griffen Jones, the carver of all the Stone inscriptions except for that on the Chowan Stone. Naturally, when he died, there would be no tombstone for him.

So the mystery of the Lost Colony had been solved. Many of the colonists had been killed by Indians or disease as they slowly made their way from Roanoke Island to Croatoan Island to South Carolina. At South Carolina, the remnant of the Lost Colony had been viciously attacked by Indians and only seven survived. These seven, with the help of friendly Indians, made their way to a Cherokee village in the Chattahoochee River Valley of northern Georgia. Eleanor had married the chief and gave birth to a daughter, Agnes. But at some point, the seven survivors were finally moved to a cave overlooking the Chattahoochee in the Atlanta area. Eleanor Dare had died in February 1599. The remaining survivors, except for Griffen Jones and the child Agnes, died off soon after.

It was an epic story, for which all Pearce needed was the archaeological evidence to back it up. He was sure that uncovering such evidence was just a matter of time. Until then, an examination of the Stones by the top academics in the country would have to suffice. If the Stones got the stamp of approval from them, then the mystery of the Lost Colony would be as close to settled as it could be without finding the actual remains of the Lost Colonists.

* * *

When he stepped again on English soil in October 1590, John White was a beaten man. He had come so close to rescuing the colonists, only to experience defeat at every turn. His family was lost, and he would never see them again. He was alone, an orphaned parent. He would make no more crossings to America. After his return, White moved to Newtown in County Cork, Ireland, to live as a tenant on one of Raleigh's estates. But not a day went by that he did not think of his family lost in the wilds of what they called Virginia.

In a last letter, White wrote miserably, "I would to God my wealth were answerable to my will. Thus committing the reliefe of my discomfortable the planters in Virginia, to the merciful help of the Almighty, whom I most humbly beseech to helpe & comfort them, according to his most holy will & their good desire."

Though White himself soon disappeared from history, his influence did not. His pictures of coastal North Carolina and its Indians became celebrated in England and so kept the fate of the Lost Colonists alive in the minds of the English people. All across England, people wondered what had happened to them.

If White was beaten, so was Sir Walter Raleigh, who had sponsored the Roanoke voyages. As a courtier to Queen Elizabeth I, his star had been at its zenith in the early 1580s. He had been one of the Queen's favorites, maybe even her lover, and she had supported his Roanoake ventures. But his Roanoke failures were not only a blow to Raleigh's finances, they also took a toll on his prestige. Whispers about the Queen's court said the whole Lost Colony disaster had been a plot to bring Raleigh down. *Master Fernandez's abandoning the colonists at deadly Roanoke instead of taking them to the Chesapeake seemed a work of sabotage. They pointed to Sir Francis Walsingham, the Queen's spymaster, Fernandez's employer, and no friend of Raleigh. But proof was impossible to come by. No matter, whether the Roanoke expedition had been sabotaged or had failed due to incompetence and bad luck, Raleigh's star began to wane. It fell even further when he married Bess Throckmorton without the Queen's permission. He soon found himself briefly imprisoned in the Tower of London. The Queen relented and released her onetime favorite, but Raleigh's time had passed. The Queen had moved on to other favorites. He found himself spending less and less time at court. He could do nothing to rescue the Lost Colonists. In fact, he would have nothing more to do with English colonization in North America.*

King James I.

In a way, Raleigh was as lost as his colonists. He found himself without a benefactor when Queen Elizabeth I died in 1603. Even worse, the new English monarch, King James I, actively disliked Raleigh and believed he'd once plotted to drive him from the throne. By early summer 1603, James had imprisoned Raleigh in the Tower of London. There the Queen's knight would languish for thirteen years. James released Raleigh in 1616 and allowed him to make an expedition to Guyana in South America. While searching for the mythical city of El Dorado, Raleigh's expedition sacked the Spanish outpost of Santo Thomé de Guayana on the Orinoco River. When the expedition returned to England and word of the attack leaked out, Spain's ambassador to England complained to James about Raleigh's attack on Spanish lands and insisted the King put Raleigh to death. James, wanting to keep peace with Spain and happy to get rid of a thorn in his side, agreed. Raleigh was arrested and beheaded at Whitehall on October 29, 1618.

Keeping his humor to the end, when showed the axe that would take his head, Raleigh supposedly said, "It is sharp and fair medicine, to cure me of all my diseases." It certainly cured Raleigh of backing colonial failures.

Fifteen years after White's unsuccessful 1590 rescue attempt, in 1605, while Raleigh sat in the Tower, a play titled Eastward Ho *was performed in London. In one scene of this comedy, a coterie of characters decide to go to Virginia for the adventure of it all. When one asked whether Virginia was already inhabited by*

The execution of Sir Walter Raleigh.

Englishmen, another replied "A whole country of English is there, man, bred of those that were left there in '87; they have married with the Indians, and make 'hem bring forth as beautiful faces as any we have in England." Though English authorities officially declared the Lost Colonists dead in 1597, most of England believed the Lost Colonists were just lost among the Indians, awaiting rescue. And England desperately wanted to rescue its missing people.

It would take almost twenty years for the next rescue attempt. In 1607, England sent another colonization effort to the Americas. This time it did what the Lost Colonists on Roanoke could not. First, this expedition actually made it to its proper destination. In April 1607, three ships of the Virginia Company, the Susan Constant, *the* Discovery, *and the* Godspeed *nosed into Chesapeake Bay. They sailed up the James River about forty miles, far from the searching eyes of the Spanish, and on the north bank of the river, the ships deposited a group of colonists who built a warehouse and a stockade. They named their new colony Jamestown after James I, King of England. Jamestown would survive, barely, where the Roanoke colonies did not, and so would become the first permanent English colony in America. The men at Jamestown were to create an English outpost in America and bring in a tidy profit for the investors of the Virginia company. But it also had a secondary mission, to locate the Lost Colonists of Roanoke. Or at least find out what happened to them.*

CHAPTER 9

Preponderance of the Evidence

Professor Haywood Pearce Jr. was ready at that moment to declare the Dare Stones as authentic, all forty-seven of them. He firmly believed the upcoming scientific conference would prove it. While he might have sometimes doubted Eberhardt and his ability to find stones almost on command, Pearce was ultimately convinced by Mrs. Jett's stone-in-the-toolbox. As Pearce had been told, it had lain in the toolbox for fifteen years, long before Eberhardt had come along. "If hoax it is," Pearce was quoted, "the hoax is more incredible, more fantastic than the story itself." Now he'd have the academics take a look and they'd be just as convinced.

In their invitations to the scholars, the Pearces told a brief version of the Stones. They also pointed out that on one Stone, lichen partially covered three letters. "These lichens are well known to be of very slow growth – hence the carving must have been done many years ago." So a select group of historians and scientists were invited to come to Brenau College for a noon meeting on Saturday, October 19, 1940. At that meeting, Haywood Pearce Jr. of Emory University and Brenau College would fill them in on the finding of the Dare Stones. After that, participants would have the chance to inspect the Stones and then there would be another 8 p.m. meeting "to discuss the problems raised by the stones." The next morning, a "special group of invited guests" would be taken to the cave on the Chattahoochee to see Eleanor's carving on the rock ledge. As an added inducement, the invitation announced that "Dr. S. E. Morison, Head Professor at Harvard University has accepted an invitation to preside at this meeting."

The academic glitterati began arriving at Brenau around October 18. Eventually thirty-four of America's best and brightest historians, geologists, ethnologists, archaeologists, linguists, and other experts gathered at the tiny women's college. Some of those attending included Drs. E. M. Coulter of the University of Georgia; J. Harris Purks, Robert E. Mitchell, Garland G. Smith, Thomas English, R. H. McLean, and J. F. Messick, all of Emory University in Atlanta; Robert Wauchope of the University of North Carolina; Count Gibson, a geologist at Georgia Tech, and C. C. Crittenden of the North Carolina Historical Commission.

Headlining the gathering was Samuel Eliot Morison, chair of the Department of American History at Harvard, president of the American Antiquarian Society, and exposer of historical frauds. Born in 1882, a son of the Boston upper crust, Morison received a privileged education and graduated from Harvard in 1908. Continuing his studies, he received his Ph.D. in history from Harvard in 1912 and returned there as a history instructor in 1915. He would remain connected to Harvard for the rest of his life, rising up through the ranks to become full professor and head of the history department. Up to 1940, Morison's most famous works were *The Oxford History of the United States* in 1927 and, with Henry Steele Commager, *The Growth of the American Republic* in 1930. His major works were yet to come. His biography of Columbus, *Admiral of the Ocean Sea,* would be published in 1942, two years after his trip to Gainesville. By the time of his death in 1975, Morison would be one of America's most celebrated historians, the winner of two Pulitzer Prizes, two Bancroft Prizes, and the Presidential Medal of Freedom. In 1940, his status as the head Americanist from Harvard lent tremendous stature to the Brenau Conference.

Finally, at noon on Saturday, October 19, with academics, newspaper reporters, and interested laymen in attendance, Pearce gave his talk on the Stones. He presented both the good and the bad. Several things challenged the Stones' authenticity. Here were forty-seven stones, supposedly lying around the region for three hundred fifty years, and had only now come to light. No other physical evidence accompanied the Stones: no bones, no artifacts, no structures. And finally, how could these carved inscriptions be made so long ago and in the middle of a wilderness?

To complicate matters, during the conference, Eberhardt's past finally caught up with him. Word now got out, probably announced by Pearce, that the stone finder had once been implicated in the selling of forged Indian artifacts.

On the side favoring the Stones' authenticity, Pearce said that the story the Stones told seem to be in "perfect harmony with facts related by history." This may have been circular reasoning on Pearce's part, as the only historical evidence that put the Lost Colonists in South Carolina or Georgia had been the stones themselves. As proof of the Stones' authenticity, he pointed to the three letters on Stone Number 37, found by Eberhardt and Turner on the old Jett place that had lichen growing over part of them. But best evidence was Stone Number 46, half of which had reportedly been found on the old Jett place and the other half in Mrs. Jett's father's toolbox. Finally, the thirty-four experts were left to inspect the Stones before the closed-door session began at eight.

Rear Admiral Samuel Eliot Morison, who later became America's most noted historian.

Crittenden of the North Carolina Historical Commission reported that the evening session went on for more than three hours with many questions asked and experts weighing in. "A geologist testified as to the types of the stones, as to the probable age of the inscriptions, as to the tools which might have been used to do the cutting, etc. A linguist discussed the type of letters used, the wording the inscriptions, and similar matters," Crittenden wrote a friend. "We also had before us a man named Jett, who testified that he had known one of the stones when he was a small boy, when it had been at his father's grist mill."

At the end of that meeting a committee was appointed to draft a statement on the Stones that could be issued to the Press. Those appointed were Samuel Eliot Morison of Harvard as chair; Dr. Thomas H. English of Emory University as secretary; Dr. Andrew L. Pickens, dean of the Paducah, Kentucky Junior College; Dr. C. C. Harrold, president of the Georgia Society for Archaeology; and Dr. C. C. Crittenden of the North Carolina Historical Commission. The next day all thirty-four scholars went out to Eleanor's cave on the Chattahoochee to look at the inscribed rock ledge. They also had a nice catered lunch, with the Atlanta skyline in the distance as backdrop.

Apparently that afternoon the committee hammered out its statement, which was approved by all in attendance. Most important in its findings was the statement that the committee "believes that the preponderance of the evidence points to the authenticity of the stones." The group, however, did not consider this the last word. "Suggestions for further study of the stones are being made by the committee to Dr. Pearce. Until this investigation is concluded, no final conclusion can be reached."

Nor was the prevailing opinion wholly unanimous. Even Professor Morison thought the Stones were authentic, but he still had "certain doubts, mainly personal, that can't be uttered yet." As Morison told the reporters, the Stones are "either one of the most stupendous discoveries or stupendous hoaxes in American history."

In less than a month, on November 12, the Conference Advisory Committee of Morison, English, Crittenden, Harrold, and Pickens sent a list of twelve suggestions that Pearce should follow up before the Stones could definitely be declared authentic:

> **(1)** The search for graves, skeletal remains, and other possible relics should be resumed as soon and pursued as thoroughly as possible.
> **(2)** The fraudulent proposals in connection with the Roanoke celebration of 1937, and the reported connection of Mr. Eberhardt with the sale of dubious Indian relics should be exhaustively probed.
> **(3)** A complete check must be made of all words and phrases found on the stones. The Oxford Dictionary will

serve as a basis for this investigation, but a special search should be made for suspect words (e.g., 'reconnoiter' and 'primaeval') in contemporary literature.

(4) A complete check must be made of all dialect or apparently dialect forms found on the stones. The English Dialect Dictionary and Grammar will be useful here. Particular attention must be paid to the consistency of dialect usages.

(5) A careful study must be made of the forms of letters on the stones. It is suggested that comparisons be made with inscriptions in stone of the period, e.g., 16th and 17th century graffiti in the London Tower and elsewhere.

(6) Further comparative study should be devoted to the names found in the inscriptions.

(7) Experts of the National Museum and of the archaeological institute at Ohio State University should be requested to study the stones for evidence of the age of the inscriptions.

(8) Topographical and ethnological maps should be made covering the regions where the stones were found and to which they relate.

(9) A genealogical study of the White and Dare families may produce clues to problems such as the name, Agnes, of Eleanor Dare's second daughter.

(10) Cooperation in this investigation should be sought from other institutions and organizations. It has been suggested that valuable advice and expert services may be obtained from the Society of Georgia Archaeology, the North Carolina Historical Commission, the Department of Archaeology of the University of North Carolina, the National Museum, the National Park Service, the Ohio State Museum, the Peabody Museum at Harvard, and from other institutions and individuals.

(11) Application should be made at once to one or more of the great foundations for money to finance further systematic investigations. The committee will gladly support such an appeal.

(12) Since it is probable that more stones will be discovered, we urge that a statement be published in the newspapers requesting that anyone who discovers a stone bearing writing or carving which might connect it with the Dare series, is requested to leave it in place and communicate with Dr. Pearce, who will then be enabled to study the stone before it has been moved, cleaned, or otherwise deprived of some of its evidential value."

The Brenau conference had been well covered by the Atlanta newspapers. The *Atlanta Constitution* ran a story titled "Scholars Study Authenticity of Dare Stones" along with a picture of Morison, Pearce, Jr., and Dr. J. F. Messick of Emory gazing at one of the Stones, magnifying glass in hand. But as the academics headed back to their respective positions, word now spread that these historians and scientists found the stones genuine. To reporters, that meant that Eleanor Dare and the Lost Colonists, or what was left of them after the Indian attacks, had wound up in Georgia. Forgetting the Advisory Committee's admonition that further investigation needed to be done and until then "no final conclusion can be reached," word that the mystery of the Lost Colony had been solved flashed to newspapers across the United States.

A sampling of clippings, retained in the Brenau archive, demonstrates the public interest in the matter. The *Waynesville (Indiana) Press*'s October 22 headline screamed "Science Gives O.K. to History of 'Lost Colony'." "Riddle of 'Lost Colony' Solved," said the *Portland (Indiana) Commercial-Review.* Even an October 21 headline in the *Raleigh News and Observer* admitted that the "Dare Stones Appear Authentic to Experts." *Newsweek* ran a short piece on the conference, quoting the conference report that the "preponderance of evidence points to the authenticity" of the Stones. Even the *Gainesville (Georgia) Eagle* crowed, "Gainesville may well become the cradle in which a new history of the America we call home will be born." The *Eagle* pointed out that the group of renowned historians and scientists "put their stamp of approval upon the stones. These authorities believe them to be true."

For Pearce, this was his moment of triumph. He had to be sitting at the top of the world during that autumn of 1940. Brenau had forty-seven Dare Stones that showed the Lost Colonists leaving North Carolina and the remnant of them winding up in Georgia. The Pearces had Eleanor Dare's tombstone. They had a play which might rival Paul

Samuel Eliot Morison (left) and Haywood Pearce Jr. (center) examine the Chowan River Dare Stone.

Green's famous North Carolina saga, *The Lost Colony*. When President Pearce heard that Paul Green was "disturbed" by the tale the Stones told, he advised that Green should "reconcile" himself to the situation and think about writing a sequel or an additional episode to *The Lost Colony*.

Pearce had sufficiently persuaded Morison and other scholars of the Stones' likely authenticity, despite the lack of archaeological evidence. Newspapers readily spread the sensational word, giving Pearce, his college, and his home state the spotlight he coveted. Not even the subsequent destruction of the inscription on the rock ledge in the cave beside the Chattahoochee persuaded the Pearces to be more cautious in their publicity. After word of the cave's location appeared in the papers, a teenaged vandal had chipped off the rock ledge bearing the inscription "Eleanor Dare Heyr sithence 1593" and stolen the stone, breaking the ledge in half in the process. Pearce was devastated. Delicate

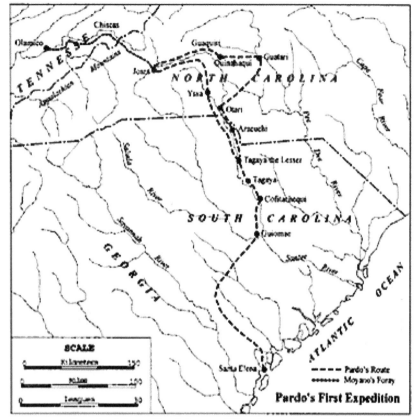

Spaniard Juan Pardo's expedition through the South.

negotiations through friends persuaded the teenager to give up the rock, however, and both pieces went to the Pearces who numbered it Stone Number 47 and displayed it among the other Dare Stones at Brenau.

To solidify their triumph, the Pearces published their third Brenau *Bulletin* devoted to the Stones on November 15, 1940. Again titled "The Dare Stones," the updated bulletin reiterated the earlier account of the Stones and their inscriptions, augmenting it with all the new information that had come to light since the previous issue, including results of the Historians' Conference.

The Pearces' good fortune was holding steady as in December Brenau acquired Stone Number 48, apparently found by Eberhardt near the cave on the Chattahoochee. He again ignored the direction to leave the stone in place until it could be archaeologically examined. The new Stone's inscription took the same form as all the other Stones found by

Eberhardt. **Stone Number 48** read: *John White manye prisoner fourtie mylles nw. Griffen Jones & Agnes Dare 1603.*

This chilling inscription seemed to be taking the Lost Colony story into a whole new direction. Forty miles to the northwest would put them in the area of present-day Cartersville, Georgia, in the vicinity of the ancient Etowah Indian Mound site, which had been occupied from about A.D. 950 to 1500. But what prisoners, and held by whom? Pearce believed that these could have been survivors of Juan Pardo's ill-fated 1567 Spanish colonization attempt of the Carolinas. Or if not that, then a later "unrecorded" 1603 expedition of Spanish gold-seekers, who, like the colonists, found themselves in Indian hands in northern Georgia. Or maybe they were the survivors of a Spanish expedition who had been sent out to search for the Lost Colonists.

Nevertheless, Brenau added this Stone to its collection, which now totaled forty-eight. Newspapers across the country took note of the latest find. Pearce reveled in this new turn the Dare Stone story was taking.

Then Professor Haywood Pearce Jr. made a critical misstep. To follow each of the twelve suggestions made by the advisory committee would take years of continuing research before the Stones could definitely be declared authentic. Pearce wasn't ready to wait that long. As he saw it, the evidence pointed to the Stones' authenticity — and that was sufficient proof. All he needed now was to get the American people to understand and accept that the mystery of the Lost Colony had been solved, and that it had led the remnants of Raleigh's colony to the Atlanta area. And the best way to do that was to get the story of the Stones published in a major popular magazine.

So in early December 1940, brushing aside the conference's recommendation that until more studies were made "no final conclusion can be reached" and ignoring all twelve points for further investigation made by the advisory committee as well, Pearce penned a manuscript about the Lost Colony, the Dare Stones, and the amazing discoveries of the past three years. In the cover letter, he explained that this was his first presentation on the three-year investigation that he and his father had done on the Dare Stones. Then he mailed it to the *Saturday Evening Post*, one of the largest and most popular American national magazines of the day, with a circulation of about 3 million readers.

*   *   *

Among those on the 1607 Jamestown expedition, Captain John Smith took seriously the orders to find the Lost Colonists. In his travels around Chesapeake Bay, Smith asked about the Lost Colonists, kept his ears open, and in doing so, kept hearing rumors of white people to the south.

On one of his expeditions Smith was captured by Opechancanough, the brother of Wahunsenacawh, the great Powhatan

Capt. John Smith.

of the Pamunkey chiefdom that dominated much of the Chesapeake Bay region. The Indians were somewhat awed and impressed with Smith, but Wahunsenacawh and Opechancanough also knew he was a dangerous adversary. Still Opechancanough treated Smith hospitably, and the two spent time talking, or communicating as best they could since neither fully understood the other's language. At some point the conversation turned toward the fate of Raleigh's Lost Colonists. Opechancanough told Smith that he knew of "certaine men cloathed at a place called Ocanahonan," *who dressed as Smith did.*

A few days later, Smith was taken to Wahunsenacawh himself. The great powhatan gave Smith a lesson on the political and geographic reality of the Indian country around the bay. Again the question arose of the lost Englishmen. "The people cloathed at Ocanahonan he also confirmed," *Smith said,* "and the Southerly Countries also, as the rest that reported us to be within a day and a halfe of Mangoge, two dayes of Chawwonock, 6 from Roonock, to the south part of the backe sea: he*

This map shows the Indian village of Occaneechee on the Chowan River.

described a country called Anone where they have abundance of Brasse,
and houses walled as ours.''

Once released by Wahunsenacawh, Smith met with
Wowinchapuncke, the powhatan of Paspahegh and a tributary of
Wahunsenacawh. This leader, too, confirmed white men living to the
south. Smith even convinced Wowinchapuncke "to conduct two of our
men to a place called Panawicke, beyond Roanoke, where he reported
many men to be appareled [like me]." The party landed on the south
bank of the James River, but Wowinchapunke deserted them after a few
days and returned home. The Englishmen do not appear to have reached
Panawicke.

Still, Smith was intrigued enough with the information that in
1608 he dispatched several search parties south into what would
eventually become North Carolina. And he sent them to the Choanoac
chiefdom down in the Chowan River area, about four days southwest of
Jamestown. He did not send searchers to Roanoke or Croatoan, the last
places associated with the Lost Colonists, nor did he send them to the
Chespian Indian villages on the south bank of Chesapeake Bay, which
had been the Lost Colonists' original destination. Michael Sicklemore
went down to the Chowan River "to seek for the lost company of Sir
Walter Raleigh's and silk grass." When he returned from the Choanoacs,

Sicklemore had "found little hope and lesse certaintie of them were left by Sir Walter Raleigh. The river, he saw was not great, the people few, the country most over growne with pynes."

This was a disturbing report as twenty years earlier, when Colonel Ralph Lane had stormed into Menatonon's Choanoac chiefdom back in 1586, he had found it large and well populated, composed of eighteen towns scattered up and down the Chowan. Menatonon's capital of Choanoke alone could put seven hundred warriors into the field. But what Sicklemore saw was a pale shadow of the Choanoac's former glory. Something terrible had happened to the Choanoacs over the past two decades.

Smith also sent out Nathanael Powell and Anas Todkill to search for the Lost Colonists in Mangoak country west of the Choanoacs, between the Chowan and Roanoke rivers. Ralph Lane, who had skirmished with the Mangoaks in 1586, saw them as a people different than the Algonquian Roanokes. They were considered some of the fiercest adversaries in the region, with a reputation as captive-takers but whose warriors could be purchased as allies with sufficient gifts. Pemisapan had tried to entice them into his plot to attack Lane's soldiers. But while the Mangoaks were warriors, they were often satisfied to trade with their neighbors. And what the Mangoaks had to trade was copper, which all Indians in the region valued. Lane said their houses were draped with copper. They also guarded the southern access to Ocaneechi town, situated on an island far up the Roanoke River. Occaneechi town — possibly the same Ocanahonan that Smith heard about from Opechancanough and Wahunsenacawh—was a trading center, well known and often visited by Indian people. But Powell and Todkill could find nothing about the Lost Colonists among the Mangoaks save that "they were all dead."

But that might not have been entirely true. Sicklemore, Powell, and Todkill did learn more about the Lost Colonists, and they reported it to Virginia Company officials. And it was sobering news. Not something that the Company wanted spread about, especially as it might make people think twice about investing in the Virginia colony. The men said that it was at "Peccarecamicke, where you shall find four of the English alive left by Sir Walter Rawley, which escaped from the slaughter of the Powhaton of Roanocke, upon the first arrival of our colony, and live under the protection of a wiroane called Gepanocon, enemy to

Powhaton, by whose consent you shall never recover them. One of these were worth much labor."

Powell and Todkill reported something similar, that "some of our nation planted by Sir Walter Raleigh yet alive within fifty miles of our fort . . . as is testified by two of our colony sent out to seek them, who, though denied by the savages speech with them, found crosses and letters, the characters and assured testimonies of Christians, newly cut in the barks of trees." Still alive but enslaved by Indians! Such news would have a chilling effect on prospective English colonists contemplating a new life in Virginia.

Captain Smith was certainly intrigued by the information his men brought back — so much so that he tried to draw a map of eastern North Carolina, complete with rivers and information on where he had heard Lost Colony survivors were being held. But Smith had never been to North Carolina and his odd map, oriented to the South, featured strangely drawn rivers and mysterious place names. Nevertheless, Smith duly recorded what he had learned. Down to the south, between a small river labeled "Pananiock" and a much larger one labeled "Morattic," he inscribed "Here the King of Paspahegh reported our men to be and wanted to go." Even further south, near the confluence of two rivers Smith calls "Caheohock" and "Pakrakwick," he noted that "Here remaineth four men clothed that came from Roonock to Ocanahonan." But where were these places? They are still a mystery.

Smith was unable to follow up on these rumors. In October 1609, he was severely burned when a careless spark set off a gunpowder keg. Returning to England for treatment, John Smith would never again return to Virginia. Scraps of tales, tantalizing hints, clues, and rumors of the lost colonists continued to trickle back to Jamestown.

C. C. Crittenden, head of the North Carolina Historical Commission, found himself helpless to prevent the public's acceptance of the Dare Stones' authenticity. Carolina Collection, University of North Carolina at Chapel Hill.

CHAPTER 10

A Blast from Tarheelia

While the Pearces were taking their victory lap, North Carolina was not yet ready to let its most sacred creation story be wrested away without a fight. As C. C. Crittenden reported, the Dare Stones had "aroused as much popular interest in North Carolina as anything which has come up since I have been in Raleigh."

Crittenden could not fault the Pearces' motives, as he believed the Georgia men were truly "conducting a serious and thorough investigation" and that they were "attempting to run down all possible clues." And though the Historical Commission director believed that right then "it would be impossible to say definitely whether the stones are authentic," he now seemed to think they were not. Repeatedly he encountered the old tale about how some fellow had prowled Roanoke Island back in 1937 offering to plant a suitcase full of fake stones so they could be "discovered." The idea was to publicize the Lost Colony aspect of Roanoke and attract tourists to the region. But even that rumor was suspect and few could agree on its details. Some said the stunt happened in 1937, but others maintained it was ten years earlier and it wasn't a box of stones, but a chest of artifacts. Tar Heels were willing to accept irrefutable evidence about the Lost Colony's journey to Georgia, but until such proof could be produced, most maintained that the Pearces were being duped and the Stones were a fraud.

North Carolina fired the first shot on October 24, 1940, just days after the Brenau Conference broke up. Bill Sharpe, editor of the Winston-Salem news magazine *Thursday,* opined "Dare Stones a Hoax That Is Too Good." Sharpe recounted the old rumor of someone offering to plant stones back in 1937. He believed the Pearces had fallen for it. "Every other explanation, no matter how fantastic, no matter how incredible, is more sensible than to suppose that the Pearce team in a period of a little over two years found, in several states, 46 stones engraved by Eleanor Dare 350 years ago and unfound until this day and time."

Nell Battle Lewis, circa 1918.

Sharpe also marveled at the "remarkable sequence" in which the stones seemed to have been found. "It was like a continued story . . . [and] highly significant that the final find wound up the purported Dare story much as a novelist would. . . . And not only did the stone-diggers find the stones – they found 'em all. Not a clue was lost and everything untoward has been accounted for. As a solution to a mystery, it is stinkingly perfect." How much sharper his wit might have been a few weeks later, when Stone Number 48 and its word of prisoners in Indian hands would offer a sequel to the story. Other Tar Heel journalists, such as the indomitable Nell Battle Lewis, columnist for the *Raleigh News and Observer*, had been skeptical of the Pearces and the Dare Stones for some time. But Sharpe's editorial seemed to let loose a flood of skepticism.

In December 1940, Crittenden at last went public with his own doubts. He may well have been facing intense pressure back in Raleigh. He was certainly catching hell from Nell Battle Lewis for participating in the Brenau Conference, which more or less gave the Stones an aura of authenticity. In a newspaper editorial, Crittenden now told of his experiences at the October Conference. He complained that he and the other experts present had never seen the Stones prior to the single, limited four-hour session for inspection and testimony. "It was impossible in so short a time to conduct an independent investigation," he wrote. He pointed out that the assembly had "agreed that the problem of authenticity of the inscriptions had not yet been solved," that more questions needed answering and so more investigation was needed. For example, Crittenden wanted to know what kind of tools could have made the inscriptions, and could the words have been made by modern sandblasting or chemicals? Could the Stones have been artificially aged? Why do most names on the Stones not match with those on the official roster of colonists? And were the words on the Stones genuine Elizabethan English? Conversely, if the matter was all a big hoax, then who might profit from finding the Stones?

In the end, even Crittenden could not make a definitive ruling on the Stones. "I believe neither that the stones are authentic nor that they are unauthentic. I do believe that a thorough investigation needs to be made. . . . If a hoax has been perpetrated, it ought to be exposed; if the stones are genuine, that likewise ought to be proved." Crittenden reminded North Carolinians that some "commonsense detective work," along with the reports of qualified experts, would "settle the matter," but that this "may require a considerable amount of time. . . . Pending such a report, I shall not attempt to solve the problem by any premature statement based upon insufficient evidence." So while Crittenden could not declare the Stones to be fakes, he could at least dust them with a little doubt.

Other North Carolinians did not hesitate in declaring the Stones a fraud. Frank Stick, Secretary of the Cape Hatteras National Seashore Commission, said he had "always looked upon the discovery of these stones with a dubious eye," and joined Crittenden's criticisms. Stick had a vested interest in keeping the Lost Colonists firmly in coastal North Carolina. In 1937, the U.S. Congress had decided to designate Cape Hatteras as the first national seashore in the National Park System. Two years later the state of North Carolina created the Cape Hatteras National Seashore Commission to acquire the necessary lands for the purpose. Frank Stick was placed in charge, and by 1941 the commission administered more than 60,000 acres, part of which included the Fort Raleigh National Historic Site on Roanoke Island. This major tourist destination, with its Lost Colony connection, was vital to the economic health of the Cape Hatteras National Seashore. Stick would be dead-set against letting the Lost Colonists be marched off to Georgia.

Now Stick questioned whether the words on some of the inscriptions were authentically Elizabethan. "I feel reasonabl[y] confident that the whole thing can be exposed," he wrote Crittenden in December. By mid-January, he was also wondering why the names on many of the Stones, particularly those found in South Carolina, did not correspond with those on the official roster. Given the glaring nature of the mismatch, Stick could not believe that the Pearces were involved in this "obvious attempt to bamboozle the public, for they would hardly have been guilty of such an error."

Frank Stick (center).

Raleigh News and Observer columnist and editorial writer Nell Battle Lewis, among the earliest and most vocal critics of the Stones, went down to Georgia for a look on her own. She wanted to check out the Stones and interview Bill Eberhardt. Her findings only bolstered her skepticism. In her "Incidentally" editorial column of Sunday, January 12, 1941, Lewis alluded to the Charles Dickens novel *Pickwick Papers* in which the title character, Mr. Pickwick, is fooled by a stone with writing on it — which turn out to be no more than the idle doodlings of a bored worker. In her opinion, the Pearces were just as gullible as Pickwick. She took C. C. Crittenden to task, as well, for writing the conference report which seemed to validate the stones.

President Pearce was incensed at Lewis's remarks. Lewis "continues her ridicule of our Dare Stone studies," he complained to Crittenden. Pearce found Lewis guilty of taking "a 'fling' at the 'pundits', including yourself, who recently studied the stones at Brenau." When Lewis had visited Bill Eberhardt during the Christmas holidays, Pearce claimed, the man had been drinking heavily and was in

bed, so he was not very polite to her. Nevertheless, despite all the bad
publicity coming out of North Carolina, President Pearce said they were
continuing their searches in the Cartersville area for more information
on the prisoners mentioned on the recently found Stone Number 48.

The escalating tug-of-war between North Carolina and the
Pearces in Georgia became, itself, fodder for the regional and national
news. On April 8, 1941, reporter Noel Yancey filed an Associated Press
story titled "Virginia Dare Novel in Stone Causes Georgia-Carolina
Row." Yancey's bylined story ran under similar headlines in several
other newspapers. "Lively Row Simmering in South Over Ownership of
Roanoke Island Recently," said the *Florence (S.C.) News*. "Virginia Dare
Stones Accepted, Rejected As Controversy Rages," said the *Wilmington
(N.C.) Star News*. "Lively Argument Is Swirling over Whether 'Lost
Colony" Belongs to North Carolina," pointed out the *High Point (N.C.)
Enterprise*. Essentially, Yancey told the story of the Stones and their
finding, but also presented North Carolina's skepticism of one colonist's
ability to leave so many stones. He reported that one Tar Heel editor
"commented acidly that Eleanor Dare must have died of an occupational
disease, that of stonecutter." Yancey repeated the rumor of how someone
back in 1937 offered to plant stones to advertise Paul Green's play *The
Lost Colony*.

"North Carolina's skeptics wondered how the colonists, beset as
they were by trouble, could have found so much time for stonecutting,"
Yancey wrote. "Eleanor Dare, they argued, keen as she was about
stonecutting, would have found a piece of bark or cloth on which she
could have written with berry juice, or with blood." It also seemed
strange to many North Carolinians that Eleanor's trail led straight to
Atlanta, where the first Chowan Dare Stone was revealed to the public.
Yancey also gave the Pearces' view that the Stones appeared naturally
aged and the inscriptions not made by modern stone-cutting tools.
Lichen had been found growing on at least three letters of one stone,
indicating age, he reported, and the language on the Stones seemed to be
Elizabethan English.

Despite the North Carolinians' protests, things did not look good
for the Old North State. Though the state's partisans might fume and
throw dirt, it appeared that the Pearces had, as Yancey said, "weathered
the Tar Heel attack." Brenau had the Stones, and the available evidence
pointed to them being authentic. Unless North Carolina could come up
with some hard proof to the contrary, it looked like American history

books were going to be rewritten. North Carolina, it seemed, was on the verge of losing Virginia Dare and the Lost Colonists to Georgia. Then Pearce Jr.'s submission to the *Saturday Evening Post* reached an editor's desk and the Stones were about to be subjected to a whole new level of scrutiny.

* * *

By the time a badly burned John Smith returned to England in October 1609, his men had gleaned three pieces of valuable but troubling information about the Lost Colony: that the colonists or some number of them had lived peacefully for a time with Indians. That at some point they had been attacked by Indians and many Colonists had been killed. And finally, that there were a few survivors of this attack who had fallen into the hands of Indians west and southwest of the Chowan River, maybe even at the Occaneechi trading town.

But when had this attack taken place, and which Indians had done it? And where were the Lost Colonists living when they were attacked? Englishman William Strachey, just as curious about the Lost Colonists as Captain Smith, was determined to find out.

At thirty-four Strachey had become secretary of the Levant Company, a joint-stock company authorized by King James to trade with Turkey and the Middle East. Strachey had a temper and it often got the best of him. In Constantinople, Strachey had argued with the British ambassador to Turkey, and so the Levant Company sacked him. Back in

Jamestown, as depicted in a U.S. Park Service illustration.

England, hoping to better his economic circumstances, he bought a couple of shares in the Virginia Company.

As a shareholder, Strachey decided to travel to Virginia. In the summer of 1609, he boarded the Sea Venture, *along with Jamestown's new governor, Sir Thomas Gates. But a hurricane wrecked the* Sea Venture *on Bermuda, where Strachey, Gates and about 150 other settlers spent ten months before they could build two ships to take them on to*

Sir Thomas Gates.

Jamestown. Strachey and Gates arrived in Jamestown in May 1610 to find the colony barely alive after their disastrous "starving time" winter. Nevertheless, the Jamestown colony hung on, and Strachey was made its secretary.*

As a colony official, he also had to deal with Wahunsenacawh, the powhatan of the Pamunkey chiefdom. He soon developed a strong dislike of the powerful leader, who stood always ready to protect his people and lands from the expanding English colony. Strachey, a tempestuous man himself, considered the powhatan "proud" and "insolent," unwilling to accept English dominance. So any enemy of the powhatan was a friend of the English, and Strachey was always ready to listen to the worst about the powhatan.

One of those willing to provide Strachey with intelligence was Machumps, an apparent brother-in-law of Wahunsenacawh who had briefly traveled to England on an earlier expedition. Relations between Machumps and Wahunsenacawh seem to have been strained. Machumps, Strachey wrote, "comes to and fro amongst us as he dares and as Powhatan gives him leave, for it is not otherwise safe for him." Powhatan had killed another Indian by having "his brains knock'd out" for selling a basket of corn to the English and for living several days at Jamestown without his permission. Certainly Machumps's willingness to visit Jamestown and Strachey regularly only caused relations between the two Indians to deteriorate further.

When Strachey asked about Raleigh's Lost Colony, Machumps told him. At Peccarecanick and Ochanahoen, the Indian said, "the people have houses built with stone walls and one story above another – so taught them by those English who escaped the slaughter at Roanoack." Even worse, "at Ritanoe the weroane Eyanoco preserved 7 of the English alive – four men, two boys, and one young maid, who escaped and fled up the River of Choanoke – to beat his copper." Seven survivors. Seven captives.

And who had done the slaughtering? Strachey had no doubt that it was Wahunsenacawh himself. "The men, women, and children of the first plantation at Roanoack were by practice and commandment of Powhatan (he himself persuaded thereunto by his priests) miserably slaughterd without any offense given him either by those first planted, who 20 and odd years had peaceably livedn and intermix'd with those savages, and were out of his territory."

Passing out the last kernels of corn during Jamestown's "Starving Time."

With a little help from Machumps and driven by his own hatred for Powhatan, Strachey had the fate of Raleigh's Lost Colony figured out. As he saw it, once White left his colonists on Roanoke Island in 1587, they soon relocated, not fifty miles into the main as they had said, but up the coast to their original destination on the south side of Chesapeake Bay, among the Chespian Indians. There they lived peacefully and happily for almost twenty years. Then in early 1607, just days before Captain John Smith and the other members of the Virginia Company established Jamestown,

Wahunsenacawh's Pamunkey warriors attacked the Lost Colonists and the Chespians. Both groups were exterminated.

Strachey believed the motive for this attack on "our nation without offense given" was to avoid a prophecy. The way Strachey told it, Wahunsenacawh's priests prophecied "how that from the Chesapeack Bay a nation should arise which should dissolve and give end to his empire . . . [and so] according to the ancient and gentile custom he destroyed and put to sword . . . all the inhabitants, the weroance, and his subjects of that province. And so remain all the Chessiopeians at this day and for this cause extinct."

Echoing Strachey's theory was Samuel Purchas, an early seventeenth-century English churchman. Though Purchas himself never came to America, he was one of the earliest to edit some of the letters and reports arriving from Jamestown. Purchas recorded that "Powhatan confessed that hee had bin at the murther of that Colonie: and shewd to Captain Smith a Musket barrel and a brasse Morter, and certain peeces of Iron which had bin theirs."

Strachey left Jamestown in late 1611 and returned to England after spending only a year in the colony. He certainly believed he had solved the mystery of the Lost Colony.

Boyden Sparkes, reporter for the **Saturday Evening Post** *who investigated the Dare Stones in early 1941. Courtesy of Elizabeth Boyden Eagles-Fouros.*

CHAPTER 11

Dupes and Crooks

W hile the experts, editorializers, and good citizens of North
Carolina and Georgia had been dueling down south over the
Dare Stones, in distant Philadelphia Pearce's manuscript had
been making its way through the editorial review process of the
venerable *Saturday Evening Post.* Founded by Benjamin Franklin in
1728 as the *Pennsylvania Gazette,* the publication had taken the form of
a political newspaper by 1821, when it adopted its present name. By the
middle of the nineteenth century it had grown to an annual circulation of
90,000, and by the 1930s, under various editors, it had become a full-
fledged illustrated magazine, the first to top a million copies sold. When
Pearce targeted the *Saturday Evening Post* for his submission in 1940,
he knew full well that it reigned supreme among general-interest
American magazines. The *Post* was an American icon, boasting a
weekly circulation of three million, some of the most accomplished
illustrators of the day, and a crack roster of editors and writers.

The magazine's editors had received Pearce's article back in
December 1940, but had been skeptical. The Stones and their story just
seemed too outlandish. Nevertheless, Pearce's academic standing, his
position at Emory, and his three-year investigation of the Stones worked
to his advantage in persuading the editors to consider it. The
endorsement of Dr. Samuel Eliot Morison likely swayed the matter.
Morison told the *Post* that he believed the Stones to be "genuine" and
explained that "some of them have been knocking around farms of

perfectly honest Georgians for these last fifty years, but were only produced when the story got around." The *Post* accepted Pearce's manuscript.

Problems arose, however, when the *Post* editor turned Pearce's manuscript over to a fact-checker — standard operating procedure for the magazine. The fact-checker was at a loss in dealing with material that hadn't made its way into the encyclopedias — and in fact ran contrary to accepted history

Nonetheless, the *Post* editors were intrigued and wanted to run something on the Dare Stones. So the magazine assigned a veteran reporter to check on the Pearces and the Dare Stones, and to see if the story was worth publishing. In January 1941, New York City writer Boyden Sparkes went down to Georgia. Crittenden and North Carolina could not have had a better champion if they had selected the reporter themselves.

Boyden Sparkes was an old-school reporter, meaning that he latched onto a story and didn't let go until he had all the angles figured and knew where the bodies were buried. At fifty-one years old, he was an imposing figure at six feet, probably pushing two hundred-fifty pounds, with a fringe of short gray-flecked hair around a smooth dome. He looked every inch a bulldog. Born in Cincinnati in 1890, Sparkes got his first newspaper job with the *Cincinnati Commercial-Tribune* at seventeen. Working as a reporter, he later moved to Chicago and then to New York. He gained a reputation for fearlessness when he was wounded by a gunshot while covering a 1921 West Virginia miner's strike. He was also well known in nation's moneyed circles, having ghost-written autobiographies of car-makers Walter Chrysler and Alfred Sloan and authored the biography *Hetty Green: The Witch of Wall Street*. During much of the 1930s he had contributed a weekly column for the the *Saturday Evening Post*. By 1941, he was spending more time on his books than he was on magazine articles. Still, he seemed eager for the assignment to investigate the Dare Stones.

Sparkes brought strong North Carolina connections to the job. In 1914 he had married Bessie Gore, a Wilmington, North Carolina girl, and when not on assignment elsewhere, he divided his time between New York City and the Wilmington–Wrightsville Beach area on the Carolina coast. As a part-time Tar Heel, he would surely have been aware of the recent hoopla about the Dare Stones.

Whether Sparkes asked for the assignment or the *Post* chose him as the best person for the job, the veteran reporter saw this as an opportunity to check out the phenomenon firsthand. It's possible that playwright Paul Green, a North Carolinian with a vested interest in authenticity of the Dare Stones, could have tipped Sparkes about the matter. A Pulitzer Prize winner, Green was a major figure on the New York theater scene — which Sparkes had once covered for the *New York Herald Tribune*. In any case Green would have been a logical source for Sparkes to interview in the course of his research.

On his research trip Sparkes took with him his son-in-law, Joe Eagles Jr., a native of Wilson, North Carolina, a graduate of the University of North Carolina and its law school, and a practicing attorney in Wilson. Sparkes hoped Eagles's legal mind would help him ferret out the truth about the Dare Stones. So in early 1941, Sparkes and Eagles traveled to Georgia to meet the Pearces and take a look at their prize historical artifacts.

At Brenau it didn't take long for Haywood Pearce Jr. to realize that Sparkes was not going to simply sign off on his manuscript without posing some hard questions. If Pearce expected the *Saturday Evening Post* to run a puff piece, he soon learned otherwise. Sparkes and Eagles were dogged in their pursuit, interviewing every contact, following every lead, and conducting background investigations on every player involved from the Pearces to Eberhardt, Turner, Bruce, and the Jetts, and even attempting, without success, to track down Louis Hammond. They traveled to Raleigh and interviewed Crittenden and to New York City to meet with Paul Green's people.

The Pearces found themselves, instead of the gatekeepers of American history, the focus of an inquisition. Sparkes and Eagles, they realized, were not necessarily buying their story of the Dare Stones. "Haywood Pearce becomes resentful when his stones are challenged," Sparkes wrote. "When I said of one of his conjectures that it must have been an exceedingly friendly naked savage who had carried a twenty-one pound stone message across hundreds of miles of South and North Carolina, he scowled." Joe Eagles, using his legal training, "pestered Professor Pearce about the lack of interest at Chapel Hill. North Carolina, Pearce said, was jealous. North Carolina people thought they 'owned' Virginia Dare." The historian was becoming defensive.

Seemingly from the first Sparkes suspected the Dare Stones were a hoax. Maybe his North Carolina roots inclined him against a threat to the state's birthright. It could have been that as a hard-boiled journalist Sparkes smelled something fishy and wasn't going to be bowled over by a few rocks the way all these academics had been. Or it might have been a touch of professional jealousy toward Pearce the historian, who had dared write a story and tried to have it published in the *Saturday Evening Post.* As Sparkes declared, "I am not an Elizabethan scholar, geologist, historian, archaeologist or paleographer, but I am a reporter. In writing an article, the professor had moved into my field. I thought we could get through in a day. It took longer. Before

Cecil B. DeMille.

the end of my investigation Pearce was calling me 'Hawkshaw'" — 1930s slang for a sharp-eyed detective. No, the Pearces did not like the hard approach Sparkes brought to his interviews.

His investigation not only led Sparkes to believe the Dare Stones were frauds, but his first impression was that they had been done by a Hollywood press agent trying to stir up interest in a movie about the Lost Colony. There had been talks between Hollywood and Paul Green about a movie of his *Lost Colony* play. However, as Pearce told Sparkes, although Cecil B. DeMille and Green had

been in communication, Green "broke off negotiations when these stones turned up." Sparkes figured that a Hollywood agent's budget could easily afford "buying the stones, having them carved, strewn around. Moreover, the "tourist" [Hammond] said he came from California."

Sparkes certainly wanted to follow up on this lead. The chief rumor circulating held that the Chowan River Dare Stone was a modern creation to publicize Green's *Lost Colony.* It would have to be put to rest. So Sparkes went to New York City to interview Anthony Buttitta, a friend of Paul Green and the former Roanoke Island publicity agent for Green's play. When Sparkes asked him about the Dare Stones, Buttitta "looked frightened." The agent declared, "Word of honor, we've never

used the stones in our publicity. I got positive orders, Mustn't refer to
'em. Everyone at Manteo knows they're fake." Buttitta told Sparkes the
story of how an unnamed person had shown up in the summer of 1937,
the first season Green's play was performed on Roanoke, and "tried to
sell a fake stone."

That often-repeated tale also had to be checked out. Sparkes
returned to North Carolina, where he interviewed Crittenden, who
provided background and leads. The reporter then drove out to Roanoke
Island to interview state senator D. Bradford Fearing, who represented
the area in the state legislature and once chaired the Roanoke Island
Historical Association. Fearing had personal knowledge of the scheme to
plant rocks. The ruse, he said, had been proposed about ten years earlier
to publicize the new Ocean Highway – U.S. 17, which linked the
southeastern coast from Virginia to Florida - by playing up the area's
Lost Colony history. Fearing told Sparkes how a fellow had come
around and proposed inscribing messages on old ballast stones, carving
the word "Croatoan" in a tree and having it chopped down, even going
so far as to "find" one of the chests left by Lost Colony Governor John
White. "He had the doggonedest ideas! He said he could get men who
could prepare the inscription, carve the rock, do the whole job." Fearing
turned him down. But that was ten years past.

Frank Stick, secretary of the Cape Hatteras National Seashore
Commission, had also been approached by the man. Stick also said it
was about ten years earlier, in the late 1920s, and not 1937. Stick was
the first to put a name to the rumor, identifying the man as "Jack
DeLisle, publicity agent par excellence." Like Fearing, Stick also
rejected the proposal.

Strangely, Sparkes did not follow up on this lead. The reporter
misspelled the man's name – it was Jack DeLysle – and during the late
1920s and early 1930s, he was the Chairman of Traffic & Publicity for
the Atlantic Coastal Highway Association. Little is known of DeLysle's
early years, but word was he was an Englishman, a former World War I
army captain, and he showed up in Fort Myers Beach, Florida about
1918 or 1919. He got a job with the Crescent Beach Road and Bridge
Company and then in the early 1920s, built the first subdivision in Fort
Myers Beach, Seminole Sands, which included a casino and hotel.
Eventually he joined the Atlantic Coastal Highway Association based in
Norfolk, Virginia and became a great supporter of US 17 – the Ocean
Highway. Always interested in local tourism near the highway, he took

Sparkes' article ran in the April 26, 1941 issue of the Saturday Evening Post.

WRIT ON ROCKE

Has America's First Murder Mystery Been Solved?

By Boyden Sparkes

particular note of Roanoke Island and the celebration of Raleigh's failed attempts at colonization. He was a charter member Roanoke Island Historical Association founded in 1932 and often visited the Island during the 1930s and the lead up to the great 1937 anniversary celebration. However, by the early 1940s, he seemed to have moved on.

DeLysle should have interested Sparkes as he certainly had the capability of being the forger. His British education and background might have given him an insight into Elizabethan language and writing. He had visited Roanoke Island during the mid-1930s when the Civilian Conservation Corps was building cottages, guardhouses, and blockhouses at the Fort Raleigh site. He could have easily gotten his hands on ballast stone, as during the construction of these buildings, "ballast stone, believed to have been left by the sixteenth-century ships, was removed from Roanoke Sound and used as a foundation for many of the buildings and for the chimneys." He had probably been at the opening night of Green's *Lost* Colony that summer of 1937. And Fearing indirectly, and Stick directly, finger DeLysle as proposing the idea of planting forged artifacts.

Though Sparkes ignored DeLysle, he kept hearing rumors that a stranger had showed up on Roanoke in 1937 with a rock he claimed was a Virginia Dare relic and offered to sell the stone to officials on Roanoke. Nobody took him up on the offer, and he disappeared. When Sparkes went to Roanoke Island, he could locate no one who recalled someone doing that in 1937. For that matter, no one on the Island could ever describe Louis Hammond, finder of the original Dare Stone, nor identify him, or remember meeting him. Despite failing to find confirmation, Sparkes continued to believe there had been a mysterious stranger on Roanoke Island, who must have been Louis Hammond. Sparkes understood that Pearce had heard of these very same rumors to plant stones in the area, but "that he never personally troubled to investigate."

Anthony Buttitta (right) with Langston Hughes in Chapel Hill, circa 1930.

Finally, on April 26, 1941, after investing considerable time and resources, the *Saturday Evening Post* published a story on the Dare Stones — not the manuscript submitted by Haywood Pearce Jr., but a highly critical article by Boyden Sparkes titled "Writ on Rocke: Has America's First Murder Mystery Been Solved?" The piece was damning. Far from a puff piece, it was an exposé.

In New York, Anthony Buttitta, Green's former press agent, got his hands on an early copy. On April 21 he sent off a letter to Crittenden in Raleigh. Buttitta was eager to inform him that Sparkes and the *Saturday Evening Post* had proven "without a shadow of doubt that the Pierce's [*sic*] Dare Stones are a fake. Without the backing of the Post and his intensive research, the article would not have been possible. We hope you feel that North Carolina owes Sparks [*sic*] a tribute – not only the state of North Carolina, the Historical Commission, the Roanoke

Island Historical Association, the University of N. C., but early American and North Carolina history."

Playwright Green must have been very happy with Sparkes' story. And it was not outside the realm of possibility that he helped shape the piece. The Pulitzer Prize-winning playwright was nationally famous, part of the Southern Literary Renaissance then flowering, and was well known and well liked in New York. Despite all the rumors that the Chowan River Stone was a hoax to publicize his play, Green knew that its transcription undercut his story somewhat. Certainly Green took a dim view of Pearce's South Carolina and Georgia Dare Stones. In a later interview, Green maintained that he had done tremendous historical research when writing *The Lost Colony* and that "the authenticity of the stones indicating that the first colonists migrated from Roanoke Island to Near Atlanta, Ga., was preposterous."

Paul Green.
Carolina Collection, University of
North Carolina at Chapel Hill.

So it would seem that a well-known dramatist like Paul Green, with connections in both North Carolina and New York, who had a vested interest in seeing the Dare Stones discredited, could have influenced a New York-based writer and former theatre columnist with North Carolina connections to accept his view. Buttitta, Green's longtime friend, was looking out for the playwright when he wrote to Crittenden in North Carolina to give him early notice of Sparkes's story. While it was possible Sparkes had been sent to do a hatchet job on the Dare Stones, it just may have been a healthy dose of skepticism and hard-nosed investigation on Sparkes's part that led him to the conclusion that the Dare Stones were fakes.

Whatever the case, Sparkes' story in the *Saturday Evening Post* essentially destroyed the Dare Stone tale and the Pearces' hopes of rewriting American history and rerouting the Lost Colonists to Atlanta.

With a map and photographs of the Stones, Bill Eberhardt, and the Pearces, the first part of "Writ on Rocke" essentially repeated Pearce's oft-told tale of the Lost Colony, the finding of the Dare Stones, and the attempts at verifying their authenticity, including the great scientific conference held at Brenau the past October.

Then, with the soft part of the story out of the way, Sparkes used the remaining pages to demolish the Dare Stones. First he went after Louis Hammond, the finder of the Chowan River Stone in 1937. Sparkes was never able to track down Hammond or personally interview him, but in trying to trace him, Sparkes came to believe Hammond was the mysterious man on Roanoke in the summer of 1937 offering "to sell a stone relic of Virginia Dare." He reported that back in 1937, the Emory faculty had been suspicious of Hammond, despite the fact that professors Lester and Purks who had actually spent a lot of time with Hammond believed him to be just what he was, a lucky California tourist.

Nevertheless, Hammond was guilty in Sparkes' mind because there was no actual evidence against him. Everything Hammond had done now fell under suspicion. Back in 1937, when he took the Emory professors back to the Chowan River, Hammond could not again find the exact spot where he had found the stone. He made only a crude map of the area on the back of a paper bag. Rather than treat the stone with professional care, Hammond cleaned and brushed the inscription to see what it was. Sparkes claimed no one ever saw Hammond's car or met his wife. A professor had tried to follow him one night in Atlanta and lost him. Someone tried and failed to get Hammond's fingerprints off a glass. He gave only a post office box for an address, and no one — including the renowened Pinkertons — could now locate Hammond or his wife, nor any reference except one mysterious Mr. Dove. This all proved to Sparkes that Hammond had delivered a fake. As Sparkes saw it, Hammond must have forged the first stone — and "if the first was a fraud, all were fraudulent."

Next, Sparkes disposed of Eberhardt, Turner, Bruce, and the Jetts, finders of the other forty-seven Dare Stones. Pearce portrayed them in his manuscript and in the Brenau *Bulletins* as virtual strangers with no connection other than they all found Dare Stones. But with minimal investigation, "Hawkshaw" Sparkes discovered that there were few degrees of separation between them. All knew each other — and in fact Eberhardt and Isaac Turner were pretty close friends and had been for over ten years. The reporter said the two often got together for bouts of drinking and dice games and planned on splitting fifty-fifty any proceeds they got from selling rocks to Pearce.

Turner, as he had told the Pearces, had found Stone Number 15 on his own in March 1939, then found Stone Number 37 with Eberhardt on the old Jett place in Fulton County in September 1940. He had then found one of the fragments of the all-important Stone Number 46, which matched with a fragment in Mrs. Jett's father's toolbox. When Sparkes questioned Turner about his finding of Stone Number 15, the Atlanta carpenter was "cautious, suspicious," and his answers "inconsistent." Turner told Sparkes that Dr. Pearce had offered to pay him ten dollars a day to look for stones with words on them. He'd searched thirty-four days, but Pearce had never paid him and so he had a lawyer ready to sue the professor for back pay. When pressed about the authenticity of the Stones, Turner replied "If those stones were crooked, Pearce knows who crooked 'em."

Turner then told the reporter another interesting bit of secondhand rumor: that not long ago a man named L. E. Martin visited Pearce and told him that the stones Eberhardt and Turner were turning up were fakes. Sparkes believed this L. E. Martin was really Louis E. Hammond and that the retired produce dealer had returned from California to Gainesville to protect the authenticity of his first stone. Sparkes may have been half right. While Hammond already had his money and does not seem to have ever personally reappeared in Georgia, he might have sent a lawyer from his neck of the woods to try to protect his Chowan Stone? If so, Leon E. Martin, known as L. E., a longtime partner in the Keyes & Martin law firm of Berkeley, California, near Hammond's Alameda home, may have been the man. While there is no firm evidence that Martin and Hammond knew each other, the coincidence is rather great.

Turner then claimed that Martin had offered him $30,000 if he could find a rock with the word "Yahoo" carved on it. The implication was that since Turner and Eberhardt were making up the Dare Stones themselves, they could produce any inscription upon request. Turner said he didn't think the man had $30,000 and so didn't take him up on the offer. Sparkes confronted Pearce with the story. The professor denied it ever happened. And if it did, Pearce said, it showed that Eberhardt and Turner were on the up-and-up since they didn't accept the $30,000 deal. To him, it proved the two friends could not be forging stones.

Maybe. But more damaging to Turner was that he was also connected to the Jetts. It had been Turner, an old friend of Tom Jett from boyhood days, who recalled a stone with "Indian writing" on it at the old Jett mill. Though Pearce, Eberhardt, and Turner had searched the mill area once, Turner and Eberhardt had gone back the next week and just happened to find the stone among the weeds. Pearce pronounced it a Dare Stone and they all went down and met with old man Jett, who acknowledged it as the stone that had been kicked around his father's mill. Then Mrs. Jett remembered that there had been another stone with writing on it at the old mill, one that had been broken in half. She, her husband, Turner and Eberhardt went to her father's place, and found the stone in the tool chest in almost pristine condition. Turner later went back to the old Jett/Campbell place, which had already been searched several times, and found the other half of the stone in a weedy ditch. It matched the tool chest fragment and "fit as neatly as a freshly broken teacup."

For Pearce, it was these two Dare Stone fragments, separated by fifty years and fifty miles and then joined again, that clinched the authenticity of the Stones, Eberhardt and Turner. So Sparkes knew that to disprove the Stones' authenticity, he would have to disprove the story behind Stone Number 46. In his interview with Sparkes, Jett told a somewhat different story than Pearce's version in the Brenau *Bulletin*. Jett only recalled the stones with "Indian writing" at his father's mill when Turner reminded him. And when Turner and Eberhardt showed up with Stone Number 37 which they said they'd just found at the old Jett place, Tom Jett was actually in the county jail for wounding a neighbor with a shotgun.

Jett told Sparkes that in jail he could not immediately identify the stone Turner and Eberhardt showed him. It was only after getting sprung that he could finally say it was one of the stones around his father's mill. It was at this point that Mrs. Jett recalled the stone in her father's tool chest. The subsequent sequence of events was all too convenient for Sparkes.

Sparkes then did what he said the Pearces never did: he actually went out to visit Mrs. Jett's father, J. H. Whitmire. Whitmire showed Sparkes the large tool chest, which was out in a barn. It was full of heavy tools, axes, knives, braces, and large hardware used for making railroad boxcars. It had been actively used over the years, with tools taken out and tossed back in on a regular basis. Whitmire admitted that there had once been a rock in it with some strange markings on it. But Whitmire, obviously literate since he read the newspaper every day, could not make out any of the letters on the rock. When Sparkes inspected the two Stone pieces, he was convinced something was wrong. The two fragments appeared too clean and fit together too neatly. "It is difficult to believe any stone could have been stored for fifteen years in that often-visited chest without becoming chipped. Heavy tools had been taken, tossed back, and taken unnumbered times." And since the chest was out in the barn under no real supervision, "anyone disposed to substitute another stone for the one Mr. Whitmire remembered could have done so."

Just as telling, the patina on the two fragments was too even. One of the fragments had been in a tool chest for fifteen years and the other had been in an open-air ditch for even longer. Sparkes believed the two pieces would necessarily have faded differently and could not have fit together so neatly. Instead, the fragments had "an evenly applied rust tone that grows gradually lighter throughout its length," Sparkes wrote. "There is no perceptible variation in that reddish tint where the halves meet; yet from the mere adventure of being rubbed together by occasional handling on the museum table, some crumbling has occurred. A blow, rock on rock, would chip it."

As Sparkes saw it, Whitmire may have once had a strange rock in his tool chest, but it had been substituted for a forged fragment made by Turner and Eberhardt. The Jetts, needing money for Tom's upcoming court appearance, jumped at the deal and told their story to the professors at Brenau in October. To Sparkes, the forgery was obvious, and Pearce, who had merely accepted what Eberhardt and Turner told him, had never really done the necessary legwork to determine the truth.

After knocking the supports out from under the Jetts, it did not take long for Sparkes to learn that William Bruce, finder of Stones Number 36 and 45, was also an acquaintance of Eberhardt. In fact, Eberhardt had admitted to Sparkes that he had known Turner and Bruce for years, "they can get together any half hour," Sparkes reported. Bruce, a grocer but also a sometime stone hauler, knew Eberhardt from that capacity. When Bruce read the newspaper accounts of Eberhardt's discoveries of stones with writing on them, he and his sons began inspecting every rock they came across. Then, as Bruce said, they found one. He called Pearce at Brenau, told him of his find, and was urged to bring it over. "There was some secret joke about Bruce's find," Sparkes wrote. "He grinned when he told us Eberhardt hadn't liked his finding it." Nevertheless, the Pearces pronounced it a Dare Stone and offered him twenty-five dollars for it. They paid him another twenty-five when he brought in Stone Number 45 soon after. Sparkes went to look at Bruce's Stone Number 36, and to him it looked "clean" and forged. "Somebody had scraped the grooves of the inscriptions as had been done with all the stones."

Then Sparkes turned his spotlight on Bill Eberhardt, the central figure in the South Carolina and Georgia stones. He zeroed in on Eberhardt's past involvement in forging and selling Indian relics. It seems that Eberhardt had, over a period of time, sold a local antiques dealer several rough soapstone effigies carved in the shape of a face or mask with a snout for a nose. For these relics Eberhardt had received $271.50, but it wasn't long before the dealer realized they were forged, artifically aged with a blowtorch. Even the Georgia state geologist thought they were recent forgeries. When questioned about the matter, Eberhardt said there was nothing to it, just a fit of pique on the part of the antiques dealer. The dealer had wanted too much profit from Eberhardt and was now angry that he would no longer sell to him. The dealer, who begged to differ, showed Sparkes the unsaleable fakes.

Sparkes now focused on the Stones found by Eberhardt. He actually visited the South Carolina site where Eberhardt had produced his first thirteen. With pictures of the Stones in hand, Sparkes met with Charles Bennett, the previous owner, whose family had owned the land for almost a century. "Never saw anything like 'em," Bennett told Sparkes. "Been around that hill all my life. They just weren't there." Sparkes even talked to Bennett's brothers and sisters, who corroborated his statement. Those Stones, it turns out, had never been on that property.

Convinced there had never really been any Stones that originiated in South Carolina, Sparkes now attacked the incredible coincidences in Eberhardt's finds. Of all thirteen stones supposedly found by Eberhardt in South Carolina, the only clue to where the Lost Colonists were going came in Stone Number 2 and Stone Number 14, both saying "Father wee goe sw." In Sparkes's view, "southwest" entailed an area of more than 50,000 square miles. Following meandering Indian trails, the Lost Colonists could have gone just about anywhere. But then, amazingly, more than a hundred miles from the

South Carolina site and not far from his own home, Eberhardt, along with his friends Turner and Bruce, located more stones. "Where Eberhardt was 'searching,' many searched; professors, students, the Pearce family, others," wrote Sparkes. "Yet only Eberhardt seemed able to find stones; and never when he was watched except for one 'find' he shared with his intimate, Turner."

Sparkes reserved his harshest criticism, however, for Haywood Pearce Jr. He did not believe the history professor and his father were in on the actual forging of Stones; that sort of lie would have been the absolute worst crime an academic could be accused of. But Sparkes did think Pearce was guilty of the second worst: playing up speculative evidence while suppressing that which countered his argument, and, further, failing to pursue the necessary research to uncover the truth. While Pearce told the *Saturday Evening Post* that the Stones "have been subjected to every scientific test I could command," it took Sparkes only a few weeks, and just a little resourcefulness, to find that was not so.

Sparkes found numerous lapses. Pearce's geologist colleague at Emory University, Dr. James Lester, who had been the first one to see Hammond and the Chowan Dare Stone back in 1937, had made a close inspection of Stone Number 25 found by Eberhardt in August 1940 along the Chattahoochee — "heyr laeth Eleanor dare 1599 seaven heyr sithence 1593". Sparkes managed to get his hands on Lester's report, which showed Stone 25's inscription to be freshly made, "cut within the past few days or weeks. . ." Quoting Lester's report in his article, Sparkes wrote that the geology professor proclaimed that he was "forced to believe less in the authenticity of this stone than in any. . . . It makes me believe it had been doctored . . . the lack of lichenous material in the grooves seems to be the first glaring drawback to any of the stones that I have seen." Lester said straight out that the stone was a fake.

Pearce, Sparkes implied, had known of Lester's report and the geologist's declaration that the Stone was a forgery. But the Emory history professor didn't mention this when he submitted his manuscript to the *Saturday Evening Post*. He had been ignoring the evidence ever since. Similarly, Pearce had declared that modern stone-cutting tools and techniques could not duplicate the inscriptions—but he had long known that stonecutters in Marietta, Georgia back in 1937 had said they could duplicate the inscriptions on the Chowan Stone.

But could they duplicate the writing on Eberhardt's stones? Sparkes took photographs of some Eberhardt inscriptions to the Mount

Airy Granite Company in New York, whose craftsmen told him that sandblasting could do the same or just about any other cutting technique. As Lester himself had told Sparkes, forming these letters would not even require carving, as "you could scratch them with your fingernail. You could do the job using the head of a tenpenny nail as a cutting tool."

As Sparkes saw it, the inscriptions and language used on the Stones alone should have tipped off the professor that they were not genuine. The language of the Stones had been a major point of controversy on which the Brenau Conference Advisory Committee had urged more research. Even Pearce admitted that some words found on the Stones did not seem in keeping with the period and gave him pause.

Sparkes took photographs of some of the Stones and their inscriptions to one of his experts in New York, Dr. Samuel Tannenbaum, an independent scholar, paleographer and a widely respected expert on Elizabethan language and writing. Tannenbaum was considered an authority on Shakespeare, but also on forged sixteenth-century writings. A glance at the writing style of the carvings in the photographs was all Tannenbaum needed to declare the Eberhardt Stones a fake. Just about everyone wrote in a gothic style back then, Tannenbaum explained, and only the upper class signed their names with Roman letters of the sort featured on the Stones. Surely the writer would "have slipped, made here and there a Gothic letter."

Tannenbaum also had problems with the words used on the Stones — not with their variation, but their too-predictable consistency. In the late 1500s, he explained, the English language, especially the spelling of words, was in transition and the same person might form the same word many different ways. Tannenbaum pointed out that Sir Walter Raleigh spelled his name forty-five different ways; Francis Bacon used about thirty different spellings. But on the Dare Stones, the word "laeth" had been used nine times; "shew" eleven times; "Father" twenty-four; "Eleanor" twenty-six; and many others as well, always spelled the same way. "Here the consistency is supposed to have been observed through twelve years of forest wandering by people shut off from white civilization," Sparkes wrote. Tannenbaum then pointed out that neither "primeval" nor "reconnoitre" appeared in the works of Shakespeare, who probably had the largest vocabulary of any English speaker of that day. Some terms, too, appeared to be anachronisms. The *Oxford English Dictionary*, a reliable record of the earliest usage of

The Lumbee students of Croatan Normal School, in Pembroke, N.C.

English words, noted the first occurrence of "primeval" as 1653 and "reconnoitre" as 1707.

Not only had Pearce ignored all this available evidence, Sparkes claimed the professor had also ignored the fact that Eberhardt's Stones ran counter to history and legend. North Carolina history was full of stories of people meeting up with English-like Indians, with gray eyes, beards, and auburn hair, speaking an Elizabethan dialect, and living and farming as Englishmen did. Sparkes pointed out that one large group who fit this description were the Croatan Indians of Robeson County, North Carolina, near the town of Pembroke. Among the Croatans, now called the Lumbees, appeared family names such as Sampson, Berry, and others that appeared on the roster of the Lost Colonists. "The case is circumstantial," Sparkes admitted, "but more convincing to me than the stones. These ask you to believe that Eleanor Dare and six white males escorted by four Indians, survived crossing a vast region inhabited by tribes mutually jealous and suspicious. By automobile today the shortest practical route is about 600 miles."

Sparked also took issue with Pearce's claim that Hollywood had come to him about making a movie of the Lost Colonists. As Sparkes discovered, it had been Pearce himself who had written Cecil B. De Mille, just days after the October 1940 Brenau Conference, to pitch him on a movie version of Maude Fiske's play *The Heritage*. Pearce promised all cooperation to the movie folk. De Mille replied that he was studying the project with interest.

Then, Sparkes found a way to drive the knife just a little bit deeper. The reporter claimed that one morning at breakfast, as he was studying a photograph of Stone Number 15, the first stone found by Isaac Turner — "Father looke vp this river to great salvage lodgment" — he discovered in the inscription an acrostic — a hidden word puzzle, where words can be found in a jumble of letters by reading up, down, diagonally, backward, or forward. In Turner's Stone Number 15, Sparkes swore, through a little "forcing," that he could find the word "Pearce," "Emory," "Shed," and "Atlanta, Ge." He saved his closing salvo for dramatic effect. "Then I found what seems to me the final word in this matter," Sparkes concluded. "It is in 'fair Roman' capital letters, beginning at the top of the stone. When a picture of it is held sidewise, a child would be able to read 'FAKE'!"

It was an intriguing, entertaining, and devastating article. Though he himself sometimes built on assumptions and committed minor errors of fact, point by point Sparkes managed to undermine the authenticity of the Dare Stones and the trustworthiness of Eberhardt, Turner, Bruce, the Jetts, and even Dr. Haywood Pearce Jr. He had also upended nearly every assumption about the Lost Colonists the Pearces had been promoting for three and a half years.

It was certainly not what Pearce had hoped for when he mailed off his manuscript last December. Nevertheless, the Pearces did not give up the cause. Sparkes had resorted to circumstantial evidence that they felt could be refuted. And all the Georgia players – Eberhardt, Turner, Bruce, the Jetts – swore they were innocent. Still, the points made by Sparkes must have given him pause and made Pearce very wary of Eberhardt and his stones.

* * *

William Strachey, the Virginia Company secretary at Jamestown in 1611, seemed to have uncovered the fate of the Lost Colonists at Roanoke. As he saw it, the colony had relocated to the Chesapeake Bay and lived peacefully for twenty years with the Chespian Indians only to be wiped out by Wahunsenacawh just as Jamestown was being founded.

In reality, once Strachey returned to England in 1611, no one really gave much more thought to the Lost Colonists. The survival of Virginia, which almost went the way of Raleigh's Lost Colony, was far more pressing. While tobacco made many Englismen rich, disease killed many, many more. And as tobacco became the poor man's way to get rich, it brought increasing conflict with Wahunsenacawh's Pamunkeys. In April 1618, Wahunsenacawh died. The next year his daughter Pocahontas died in London, severing important kinship links in the Indian-English relationship. In 1622, Opecanchanough, now powhatan of the Pamunkeys, attacked the Virginia plantations and nearly destroyed the colony. Jamestown weathered the attack, but barely. Few could spare a moment's thought for what became of the Lost Colony.

Mátooks ós Rebecka daughter to the mighty Prince Powhatan Emperour of Attanoughkomouck ots Virginia converted and baptized in the Christian faith, and Wife to the Wor' M' Tho: Rolff.

Pocahontas as she looked in England.

Those who did tended to accept the version of events put forth by Strachey and Purchas. But others doubted the Lost Colonists could ever have made it to the Chesapeake Bay.

Though it seems just a short run up the coast, in the 1580s the way for the Lost Colonists to get to the Chesapeake from Roanoke Island was not by boat up the coast. That was too dangerous. In 1586, Ralph Lane at Roanoke, even with veteran soldiers and more and better boats, determined he could not undertake a major coastal expedition northward. He had written that the coastal passage to the Chesapeake was "very shallow and most dangerous, by reason of the breadth of the sound and the little succour that upon any flawe was there to be had." The colonists also recalled stories of shipwrecked sailors, including the fifteen men they had come to rescue, who had set sail from Roanoke or the Outer Banks never to be seen again. Besides, the Chesapeake would not be "into the maine" as they had agreed. And the Chespian Indians were not necessarily friendly—they had once allied with Pemisapan against Ralph Lane.

Still, if the Colonists had hoped to relocate to the Chesapeake, then the only way to reach it was to go west — into the maine. Lane had showed the way in 1586: row up Albemarle Sound, then up the Chowan River to Menatonon's Choanoac towns. From there it was four days' march overland to the Chesapeake. However, once on the Chowan River, they would find that it was not an easy four-day stroll to the Chesapeake, but a hard, dangerous journey through forests and swamps inhabited by not necessarily friendly Indians.

Menatonon had warned Lane about going overland to the Chesapeake, where the rising young Wahunsenacawh was just beginning to solidify his power among the Pamunkey Indians. To go to the Chesapeake, Lane learned he should "take a good store of men with mee, and good store of victuall, for he sayd, that king [on the Chesapeake] would be loth to suffer any strangers to enter into his Countrey, and especially to meddle with the fishing for any Pearle there, and that hee was able to make a great many of men into the fielde, which he sayd would fight very well."

No, the Chesapeake was not the place for the Lost Colonists. Even Strachey himself had said that the Lost Colonists "were seated far from him" and were "out of his territory." And other than Strachey's rather indirect placement of the Lost Colonists among the Chespians, there is really no evidence that the Lost Colonists relocated to Chesapeake Bay.

Others have also doubted Wahunsenacawh's role in an attack on the Lost Colonists. Again, it was only Strachey and Purchas who accused the Powhatan. Purchas said Wahunsenacawh had "confessed" to John Smith that he had destroyed the Lost Colonists and even showed him a musket barrel, a pharmacist's mortar, and some metal that came from them. But Smith mentions no confession by Wahunsenacawh. Surely an attack of this scope and one done so recently would have generated much more talk and harder information for the keenly interested Captain Smith. But in none of his writings does Captain John Smith accuse Wahunsenacawh of massacring the Lost Colonists. On the contrary, Wahunsenacawh and his brother Opechancanough openly told Smith about Lost Colony survivors to the south and encouraged him to go find out what he could — hardly the actions of a man guilty of their extermination.

As for the gun barrel, brass mortar, and pieces of iron in Wahunsenacawh's possession that Purchas put forward as evidence, they could just as easily have been acquired through the Indian trade network. Indians were fascinated with the manufactured goods that the English brought. Some of these items had utilitarian value, while others possessed spiritual power or bestowed status on the owner. European goods had been passed through Indian hands along the East Coast since the first Spaniards had come with Pánfilo de Nárvaez, Lucas Vázquez de Ayllón, and Hernando de Soto in the early 1500s. All the Roanoke Island expeditions, including that of the Lost Colony, deposited a number of goods into the trade networks. Some such items probably showed up at Occaneechi town. So it would make sense that the great Powhatan would have some English manufactured goods, even some from the Roanoke expeditions, in his possession.

The **Susan Constant II,** *a working replica of the ship that carried settlers to Jamestown in 1607.*

But why would Wahunsenacawh suddenly attack the Lost Colonists, and why in April 1607 just as the Jamestown colony was landing in Virginia? As Strachey said, the Lost Colonists had been living peacefully with other Indians outside of the powhatan's territory. The most obvious answer would be that Wahunsenacawh feared that there would now be two colonies of Englishmen in the region and that they would ally against him. To prevent this, the powhatan decided to exterminate the Lost Colonists first.

Of course, that would give the powhatan the ability to foretell the future. Ever since the early 1500s, European ships had been sailing up and down the East Coast, with many nosing into the Chesapeake Bay. In the 1560s and 1570s, Spain had even established a few short-lived missions in the Chesapeake, but the Indians had wiped them out. That the Lost Colonists knew of the Chesapeake and planned to colonize there meant that English ships had been there before. And after 1590, even more English ships ventured into the Bay. So by the time the Susan Constant, the Discovery, and the Godspeed entered the Bay in April 1607, there had been many English ships inside of Chesapeake Bay. So how would

Wahunsenacawh know that this expedition was anything more than just another set of ships venturing into the area? It would not be until months later that the powhatan realized just what a threat Smith and the English posed to his chiefdom.

Of course, there was the prophecy that Wahunsenacawh's priests kept whispering to him that out of the Chesapeake would come a people to destroy his chiefdom. Was a hard-bitten political leader like Wahunsenacawh that likely to listen to stories by his priest? And prophecies predicting the arrival of Europeans who would overthrow Indian rulers were common in all places Europeans took by force. The Spanish spouted them to justify the destruction of the Aztecs and Mayas. Now English officials were offering up the same.

Strachey and Purchas may have been doing something similar by accusing Wahunsenacawh of killing the Lost Colonists. Strachey certainly had no love for the powhatan and hated the way he stood up to English demands. For some, Strachey and Purchas's charge was merely unsubstantianed, anti-powhatan propaganda. Claiming that Wahunsenacawh had murdered Raleigh's Lost Colonists allowed Strachey and Purchas to justify an English war on the powhatan, giving the English legal right to subjugate him and take his lands.

But if the Lost Colonists did not reach Chesapeake Bay and if they were not murdered at the order of Wahunsenacawh, then what happened?

The Thursday, May 15, 1941 evening edition of the **Atlanta Journal.**

CHAPTER 12

Acid and Extortion

The *Saturday Evening* Post article hurt. But Haywood Pearce hoped that Boyden Sparkes had gotten bad information. He dreamed of finding a way of proving the reporter wrong and vindicating his theory. Then the bottom fell out for Professor Pearce.

Toward the end of April 1941, Bill Eberhardt brought another rock to Brenau. But Pearce refused to accept any more stones removed from their setting. He declined to purchase the stone from Eberhardt, and its inscription remains unknown. Pearce would only pay for stones he could inspect in their setting.

Within days Eberhardt informed the Pearces that he had discovered another carved rock on a bluff above the Chattahoochee River, not far from his Eleanor Dare cave. And this time he was leaving it where he found it for Pearce to come see.

Pearce drove out to the bluff and Eberhardt showed him a stone with the inscription "Father, Five are buried on the hill." Pearce was suspicious. Something didn't ring true. If only seven colonists had survived the attacks in South Carolina — and these were all now accounted for — then who were these five? The professor was becoming ever more distrustful of the stone hauler.

Something else about this new stone bothered him, too. Stung by Sparkes's recriminations, Pearce decided to do further checking. He went back out to the river bluff when he knew that Eberhardt would not be around, and took with him Dr. Count Gibson of the Department of

162

 THE LOST ROCKS

Geology at Georgia Tech. Together they examined the inscription above the Chattahoochee and both declared it to be a fake. Then, while they were poking around the bluff, Gibson made an incriminating discovery: a glass bottle of sulfuric acid "which had been used to smear on the rock to give it the appearance of age. That accounted for the suspicious dark color." Pearce and Gibson then confronted Eberhardt and gave him "a good scolding." Pearce now told Eberhardt that he would purchase no more Stones from him.

Eberhardt realized the game was up. There would be no more cash coming in from the Pearces. Still, he had enjoyed the money he'd gotten and wasn't ready to let it go. He decided to put one last squeeze on the Gainesville family. Eberhardt called up Mrs. Haywood Pearce Sr., the wife of the Brenau President and mother of the Emory history professor, and asked her to meet with him as he had something to show her. Lucile Pearce had become very interested in the Dare Stones, and had often accompanied her son and husband when they went looking for evidence of the Lost Colony. So Mrs. Pearce agreed, hoping for a good stone.

At their rendezvous, said Mrs. Pearce, Eberhardt did produce another stone similar in appearance to the ones he'd been selling them the past couple of years. But there was a twist to the inscription. This time, instead of a message from Eleanor Dare, the words read *"Pearce and Dare Historical Hoaxes. We Dare Anything."* Now Eberhardt played hard ball. If the Pearces didn't give him two hundred dollars, he intended to turn this stone over to the *Saturday Evening Post* and admit to faking all his stones. She should go back and tell that to her son and husband.

Crestfallen. Glum. Embarrassed. Sickened. These terms must have described the Pearce household that evening when Lucile Pearce returned with the blackmail demand from Eberhardt. Though the family now had reliable proof of Eberhardt's guilt, the blow must have hit Pearce the historian like a Joe Louis roundhouse. If Eberhardt was indeed a charlatan, Pearce had to face many things in a new light. The thousands of dollars he'd talked his father into wasting. The time he squandered on this crazy chase when he could have been doing more legitimate historical research. The likelihood that his opponent, Sparkes, was right. And that hurt. But what hurt the worst was that he now had to admit that he'd been taken. Flat out fooled. The Ph.D. hoodwinked by the country boy with no education. It was as American as snake-oil.

Though Pearce might have been gullible, he was still an honorable man. He may have been bamboozled by the stone cutter, but he was not about to be victimized by Eberhardt's blackmail. The Pearces went on the offensive, determining to gather evidence against him. Pearce Jr. contacted Eberhardt and asked for a meeting. Eberhardt agreed. Pearce drove down to north Atlanta and talked with Eberhardt at his shack, taking Count Gibson with him as witness. The mood was tense. Pearce claimed Eberhardt kept a rifle across his knees the whole time and wouldn't let Pearce come near him.

Out of the meeting came two documents, one signed by Eberhardt, the other unsigned. The unsigned document, which Pearce had apparently prepared before going to meet Eberhardt, read "In consideration of $200 paid to the undersigned I agree not to divulge anything regarding the fraudulent character of stones delivered to H. J. Pearce in the past and not to deliver any other carved stones to other parties than said H. J. Pearce and not to discuss with or communicate with other parties any matter pertaining to the so-called Dare stones." Cagey fellow that he was, Eberhardt refused to sign this paper until he received his hush money. Pearce wasn't going to pony up any more money to Eberhardt. Still, the professor needed something, some evidence that Eberhardt had faked the Stones and was trying to blackmail him. So he wrote up another contract there on the back of an envelope. It read "I agree to accept from H. J. Pearce Jr. $200 on Thursday night, May 13, in connection with the matter between us." In the absence of anything he considered incriminating, Eberhardt signed this one.

Though Pearce could not get Eberhardt to admit on paper he had forged the stones, the professor came away convinced that Eberhardt had been hoaxing him all along. So instead of giving Eberhardt the $200, Pearce took the story to the newspapers. He explained how he had been taken. He showed the two contracts – the one Eberhardt signed and the other the stone hauler refused to sign — to reporters from the Atlanta newspapers. He confessed that Eberhardt was a hoaxer and extortionist, and that most of Brenau College's Dare Stones were forgeries. It must have been a hard press conference for the historian.

The front page of the Thursday, May 15, 1941, edition of the *Atlanta Journal*, in huge all-capital headlines, blared, "Hoax Claimed By 'Dare Stones' Finder in Extortion Scheme, Dr. Pearce Charges." The Pearces told their side of the story.

When the news first broke on May 15, Eberhardt went to ground and disappeared from his usual North Atlanta "haunts." But once the newspapers located him, Eberhardt told an entirely different story. He had never faked the Stones, he said, but only looked and found Stones where the Pearces told him to look. If anything, he implied, it was the Pearces who were faking the Stones, and he was just a pawn in their crooked game. "I smelled a rat," Eberhardt said, "but I was being well paid, so why not." As for the phony "Pearce and Dare Historical Hoaxes" stone and his meeting with Mrs. Pearce, Eberhardt denied any attempt at blackmail. He had actually discovered that Stone, he claimed, just as he had found all of them. He was as surprised to find it as the Pearces, and $200 was a reasonable reward for such an interesting stone. When asked to produce the controversial rock, Eberhardt couldn't. He claimed it had been stolen by someone right out from under his bed.

The Pearces considered Eberhardt's outlandish story sour grapes. Eberhardt was angry because the Pearces had found out that he'd been fleecing them for years —at fifty dollars a stone, Eberhardt had earned about $2,000 from his efforts, as he told the papers. What he did not tell the papers or the Pearces was that he'd netted even more on the deal as he had secretly sold his half interest in the South Carolina hill where his first thirteen stones had been found. It truly had been a good move when Eberhardt turned down the $500 reward for the Second Stone and accepted $100 and half interest in the hill. The Dare Stones had been very good to Bill Eberhardt. But now his steady income had dried up.

The unfolding controversy of the Dare Stone Hoax made great front-page copy for several days in the *Atlanta Constitution* and *Atlanta Journal*. Reporters went into high gear trying to determine for themselves whether or not the Stones were fakes. They even tracked down William Bruce, who had found Stone Number 36 and Stone Number 45 along the Chattahoochee River. While Bruce would not confess to faking the stones, he allowed that he was "in the rock business" and that he knew Bill Eberhardt. And when Eberhardt was finding all the stones, which were selling for twenty-five dollars each, a sort of "Klondike fever" hit the neighborhood. "Everybody was out clawing off their nails in eagerness to get in on the bonanza," one of Bruce's neighbors said. But none of the neighbors ever succeeded in discovering a Stone — only Bruce himself did. And while Bruce made "no claims as to authenticity of the specimens he discovered," he told the paper the Pearces paid him fifty dollars for the two he found.

Assailed by claims and accusations of hoaxing and extortion, the Dare Stones were dead. Still, Pearce and Gibson tried to salvage something. The *Atlanta Journal* reported that "the Pearces recognized, of course, that Eberhardt's story complicated their problems and discredits the stones. They believe that in an endeavor to extort money, he is seeking to discredit the entire story of the stones." Pearce pointed out that Eberhardt had not found all the Dare Stones and so some of them, maybe five, could still be genuine. They offered arguments in support of their position: that while some stones, under fluorescent lighting, did show evidence of acid, others did not; that micro-particles had been found in stones which showed they were not recently cut; that history corroborated much of the story of the Stones, though in what way was not specified; and that the linguistic studies of the stones showed them to be plausibly Elizabethan.

Pearce also said that one of the Stones, he did not say which, had been sent to Dr. Colin Fink, head of the department of electrochemistry at Columbia University, for further testing; results were pending. Dr. Fink had earned an international reputation as being the professor who "established the authenticity of the famous 'Drake Plate' that was found near San Francisco in 1936." While Fink's opinion may have carried substantial weight in his day, scientists in the 1970s ruled the Drake Plate a forgery and the whole matter a great hoax.

Pearce's claim of partial authenticity of the Stones was not sufficient to right his rapidly sinking ship. The Dare Stones were now tainted by fraud, and there was nothing Pearce could do to undo the damage. The Associated Press picked up the story from the Atlanta papers and flashed it around the country. Headlines dismissing the Dare Stones peppered the national press: "Expert Says Some Dare Stones Are Fraud: Accuses Georgia Mason of a Playing Part," wrote the *New York Times*. "Eleanor Dare Stones Are Branded Fraudulent," said the *New York City Herald Tribune*. "Virginia Dare Stone Hoax Alleged by Georgia Savant," screamed the *Detroit News*. "Stone Mason Reportedly Admits Faking 'Eleanor Dare Messages'," said the *Indianapolis News*.

To add insult to injury, the Dare Stones came to stand as a symbol of fakery. In August 1941, T. W. Samuels Bourbon used the Stones in a newspaper ad. "Easy To Be Fooled," proclaimed the headline over a picture of the front and back of Isaac Turner's Stone Number 15. "Recently thousands were spent for stones inscribed with 'messages' from the lost colonists. It now seems that these stones are hoaxes – another example of how easy it is to be fooled," read the ad copy. So "Those Who Know Their Bourbon Best" should know that with T. W. Samuels Bourbon there is "No Better Bourbon in Any Bottle."

By the summer of 1941, the Pearces' triumph had been shattered. The rocks were rendered worthless, as was Maude Fiske's play. The time and money the Pearces had invested in the project had gone for naught. At least they owned a hill near Pelzer, South Carolina, and a room full of rocks. But their reputation, especially that of Professor Haywood Pearce Jr., was in tatters.

Pearce's old journalist-nemesis from North Carolina, Nell Battle Lewis, dealt the death blow to the Stones. "The 'Lost Colony' Is Still Lost – Much To the Amusement of North Carolina," she wrote, reviling the Stones and their champions, and reveling in the victory. Lewis wrote that the Pearces' attempt to "appropriate North Carolina's Lost Colony has failed and many Tarheels are chortling heartily over the failure." The exposure of the Dare Stones as frauds was "so welcome in Tarheelia where from the first these four dozen ridiculous rocks have been under the darkest of suspicions." She lambasted Crittenden of the North Carolina Historical Commission, Professor Morison of Harvard, and other scholars who had fallen for the hoax, saying the "exposé ma[de] monkey" of them. From the first, the rocks had "looked extremely fishy, and never were taken seriously in North Carolina," except by Crittenden, whom Lewis scorned for not standing up more forcefully for the Old North State. Despite all this, "North Carolina's Lost Colony still belongs to Roanoke Island."

The mere idea of Eleanor Dare leaving behind all the Stones was far-fetched enough and should have tipped off the experts that they were faked, Lewis believed. It was so foolish, that "one Tarheel rhymester indited verses to 'Our El' beginning:

> 'Dame Eleanor Dare by her log-cabin door,
> With mallet and chisel and tomb-stones galore,
> Sat busily knocking out tender adieux
> In dozens of delicate stone billets-doux.
> Virginia Dare squalled and the pot bubbled o'er,
> But Eleanor only did hammer the more!

With rare intuition, to which she paid heed,
She felt that some day she would probably need
A few such mementoes to sprinkle her trail
To tell future searches the pitiful tale'
And, knowing with Indians behind ev'ry pine,
She'd never have time to drop papa a line,
So like the wise babes in the wood she did plan
To carve a few letters to strew as she ran.'

Still, the hoax was an amazing one, Lewis admitted. That Eberhardt, with only three years of formal education, "was able to compose pseudo-Elizabethan which could deceive the erudite . . . suggests that he has a grinning and scholarly confederate still hiding somewhere in the bushes who helped him to perpetrate the colossal hoax."

King Charles II.

That aspect of the mystery remains unsolved. If Eberhardt did have an educated accomplice who told him what to write, he was never found. But it didn't really matter. The Dare Stones and their story seemed as dead as Eleanor and Virginia Dare.

*   *   *

The English colony in Virginia survived its early troubles. Opechancanough had launched one last attack on the Virginia settlements in 1644, but these had been beaten back. Opechancanough was captured and executed. Since then Virginia had prospered and its population had grown. Every now and again a rumor would emerge of some English people living among the Indians. But no more search parties were sent out, and most forgot about the Lost English Colonists. In 1663, King Charles II created the colony of Carolina and gave it to the eight Lords Proprietors. Soon colonists were moving south out of Virginina to the banks of the Albemarle Sound and along the Chowan River.

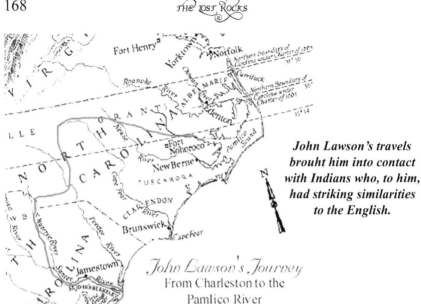

John Lawson's travels brouht him into contact with Indians who, to him, had striking similarities to the English.

John Lawson's Journey
From Charleston to the
Pamlico River

In 1701, more than a century after the failed Roanoke colony, renowned surveyor John Lawson made a trip across the Carolinas. He was astounded to find Indians with distinctly European traits and customs. Lawson reported that the Hatteras Indians, who often moved between Croatoan and Roanoke islands, said that "several of their Ancestors were white People, and could talk in a Book, as we do: the Truth of which is confirm'd by gray Eyes being found frequently amongst these Indians, and no others. They value themselves extremely for their Affinity to the English, and are ready to do them all friendly Offices." As Lawson saw it, these must have been the descendants of the Lost Colony, which had "miscarry'd for want of timely Supplies from England; or thro' the Treachery of the Natives, for we may reasonably suppose that the English were forced to cohabit with them, for Relief and Conversation; and that in process of Time, they conform'd themselves to the Manners of their Indian Relations."

For many years, this became the main explanation of what happened to the Lost Colonists. Lawson's theory directly refuted Strachey's and Purchas's assertion that the Lost Colonists had relocated to the Chesapeake Bay, to meet their eventual doom. Now the clues found by Governor John White inscribed on the fort post at Roanoke in 1590 became paramount – CROATOAN.

Some now believed that the Lost Colonists, realizing that they could not remain on Roanoke, relocated to Croatoan Island, just as their sign indicated. There they awaited Governor White's return. But when he did not arrive after six months, after a year, after a second year, never, they were eventually absorbed into Croatoan Indian society. This assumption seemed logical, as there were no other peoples to whom the Lost Colonists could turn for assistance. Indian peoples were known to be very inclusive, and adoption and marriage of outsiders was common as it turned strangers into family. The idea only made sense.

But Croatoan Island, now Hatteras Island, posed problems of its own as a destination of the Lost Colonists. Even smaller in area than Roanoke, Croatan — the long, narrow strip of dunes known today as Hatteras — was a rather barren, sandy barrier island. If 117 colonists could not find enough food for the winter on Roanoke, they surely could not on Croatoan.

But that doesn't mean there were no colonists on Croatoan Island. There was a good-sized Indian town on the island, whose residents were friendly toward the English. It was Manteo's town, a safe haven for the colonists where his mother was wiroans. Furthermore, the shape and situation of the island, jutting out into the Atlantic, made it a perfect place to watch for ships. Lane had sent a contingent of men there in the spring of 1586, not only to relieve pressure on his dwindling food supplies, but also to keep a look out for the long-awaited supply ship. When the Lost Colonists, abandoned on Roanoke in 1587, begging Governor John White to return to England for help, they surely imagined that he would return in only a few months, maybe a year at the most. Where better to await him? And where better for him to find them—and easier, surely, than "fifty miles into the maine."

Following in Lane's footsteps, it would seem logical that they dispatched a small contingent of colonists to Croatoan, probably no more than twenty. The group would await White's return. They would even leave clues carved on fort posts and trees on Roanoke to direct him back to Croatoan. Once he'd made his way there, just a few miles south of Roanoke by water, they would show him where the rest of his colony was living along the Chowan River.

Ships sailing up and down the East Coast often anchored off Croatoan Island. John White's ship did so on the night of August 12, 1590, before he returned to Roanoke to find his colony gone. His journal made no mention seeing any signal or evidence of people, English or

Indian, on Croatoan Island. If a party of colonists had been sent there to wait for John White, then they missed their mark. More than likely, they were not there at all. The Croatoan Indians did not spend all the year on that narrow strip of sand. Periodically they moved inland for better hunting and farming. And with John White gone so long, the small party of Lost Colonists with the Croatoans eventually moved off with them. Never rescued, they intermixed with the Indians as John Lawson said, and brought forth the reports of "white" Indians in the Carolinas.

By the 1880s, historians and the general public had come to

share this explanation of the Lost Colony's fate. The colonists had moved to Croatoan, but when help did not arrive, they intermarried with the Croatoans, now known as the Hatteras Indians. Eventually they all moved southwest to the Neuse River area or down into the swamps of southeastern North Carolina. There these survivors married into Indian families and so created a new people that came to be called the Croatan Indians of Robeson County, but are now known as the Lumbee Tribe of North Carolina.

Nineteenth- and early twentieth-century investigators found the Lumbees using a variety of Elizabethan English words in their dialect. North Carolina historian Stephen B. Weeks pointed out that about forty-one of the ninety-five English surnames of the Lost Colonists

Could Lumbees like Henry Berry Lowry have ties to early English colonists?

could be found among Lumbee Indian families in Robeson County, such as Berry and Sampson. Even the Lumbees themselves claimed a connection between them and those earliest of English settlers. Many still do.

For many North Carolinians, the fate of the Lost Colony had been solved. But it seemed a peaceful assimilation, devoid of the dramatic accounts of attack and death that John Smith and his men encountered. The Neuse River and Robeson County were located far south of the Chowan and Roanoke Rivers and Occaneechi town, where rumors put some survivors. Perhaps, some conjectured, the Lost

Colonists had divided into two groups. A smaller group went to Croatoan and when help never arrived intermarried with the Croatoan Indians, and whose descendants eventually migrated to the swamps of southeastern North Carolina. But a much larger group of colonists went elsewhere. Just as they said they would do when they worked out their plan with Governor John White.

When Eleanor Dare and the other surviving Roanoke settlers turned in to the interior, they gave birth to an American mystery that resonates with people even today.

CHAPTER 13

The Stones Roll On

For a while, the Pearces kept up the battle, trying to convince the world that just because the Eberhardt Stones were fake, the whole story was not wrong. As early as July 1941, just weeks after Eberhardt had been exposed as the Stone forger, newspapers were still running stories about the Dare Stones as the last word on the Lost Colonists. The *Providence (R.I.) Journal* headlined with "Inscribed Stones Revive Mystery of Lost Colony." Nothing was said of Eberhardt's extortion or the Pearces' claim he had faked the Stones. As late as the 1960s, American encyclopedias continued to include the episode of the Dare Stones in relation to the history of the Lost Colony. Nevertheless, though interest waxed and waned over the years, for most people, certainly historians, the Dare Stones were considered fakes and the story they told was discredited.

Though the Pearces still wanted to believe that at least some of the Stones might be genuine, even they had to accept that they had been hoodwinked. The Stones, which had been on display at Brenau, were taken down. Only the original Chowan River Stone remained accessible, as it was the only one definitely not associated with Eberhardt.

Two years after the revelation of Eberhardt's scam, in 1943, Brenau president Haywood Pearce Sr. died. The presidency of the college went not to Pearce Jr., but to Dr. Josiah Crudup, who was not all that interested in the Stones or the story they told. During World War II, Pearce Jr. left his family and his teaching job at Emory and Brenau and entered the Army. His research skills were put to good use in co-authoring a history of the Army Signal Corps. After the war, he went back to neither institution but instead took a position as professor of history at Eastern Michigan University at Ypsilanti. He retired to Pompano Beach, Florida, in 1963. Supposedly he was working on a book concerning the Dare Stones at the time of his death in 1971. Maude Fiske's play, *The Heritage,* was performed a few more times at Brenau commencement exercises, and then was put on permanent hiatus.

Boyden Sparkes could never really let the Dare Stones go. After World War II ended, Sparkes kept up a correspondence with various Emory faculty on the subject. The issue that seemed to weigh most heavily on him was that of the original Chowan River Dare Stone. If there was one among them that might be authentic, then it would be that one. Sparkes continued his efforts to track down Louis Hammond. In 1946, he discovered that there had been a fellow named Hammond in New England, a trained historian, who prior to 1933 had been involved in the forging of Indian relics. Sparkes wrote to Dr. J. Harris Purks of Emory to wonder if this could have been the same Hammond or maybe a "stupid brother."

Sparkes managed to get a photograph of the New England Hammond and had it flashed at some of the Emory faculty. Neither professors Purks nor English, nor university treasurer George Mew, could identify the man, but once told that it might be Louis Hammond, they all admitted that there was a likeness. Geology professor Lester, who had been told up front that it might be Hammond, admitted that it looked somewhat like the man he once spent time with traveling back and forth to North Carolina, but only if you added about forty pounds. Still, "the man's face shows more intelligence than I remember in Mr. Hammonds [*sic*]," Lester said.

Sparkes did not bother to show the picture to Pearce. Unfortunately, the reporter never followed upon this lead and so never completely eliminated the possibility of a New England Hammond who might have been pulling a hoax. And despite his other efforts, Sparkes never did track down the California Hammond. The hardboiled reporter retired to Wrightsville Beach, North Carolina, and on May 18, 1954, died of heart failure in Wilson, North Carolina, an adopted Tar Heel to the very end.

The unsolved mystery of the Dare Stones, however, was just too compelling to stay dead. The 1960s, when newcomers came across the intriguing threads of a forgotten story, saw a resurgence of interest. Dr. Crudup, the president of Brenau, received numerous letters from people around the country asking for information. Crudup would patiently explain the bare facts of how Brenau came to possess the Stones, but would often remind the writer, "Since atomic physics is my academic field of interest, I have not attempted to persue [*sic*] any further research into the Eleanor Dare Stone."

Newspapers and magazines would periodically retell the story of the Stones and how they may be the key to the mystery of the Lost Colony. Even the *Raleigh News and Observer*, ignoring the hefty file it must have maintained in its own morgue, in July 1964 published an article headlined "Clue to Lost Colony's Fate Lies Forgotten." The piece implied that stone clues remained hidden in storage lockers in the bowels of Brenau College, and that historians were fools for ignoring them.

In the 1979, the popular television show, *In Search Of . . .*, with host Leonard Nimoy, who had played Mr. Spock in the *Star Trek* series, presented a segment on the Dare Stones. Again, the show asked whether the Stones at Brenau might provide a clue to the disappearance of the Lost Colony. It did not devote much attention to Boyden Sparkes's 1941 verdict of forgery.

Others wanted to write a book on the Dare Stones and the Lost Colonists. Prospective authors often contacted Brenau requesting information or permission to come view the Stones. Brenau librarian Lucille Adams, the daughter of President Pearce and half-sister to Pearce Jr., replied in a polite near-formula, defending her family and admitting they were duped by Eberhardt. "The [*Saturday Evening Post*] article seemed to imply that they had worked up this hoax in order to promote Brenau. Nothing could have been further from their minds. While the Stones have never been proved authentic, they have never been completely disproved either," she wrote. "I myself feel that the first one, at least, is probably authentic. But I am sure that a lot of the later ones are fakes."

There was enough interest in the Stones that Brenau officials decided to have some of them examined by an expert. In late 1982, they allowed the South Carolina State Archeologist, Dr. Robert L. Stephenson, director of the Institute of Archeology and Anthropology at the University of South Carolina at Columbia, examine the Stones. Dr. Stephenson had complete access to the Stones and the extensive newspaper file the Pearce family had kept. He concentrated on four of the collection: the Chowan Stone and three Eberhardt Stones.

From the first, Stephenson found that his expertise as a scientific archaeologist was useless in determining authenticity of the Stones. "Frankly, I have not been able to suggest a single test or line of scientifically demonstrable evidence that would be helpful," he wrote. Stephenson ticked off the problems. Microscopes had told them nothing; an electron microscope would examine an area too small to be of any relevance. Archaeological excavations of the few known sites had been done, but with no luck, and repeating them now would be even less helpful. Nor could Stephenson imagine any chemical or physical test that would provide any solid clue. "This leaves me able only to offer an opinion based on the not very good documentary evidence that I have seen. The opinion is that 'The Dare Stone' is a hoax perpetrated on the public, and on Dr. Pierce [*sic*], by a combination of persons for reasons publicizing 'The Lost Colony' of Roanoke." Stephenson, as he admitted, had no hard facts to back up his idea, just an opinion.

Without much trouble, Stephenson declared the three Eberhardt Stones as fakes. He noted the obvious difference in writing style and technique between those and the Chowan Stone. "One, of the three, clearly appears to have been freshly carved with no weathering in the grooves. . . . I am, therefore, convinced that all of these stones are fakes and will consider only the original [Chowan] stone."

As for the Chowan Stone, Stephenson didn't think much of it either. The absence of signs of stream erosion made him dubious. Though the Stone was not found in a stream, Stephenson said he would still expect it in that part of North Carolina. Laying aside his scientific expertise, Stephenson then offered his opinions on Hammond, just as Boyden Sparkes had. He ticked off the same questions the Emory professors and others had asked fifty years earlier. How could Hammond, a California tourist, just happen to be in the area for a couple of months? How could he take such a long vacation? Just who was Louis Hammond anyway? It was Sparkes' old circumstantial evidence and faulty logic all over again, lack of evidence indicating proof of guilt.

Next, Stephenson took a more practical view of why the Chowan Stone was not Eleanor Dare's last word. If the Lost Colonists were under attack by Indians, "whatever they took with them (if anything) would have been only what they could grab quickly and run with. It is extremely doubtful that this would have included tools [with] which they could carve a message on a quartzitic stone." Finally, Stephenson believed that the Chowan Stone was part of some promotion, maybe the newly opened Ocean Highway, but more likely for "the renowned play 'The Lost Colony' and the possibility of a motion picture resulting from it. Any of these or any combination of them would have provided ample incentive for a fake 'tourist' to create and 'find' a fake 'Dare Stone.'" The archaeologist did not seem to appreciate that the Lost Colonists might easily have had a chisel with them, or that they might have had more time to carve the stone than some believed. Like others before him, he skirted the issue that the Chowan Stone essentially contradicted, rather than supported the plot of Green's *Lost Colony* and would hardly have served as an effective promotion.

Stephenson summed it up for the Brenau officials. "I do not know of any positive means of identifying the unquestionable authenticity, or lack of authenticity, of 'The Dare Stone'. However, from the above, it seems quite clear to me that 'The Dare Stone' is a forgery. Admittedly this opinion is based upon logical reasoning and a combination of contemporary documentation and hear-say evidence but not one line of reasoning leads to a logical conclusion of authenticity of 'The Dare Stone'." Stephenson concluded that Dr. Pearce was not in on the forgery, but was "an innocent pawn in the whole matter."

The archaeologist then urged Brenau officials to back away from any attempt to exhibit the Dare Stone anywhere, as there "would be a high potential for embarrassment to both Brenau College and the exhibitor." He suggested it just be kept stored away at Brenau "as a memento of a hoax and a symbol of 'what might have been.'" If the Stone should ever be authenticated, however — and he thought that highly unlikely — it would "become a part of the national heritage and be placed in the Smithsonian Institution as one of the major national treasures."

Brenau officials were not happy with Stephenson's report. But while it was not the answer they had hoped for, as John Sites, the executive vice president of Brenau who had authorized the investigation, punned, "We did the best we could, even though hoax springs eternal." In the end, physical evidence was insufficient to swing the question of authenticity one way or another. So the Stones were returned to their storage areas and pretty much forgotten for some while.

In April 1987, the *Atlanta Weekly*, the Sunday supplement magazine for the *Atlanta Journal* and the *Atlanta Constitution*, revisited the matter in a fifty-year retrospective. Gerdeen Dyer's "The Dare Stones Mystery: A Fascinating Chapter in Georgia History" retold the story of the Lost Colony, described the discovery and investigation of the Stones, and concluded with Boyden Sparkes's disposal of the matter.

Then in 1991, more than half a century after the Stones first emerged in the scene, a full-blown book devoted to the Dare Stones came out. *A Witness For Eleanor Dare: The Final Chapter in a 400 Year Old Mystery* was written by Robert W. White and published by Lexikos, a small, now-defunct press in San Francisco that specialized in local histories and miscellaneous nonfiction. About White, nothing is known. Apparently not an academic historian or an investigative reporter, he may have been a layman who became interested in the Dare Stones when he read about the Lost Colony in the *Encyclopedia of American History*. White approached the story in a novel way. Accepting all the Dare Stones as authentic and the story they told as absolute fact, he set out to discredit Boyden Sparkes's 1941 *Saturday Evening Post* story.

Robert W. White's book.

White had little use for the reporter. "Sparkes was interested in neither reason nor justice," White wrote. "He was interested in lynching Pearce in public and did just that." He criticized Sparkes's use of circumstantial evidence. Just because someone was trying to peddle carved stones on the 350th anniversary of the Lost Colony and the opening of Paul Green's play on Roanoke Island, he argued, did not mean that it was Hammond. Just because Eberhardt, Turner, Bruce, and the Jetts may have known each other through normal everyday activities, it did not mean they were all conspirators in a forgery. As for the Stones, the weathering seemed to be genuine enough, and the presence of lichen on one proved they were authentic. And would not a forger have been smart enough to check the

Oxford English Dictionary to ensure they got their words right? "Trale" and "reconnoitre" seemed to go back to the twelfth and thirteen centuries, White claimed, neglecting to consider the test case of "primeval."

However, in piecing together a history from the artifacts, White soon ran into the same problems that had bedeviled Pearce: how to reconcile the original Chowan Stone with the other Stones found in South Carolina and Georgia. To White, the first Stone found on the Chowan River by Hammond in 1937 made sense, as this was where the Lost Colonists had told Governor John White they would relocate. But that put it at odds with Eberhardt's Stones found in South Carolina, which indicated Virginia had been killed there.

Even White could not accept Pearce's explanation that an Indian had carried the original Stone from South Carolina up to the Chowan River. But White also had to admit that when it came to the divergent discovery sites of the Chowan Stone and Eberhardt's South Carolina "Second Stone," "It's a mystery how these stones with the same message referred to places hundreds of miles apart." White was troubled that Eberhardt's "Second Stone" not only told of the deaths of Ananias and Virginia Dare, which were also told on the Chowan Stone, but it also listed the name of fifteen colonists, none of which appeared on the official roster of the Lost Colonists.

To tie all these loose ends together, White had to weave a complex explanation. As White saw it, after the colonists were abandoned at Roanoke in 1587, they realized they could not stay there and removed to the Chowan River area. The first two years were times of war, and around 1589, a large group of the Lost Colonists, fed up with the dangerous life on the Chowan and eager to find gold in "Apalatcy," decided to head south. This "Southern Group" went back to Roanoke Island, strengthened the fort there, deliberately misdirecting the Spanish by carving "CROATOAN" on a post. Then they moved west to the Saluda River in South Carolina.

In South Carolina, this "Southern Group" may have met up with the missing thirteen Englishmen who had been chased off Roanoke in 1586, never to be seen again. Along the Saluda River, the "Southern Group" was attacked by Indians and left carved stones to mark their attacks. As for the names on the "Second Stone" that did not match the official roster, White believed these might have been the missing thirteen men from Roanoke or additional colonists omitted from the roster. The

White's theory postulated that friendly Indians took Eleanor to the safety of the Hontaoase village.

members of the "Southern Group" were eventually captured by Indians, and their survivors became the prisoners mentioned by Griffen Jones in Stone Number 48.

A "Northern Group," consisting of Eleanor, Virginia, and Ananias Dare and others, remained for a few more years on the Chowan River. Virginia, Ananias and others were killed there in 1591. From that point, Eleanor and others decided to head to South Carolina in search of the "Southern Group." However, a small group did not leave the Chowan, but actually moved further north into southern Virginia. In South Carolina, Eleanor's "Northern Group" did not find the "Southern Group," but discovered that group's messages carved into rocks. In South Carolina, Eleanor left another stone telling of Virginia's and Ananias' death on the Chowan. Fortunately, four friendly "Muskogee" Indians appeared to lead the "Northern Group" to the safety of the Hontaoase Indian village.

From there, the seven survivors of the "Northern Group" journeyed to Hontaoase in northern Georgia, where Eleanor married an Indian king, gave birth to daughter Agnes, and in 1599 finally died in a cave north of what would become Atlanta. As for the small remnant left in southern Virginia, they built Old St. Luke's Church in Isle of Wight County on the south side of Chesapeake Bay — an old brick church

whose origins had long been shrouded in mystery — even before
Captain John Smith and the English arrived there. But these lost English
were eventually slaughtered by Wahunsenacawh, the famed and
powerful powhatan of the Pamunkey Indians in the very month that the
English established Jamestown in 1607.

White's fancifully embroidered story offered an intriguing but
far-fetched explanation, and it led to no change in prevailing thought. A
few partisans adopted White's theory. But among the few historians who
gave the matter any attention at all, the Dare Stones were still widely
accepted as fakes and forgeries.

At the turn of the twenty-first century, the Dare Stones have
been consigned to obscurity. The heated debate that once surrounded
them stirs every now and again: a researcher or two will read something
about them, take an interest, and go see for themselves. One can still
visit Brenau, a university since 1992, go to the campus library Special
Collections room, and view the original Chowan Stone found by
Hammond in 1937. The forty-seven other Stones are stored in a furnace
building, stacked in a corner like surplus building materials. Brenau
officials do not usually advertise the existence of the Stones or promote
their story, though they will answer questions about them.

Though C. C. Crittenden died in 1969, he would be happy to
know the Lost Colonists and their legend have become firmly
entrenched in North Carolina and probably will not move from there
anytime soon. Except for a four-year hiatus during World War II, Paul
Green's *The Lost Colony* has been performed every summer since 1937.
One of the Outer Banks's most enduring attractions, it draws large
crowds every weekend during the summer. An entire culture of outdoor
theatre has been generated by the production, and the play has by now
involved multiple generations of families, as well as many famous
theatrical figures, as cast and crew. For most Americans these days,
especially North Carolinians, there is no controversy whatsoever about
where the Lost Colony belongs — only the nagging question of what
happened to them. It is still America's number-one historical mystery.

But tracing that mystery always leads back to the Chowan River
Dare Stone and the enduring question: factual artifact or artifical fake?
Many who studied it – historian Pearce, geologist Lester, English
professor Purks, and others – believed it to be authentic. Though Boyden
Sparkes suspected it to be a worthless fake, he was uncertain enough
that he spent the rest of his life searching for the forger. Even South

Carolina archaeologist Stephenson could offer no conclusive evidence. So which is it?

* * *

Fifty miles "into the maine" was the plan. Take their small boat and, over several trips, gradually move the entire colony west up the Albemarle Sound to where it was joined by the Chowan River.

In that direction, up the Albemarle, lay their only politically

expedient route to survival. With the ocean at their backs, Roanoke and Croatoan islands too small, the angry Roanokes Indians and their allies immediately to their west and the equally angry Weapemeocs to the north, safety could only be found by going further west to meet up with Menatonon's Choanoacs, some of the few pro-English Indians around. There also lay good land, spacious and fertile enough to support them. Ralph Lane had called the west bank of the Chowan "goodly high land" which "hath a very goodly corne field." And if the colonists actually were thinking of trying to make it to the Chesapeake Bay, then as Lane had shown, going

A typical example of a pinnace.

to the Choanoacs was also the way to do it.

At some point after Governor White sailed off with Fernandez's small fleet, the Roanoke colonists put their plan into motion. How long they remained on Roanoke is uncertain. Did they stay the winter on Roanoke, living off supplies? Did they move immediately? There were, after all, two infants to consider. Still, at some point, the party of colonists split up. A small contingent, probably no more than twenty, were dispatched to Croatoan Island, there to live off Croatoan hospitality and await the return of John White.

The much larger group of colonists then began moving up the Albemarle fifty miles, to Choanoac territory near the confluence of the Albemarle Sound and the Chowan River, near what is today Edenton, North Carolina. It seemed to be a thorough, well-planned, and well-

executed relocation. Using their small boat—possibly a pinnace—they
carefully took down their houses so they could be reassembled in their
new home, packed up their supplies and equipment, and then, in the
course of a few weeks, moved inland to the Chowan River and the
protection of their friend Menatonon of the Choanoacs.

    It would be nice to think that the Lost Colonists achieved
something of their dream. That along the Chowan River they built their
little English farming town and lived together as a people awaiting the
return of John White. Maybe, for a time, they did. Then disaster struck.

*Some critics of Dr. Pearce felt he had been as gullible as Charles Dickens'
Mr. Pickwick, who was also taken in by faked stones.*

CHAPTER 14

As Gullible as Pickwick

s a hoax and a fraud, the South Carolina and Georgia Dare Stones were truly magnificent. The old showman P. T. Barnum would have been proud. Such classic schemes played on the belief that good, old-fashioned American common sense could discern real from fake. Barnum made a fortune on Americans' errant common sense and their inability to tell the difference between authentic and imitation. And what made the Dare Stones all the more delicious was that a country charlatan like Bill Eberhardt could fool some of the top scholars in the nation.

Pearce, still clinging to the hope that some of the Stones might prove genuine, concluded that somewhere along the line the stonecutter had figured out how to imitate Elizabethan writing. A closer looks shows that there was precious little genuinely Elizabethan writing on those Stones produced by Eberhardt, Turner, and Bruce. Some words, a few phrases, and many of the words and spellings were English, but not necessarily Elizabethan. And these bore little resemblance to the vocabulary of the Chowan River Stone, which for the most part do appear to be Elizabethan. Still, a grudging nod of admiration must be given to Bill Eberhardt for his ability to use a little sandblasting, a little scraping, and a smear of acid to pull off one of the great hoaxes of the twentieth century. Even better, he actually made money from it. And selling off his half interest in the worthless South Carolina hill elevates Eberhardt into the upper echelon of American con men. A good hoax works because people who should know better want to believe it. The Pearces — naïve, wishful, downright gullible — certainly fell into his snare.

That's what makes the Dare Stone story such a cautionary tale. Dr. Haywood Pearce Jr., the Emory history professor, simply wanted to believe too much. He was on the trail of America's greatest mystery and convinced himself he had solved it. He had Hammond's Chowan River Stone — which fueled a burning urge to find the predicted Second Stone. At the outset Pearce conducted his research in an orthodox manner, gathering clues, investigating them, and discarding those that didn't make sense. But Pearce grew desperate of finding that Second Stone. He was vulnerable to a scam — in fact, had advertised a reward that practically invited it — when Bill Eberhardt turned up with his South Carolina Dare Stones. From that point on, Pearce ignored what should have been an academic's natural skepticism. He began concocting convoluted explanations, back-tracking on everything he had previously written, predisposing him to accept the story he wanted to believe.

Good old American common sense should have made Pearce suspect Eberhardt's stones from the start. The vast differences between the original Chowan River Stone found by Hammond and the stones found by Eberhardt and others in South Carolina and Georgia should have been a tip-off. The inscriptions could not have been made by the same carver.

Once Pearce accepted Eberhardt's South Carolina Stones as valid, he had to jettison all he had written earlier about the Chowan River Dare Stone. To support his own hypothesis, Pearce had to create an almost outlandish story that should have given pause. Certainly his critics found Pearce's idea that an Indian would carry a twenty-one pound stone for several hundred miles through forests and rivers only to drop it on the Chowan River preposterous

Eberhardt's "discovery" and presentation of his Stones should have raised red flags, even before dozens of similar stones began to turn up. When Eberhardt appeared in 1939 with his first Stone, the Pearces had told him it was not the "Second Stone" they were seeking. Eventually they described to him what they were looking for: a large stone with seventeen names on it, two of which were of Ananias and Virginia Dare, and a date of 1591. It should not have been much of a surprise when Eberhardt showed up with exactly what they were looking for. And when a majority of the names did not match the historical record, they should have wondered if the stone was more likely the work of a forger who needed fifteen English names and didn't realize an official roster existed.

Many other inconsistencies should have worried the Pearces. Eberhardt never left the Stones where he found them, as the Pearces instructed, but always brought them in. And how could Eberhardt have found so many of them when so many other people were also looking for them? The Stones also seemed to be found in a logical, almost narrative order—a "novel in stone," one newspaper called them. Could a group of people under such stress from the loss of their loved ones, the constant sickness, the constant Indian attacks, have the tools, time, and inclination to carve inscriptions on so many stones? And considering the effort it must have taken to carve them, many of those inscriptions — "Father, wee ben heyr 5 yeeres in primaeval splendour"; "Father, hab mercye." — said little of importance. In all, a little bit of hard questioning and research in the mode of Boyden Sparkes might have saved the Pearces a lot of money and embarrassment.

Had historian Haywood Pearce Jr. continued to pursue a thorough, methodical study of the original stone that so unexpectedly came his way — had he not accepted the Eberhardt, Turner, and Bruce Stones at face value as authentic — the picture today might be quite different. To this day there is no way to say unequivocally whether the Chowan River Stone was an authentic message left by Eleanor Dare in 1591, or was just a magnificent fake, ranking up there with Drake's California brass plate. That it had been used as a ship's ballast stone works both for and against the Chowan Stone. One can imagine that the Lost Colonists would have seen the usefulness of having several good-sized stones that could serve as a hard surface in a coastal region that had no hard surfaces. However, ships disgorge ballast stone when they take on cargo and so need fewer stones. But there was no cargo to take on at Roanoke in 1587. In fact, the ships were unloading people and supplies, so it would need to keep what ballast it had. And since the Lost Colonists were some of the first settlers in the area, there would not be any piles of ballast stone around. However, there might have been a few stones left by some of the ships wrecked on the beaches or from earlier voyagers to the area, such as the expeditions of Amadas and Barlowe in 1584, Richard Grenville in 1585 and 1586, or Sir Francis Drake in 1586. One can imagine it would have also been possible for a savvy colonist to pilfer a stone or two from the *Lion's* hold to serve as a hard surface. It certainly could explain why the Colonists on the Chowan River would have had such a stone with them.

Nevertheless, if the Chowan Stone is a fake, it is truly masterful. Creating it would be only somewhat difficult. Find a flat piece of English ballast stone and a mason with basic skills who could cold-chisel the inscription. Apply considerable skill and intelligence, and research to mimic the language of the 1580s. But to invent the story itself: that would require true cunning.

R.D.W. Connor.

Whoever might have forged the Chowan River Stone would have to have possessed a detailed and thorough knowledge of the Lost Colony consistent with John White's journal, the writings of Captain John Smith, and the records of the Virginia Company and some of its officials, such as William Strachey, documents at the time not readily accessible to general readers in the United States. Even at that, references to the Lost Colony in these primary records are scant and scattered. Anyone looking to form a cohesive account would have to have read most of them to glean the few crumbs found there. That means the forger would have to have been a superior scholar of North Carolina, Virginia, and Lost Colony history—an academic historian, or an extremely keen amateur with academic training and access to source materials. In the 1930s, the known list of such scholars was short indeed.

And placing the Stone on the Chowan River would have proposed an interpretation that was not in vogue in 1937 or earlier. At the time of the Stones' discovery, prevailing thought on the fate of the Lost Colony ignored the Chowan River connection. Until the middle of the twentieth century, most scholars believed the Lost Colonists had gone to Croatoan, precisely where the clues found by John White pointed them and where the Colonists eventually merged with the regional Indians.

By 1919, North Carolina historian R. D. W. Connor, in his three-volume *History of North Carolina*, had enshrined the theory that English genes were passed on by the colonists' intermarriage with North Carolina Indian peoples. Connor makes no mention of Virginia Dare's death or the Chowan River, and while he might have been smart enough to create the Chowan Stone forgery, it would be hard to accept that the future archivist of the United States would stoop to faking historical evidence.

Only one professional North Carolina historian of that time had ventured to link the Lost Colonists with the Chowan River: Samuel A'court Ashe. The entry for "Virginia Dare" in Ashe's 1906 *Biographical History of North Carolina* poses an unconventional view. "White's Colony, after his departure, did remove into the interior, and located in either what is now Bertie County, or south of Albemarle Sound"—an area situated along the west bank of the Chowan River. Certainly the former Confederate general turned historian would have been sufficiently knowledgeable to have forged the Dare Stone, but his involvement would be highly doubtful. Ashe, son of a U.S. Congressman, was one of North Carolina's most distinguished historians, with a sterling reputation on a national scale. He was ninety-seven when the Dare Stone was found in 1937 and he died the next year after a long and distinguished career as attorney, writer, newspaper publisher, civil servant, and state legislator.

Playwright Paul Green, author of *The Lost Colony* symphonic drama, had done admirable research in the preparation of his play. Many people suspected a publicity link between the Chowan River Stone and the debut of *The Lost Colony*. But Green consistently denied any connection to the Stone, which would have ill served the play's purposes in any case.

If Paul Green or his publicity man wanted to plant a fake relic to publicize the play, they surely would have drafted an inscription that corroborated their script. Green has Wanchese and his Indians attack the Colonists, and while Ananias is killed, Virginia Dare remains very much alive. Manteo and his people come to the Colonists' aid. Wanchese is eventually killed and peace is made with the Indians. So in Green's play, it was not Indians who forced the Lost Colonists from Roanoke, but the arrival of a Spanish expedition. As the Spanish approached, the Lost Colonists relocated to Croatoan where they would be safe. The play ends there and nothing is suggested about the Chowan River area.

The name of Hugh Talmadge Lefler, respected member of the University of North Carolina history faculty, might appear on any list of Lost Colony experts of that generation. But Lefler was on the committee in 1938 called by C. C. Crittenden to investigate the stones Tom Shallington pulled from the Alligator River. Crittenden, Lefler, and a host of others had declared those stones to be fakes. During the 1950s and 1960s Lefler would go on to occupy the Kenan chair of history at the university and to take up Ashe's mantle as the premier historian of North Carolina. But at no time did he ever advocate the Chowan River theory of the colonists' fate. On the contrary, Lefler in his 1956 *History of North Carolina* wrote that "one of the most plausible theories – though seldom advanced by writers – is that the group, finally despairing of relief, sailed for England in a boat which had been left with them by White in 1587, and were lost in the Atlantic."

Dr. William S. Powell.

Several other historians may have known enough about the intricacies of the Lost Colony to have forged the stone. Crittenden of the North Carolina Historical Commission was well known to be the Dare Stones' most vigorous opponent. Dr. Douglas L. Rights, who a decade later published the classic *The American Indian in North Carolina*, was an expert on the subject. A theologian and minister by training, Rights held that the Lost Colonists had gone to Croatoan and intermarried with Indians there. Dr. William S. Powell, who later became a history professor at the University of North Carolina, and David Beers Quinn, who by the late 1950s was considered the dean of Lost Colony studies, both dismissed the Stones as fakes in 1959. Quinn accepted Strachey's theory and contended the Lost Colonists moved in with the Chespian Indians on the south side of Chesapeake Bay, not the Chowan River, and were wiped out by Wahunsenacawh in April 1607.

Among the many characters involved in the discovery of the Stones, none would appear sufficiently learned to have forged them. Certainly not a retired produce dealer — if in fact Louis Hammond was what he claimed. Not the backwoods Eberhardt, Turner, or Bruce, however clever they were in creating knockoffs. Not a Hollywood agent, as Boyden Sparkes believed. Nor, necessarily, the New England Hammond, whom Sparkes later investigated. And though Jack DeLysle the publicity promoter out of Virginia may have been a little more educated and capable of pulling off such a hoax, we can't be sure even he knew enough of the history to be able to do it. And why would a promoter forge a stone that killed off Virginia Dare, North Carolina's most beloved historical figure?

Likewise, the obscure location of the Chowan River Stone defies any sensible motive — publicity, personal fame, financial gain. If there existed in 1937 a well-read history buff with sufficient time and access to do the research, the ability to concoct the transcription, enough proficiency with a chisel to hammer it out or acquaintance with someone who could, no such person has surfaced in more than seventy years. But if such a hoaxer were ever to be revealed, the most pressing question might still be that after going to all that trouble, why plant the forgery on the swampy bank of the Chowan River, where no one knowing the Lost Colony would look, and where it could be found only by lucky happenstance?

Rule that out, then, all the known suspects who might've perpetrated a forgery. Rule out anyone who might benefit from a faked relic. What if — just if — the original Dare Stone were not a forgery at all? Read the details from the Stone's inscription, consider once more the record left by White, Smith, Strachey, and other witnesses, and apply the same dose of conjecture that all historians must use in writing a history of the Lost Colony, and a new and very plausible interpretation of what happened to the Lost Colonists comes about.

* * *

Once Governor John White sailed for England in August 1587, the colonists on Roanoke found themselves in dire straits. Too late to plant crops and surrounded by hostile Roanokes, Dasemunkepeucs, and Weapemeocs, the colonists soon put their plan in motion.

A small party, probably no more than twenty, sailed to Manteo's town of Croatoan to await the return of John White, whom they expected back within a year. The clues on Roanoke — CRO and CROATOAN *— would direct White to them. Once he located them, they would tell him about the situation and show him where he would find his daughter, granddaughter and the others.*

  The larger group of colonists now did what they told White they would do: relocate about fifty miles "into the maine." That would take them up the Albemarle Sound to the Chowan River area, where Menatonon of the Choanoacs was their only friend. **Father soon after you go for England we came hither.**

  For four years the hundred or so English colonists lived among the Choanoacs. Since a hundred colonists would have severely strained a single town, they were hived off among several towns so as not to overburden a single community. During those years the English and Choanoacs would have certainly influenced each other. The English, with the dwindling supplies they'd brought from home, would have out of necessity adopted Indian customs. As clothes wore out, they would have turned to hides and grasses. Indian foods became English fare. As gunpowder and shot ran out, English hunters returned to the bow and arrow. Bachelor Englishmen took Choanoac wives. The Choanoacs watched while the English tried to recreate their familiar two-story houses, as Strachey would later report.

  Their sojourn along the Chowan River did not appear to be a pleasant time for the English or the Choanoacs. **Only misery & war two year. Above half dead here two year more from sickness being four & twenty.** *War, Sickness, Misery, and Death — the Four Horsemen of a New World apocalypse — decimated the Lost Colonists. Raiding and feuding were common in eastern North Carolina Indian society. Raids were made to take revenge, but sometimes to obtain shells, copper, hides, even captives. They were also ways in which young men who showed bravery and fortitude in combat gained prestige, which led to political power. So the Lost Colonists, essentially a nation of strangers in an area where they had no kinship, economic, or military ties other than with the Choanoacs, found themselves the targets of small-scale raids. These may have come from the Mangoaks to the west who feared the English would upset their control of the copper trade with their own manufactured goods. Roanokes, Weapemeocs, and Secotans in the east and south, with revenge in mind, may have made their own raids. Possibly some came* *from Virginia peoples to the north. These years of constant low-level feuding, surprising and disconcerting to these English civilians, may have picked off many of the Colonists. The Choanoacs, as the hosts and new families of these English, would be hit as well. Certainly at some point some Choanoac families, themselves the victims of raids, began to wish the Colonists had not settled among them.*

Sickness did not help matters. Back in 1585 and '86, when Colonel Ralph Lane and his Irish War veterans rampaged across the Albemarle Peninsula, wherever they went they left a trail of illness that hit the Indians hard. Thomas Hariot admitted that in every town the English visited, a few days after they left, its people would be hit with disease and start dying rapidly, "in some townes about twentie, in some fourtie, in some sixtie & in one sixe score, which in trueth was very manie in respect of their numbers." Pemisapan blamed the English, who could kill whomever they would "without weapons and not come near them." Now Choanoac towns suffered. By this time malaria was beginning to settle in the Carolina sounds. It could easily kill off the very young, the old, and those with bodies weakened by hunger and hardship, Choanoac and English alike. Similarly, sanitation diseases brought by the English, such as typhus and typhoid fever, seemed to hit hardest in crowded villages. The Choanoac chiefdom was deteriorating. When Sicklemore, Powell and Todkill visited in 1608, they reported the Choanoacs to be a shadow of their former glory.

Amid all this, Choanoac society was undergoing great stress. The raids, the sickness, the deaths, and the English influence among them were dividing the Choanoacs into anti-English and pro-English factions, just as Lane had done among the Roanokes. As long as Menatonon was alive and in power the Lost Colonists had a protector. But if Menatonon, already old and lame in 1586, died during this time, then it's possible the anti-English faction gained power. Certainly these Lost Colonists were not the hardened soldiers Lane had used to cow the Choanoacs in 1586. These were men, women, and children, lost from their people, weak and in need of assistance. And so by 1591, the Choanoacs may well have been ready to be rid of these difficult guests.

During this same time, Wanchese was rebuilding Pemisapan's Roanoke chiefdom and creating a military alliance with the Dasemkepeucs, Secotans, Aquascogocs, and Pomeioocs, all Indian peoples on the Albemarle Peninsula. Powell and Todkill, after their 1608 search along the Chowan, reported that the "slaughter" of the Lost

Colonists was done at the command of the "Powhaton of Roanocke."
The term "Powhatan" is not a name, but a title, and the "Powhaton of
Roanocke" at that time was most likely Wanchese, who probably
inherited the position after the murder of Pemisapan by Ralph Lane in
1586. Wanchese was likely a nephew of Pemisapan and had been named
by John White in 1587 as one of the Indian leaders making attacks on
them. Now Wanchese, the Powhatan of the Roanokes, was able to exact
revenge on the English.

Up to this time, with the Lost Colonists isolated in Choanoac
territory, Wanchese may have allowed his warriors to make a few raids,
but he made no real effort to overwhelm them. Then John White returned
to Roanoke in August 1590. **Savage with message of ship unto us. We believe it
not you.** Since the ship did not stay long and did not search for them, the
Colonists, once they learned of this, did not think it was John White.
After all, they imagined White would initiate a major hunt for them, not
just turn around and sail off, which was what happened.

Like the Colonists, Wanchese could not know that White left
never to return again. Instead, White's return worried him; made him
think the English had returned to re-create their Roanoke colony. But
Wanchese could not allow this.. He could not chance the reunion of the
Lost Colonists with another English colonization effort. To have two sets
of English colonists bracketing his chiefdom was unthinkable. So now he
determined to rid himself of the weakened but still threatening Lost
Colonists. Eliminate the Chowan River threat first and then deal with the
English re-colonization of Roanoke when it came.

Wanchese's ambassadors now contacted the Choanoacs to tell
them of his plan. He may have explained his need for revenge, the
looming threat of another English colony bent on vengeance of its own,
and reiterated the problems that the Lost Colonists had brought to the
region. And if an anti-English faction was in the ascendancy among the
Choanoacs, they may have been amenable. Especially when Wanchese
explained that the Choanoacs would not have to lift a finger against
their guests – just withdraw and allow Wanchese and his warriors to do
the job. Withdrawal was a common Indian strategy of the day.
Pemisapan had done it in the spring of 1586, when he ordered his
people to withdraw from Roanoke Island and leave the English to starve.
Now the Choanoacs would withdraw as well. And the explanation to the
Lost Colonists was that angry spirits demanded their withdrawal from
the Colonists. **Soon after the savages fain spirits angry.**

So on the given day, the Choanoacs deserted the Lost Colonists, leaving them exposed and alone. Small space of time they afright of revenge, ran all away. *Now Wanchese, the "Powhaton of Roanocke," and his allies attacked.* Sudden murder all save seven. *It was a "slaughter," with most of the Lost Colonists killed in their fields, woods, and homes. Ananias and Virginia Dare were two of the casualties.* Mine childe Ananias too, slaine with much misarie. *Had Ananias been captured, it would not have been unusual for him to have been tortured to death, and that would certainly entail "much misarie." In 1711, North Carolina surveyor John Lawson was captured by the Tuscaroras and tortured to death by having small splinters of woods stuck in his body until he looked like a porcupine. Then these were set on fire. As for Virginia, the raiders may have deemed a small child of three or four years old a hindrance, especially if they meant to move fast. A crying child could bring enemies down on them. So the death of the first English child born in America may have been something as quick as dashing her brains out against a tree.*

At least seven in Eleanor's party survived the attack. How they survived is not known. Maybe they were not there when the attack took place, or hid themselves or were hidden. Somehow these few had survived. Now they had to bury their dead. Bury all near four miles east this river upon small hill. *And they had time to do it. Raids were fast-moving affairs, with warriors striking quickly and withdrawing quickly. Wanchese's warriors would not dally in Choanoac territory, but after achieving their goals would have quickly returned to their villages. The Choanoacs who deserted them would probably not immediately make a move against the surviving Colonists. So the survivors were not immediately chased up the Chowan River, but had time, maybe days, to bury the dead and prepare to the leave area. Certainly the survivors would have understood that they could not stay any longer in Choanoac territory. Withdrawal by the Choanoacs had shown the survivors they were no longer welcome among them.*

Now they carved their last message to John White, whom they imagined would come looking for them. One rock listed the names of those killed in the attack and was placed on the small hill where they were buried. Names writ all there on rock. *Next Eleanor had the Chowan River Stone carved, which described the attack. On the front of the Stone was inscribed* a Cross, *the signal of distress that White and the Colonists had agreed upon. And Eleanor was certainly in distress as the Colonists had been wiped out along with her husband and daughter. She memorialized them here.* **Ananias Dare & Virginia went hence unto Heaven 1591.** *Imagining her father still looking for her, she hoped the Stone would fall into his hands.* **Any Englishman shew John White Govr Via.** *John White was still the governor of the Lost Colony and this country was then called Virginia by the English. To ensure he got it, she promised recompense.* **Savage show this unto you & hither we promise you to give great plenty presents.** *Here was a final message to John White, binding him to give lots of gifts to the Indian who brought this stone to him. Again, this was very much within Indian culture. Gift-giving was an everyday and essential part of Indian life. That Eleanor would promise presents to any Indian who got this into the hands of John White would be normal. And she surely thought she could promise this and that White would abide by it.*

    Then she had it signed **EWD** *– Eleanor White Dare. Though she did not carve the stone herself, she ordered it done, and her signature initials would have meant much more to John White than those of the actual carver. And as to why she spent all the time and effort carving the message in stone rather than using a piece of petticoat, pottery, or tree bark, it was because this really was the last word from Lost Colonists. The never-found Second Stone was to serve as a tombstone for those killed in the raid, while the Chowan River Stone was the last testament of what happened to them. Then she left both Stones there near the Chowan River.* **Put this there also.** *Certainly she hoped the Stone would make its way into her father's hands, but she knew now that he would never find her. The Lost Colony was dead after four years of war, sickness, misery, and death.*

    Then the seven survivors, as Strachey later reported, the "four men, two boys, and one young maid . . . escaped and fled up the River of Chaonoke." North up the river was the only logical way to run as Wanchese's attack had come from the south and east. They probably did not get far before they were scooped up by Indian warriors, possibly Mangoaks or even unfriendly Choanoacs. Now they were captives, the property of the man who took them. He might take them back home to become part of his family, working alongside his wife and children in the fields or with him on hunting or fishing trips. He might take them to Occaneechi town and exchange them for seashells, copper, or whatever might be offered. This might explain why Smith and others learned that some of the Lost Colony was there. At Occaneechi town, Gepanocon and Eyanoco, probably one in the same person, exchanged copper for them.

He took these captives back to his town of Ritanoc in the west, where they became "worth much labor," and "beat his copper." Others wound up at Anone and Panawiok, probably other Mangoak villages west of the Chowan, or at Peccarecamicke down on the Tar River.

And what of those Colonists at Croatoan? We know nothing about their fate. Were they killed in a similar attack? Did they ever join their fellow Colonists on the Chowan River? Did they despair of John White ever returning and so assimilated with the Croatoans and followed them inland? Probably this last as they never returned to England nor seemed to have been picked up by the Spanish. Still, for those who survived any length of time, assimilation into Croatoan society through adoption or marriage would have been the most logical answer. It was possibly their gray-eyed descendants who John Lawson found on Hatteras Island in 1701.

And that was probably the same fate for those few Colonists who survived the "slaughter of [the] Powhaton of Roanocke." They were eventually absorbed into North Carolina Indian society. Even those enslaved to hammer copper for Eyanoco may have been adopted by an Indian family. Others married Indian women and Eleanor may well have had a second, but this time an Indian, husband. So it is quite possible that a small rivulet of Lost Colonist genes trickles through eastern North Carolina Indians today.

But for all intents and purposes, by 1591 Sir Walter Raleigh's Lost Colony of Roanoke was dead after four years of war, sickness, misery, death and one last Indian attack. And the last we see of the Lost Colonists are seven desperate survivors scurrying up the Chowan River to their captivity and immortality.

AFTERWORD

W hile the only evidence to support the Chowan River Dare Stone's account is purely circumstantial, so is the only evidence to disprove it. No archaeological discoveries have come to light that prove it genuine — but none, on the other hand, that prove it false. For that matter, no artifacts of any kind have been conclusively linked to the Lost Colonists. Though artifacts have been found on Roanoke and Hatteras Islands that are linked to the Roanoke voyages, they seemed related to Ralph Lane's earlier expedition.

When I saw the original Dare Stone at Brenau I was drawn to its aura of antiquity. The small, crabbed letters and uneven lines seemed a message carved by someone in haste. As a historian who has immersed himself in the Dare Stone story and as a North Carolina resident, I feel the tug of wanting to believe the Chowan Dare Stone to be true. And it might well be as the story it tells is certainly plausible. But then the image of the disgraced Professor Pearce rises up before me. The historian should always be skeptical, above all, even while tapping the full power of imagination. The subsequent South Carolina and Georgia Stones purchased by the Pearces are certainly fakes, seemingly perpetrated by Bill Eberhardt and friends. And if the uneducated Eberhardt had a more knowledgeable accomplice helping write the inscriptions, that person has never been identified. But Pearce fell into their trap. The good professor allowed himself to become so enamored with his subject that he abandoned his professional skepticism — and risked everything for the sake of a few crude forgeries. He just wanted to believe too much. And just when I want to put away my own skepticism and do the same, I hear Jack DeLysle, "publicity man par excellence," laughing from beyond the grave.

Still, in considering a case like the Lost Colony, every historian must rely on the same few existing sources. And each of these nuggets is subject to interpretation and may be bent to support the writer's chosen position: intermarriage with Indians, gone to the Chesapeake, gone to the Chowan River, attacked by Powhatan, the Mangoaks, by Wanchese and his Roanokes, sold at Occaneechi Town, enslaved to hammer Indian copper, lost at sea, or rotting away in a Spanish prison. Eleanor, Ananias, Virginia Dare and the Lost Colonists will always be frozen in time and memory, until harder evidence is found.

ACKNOWLEDGEMENTS

I owe a tremendous amount of gratitude to a host of people who helped me with the researching of this book. I happened upon the Dare Stone story by accident while researching the Lost Colony and wondered why I had not heard more about the Stones. In tracking down the story, I turned first to Ginger Cain, archivist at Emory University in Atlanta. Ginger was wonderful in taking my calls and was gracious enough to mail me copies of some of the information Emory had in its archives. When I visited Emory for more research, Kathey Shoemaker was very kind to help me find as much information as I could on the topic.

Of course, much of the information on the Dare Stones came from small Brenau University in Gainesville, Georgia. Debbie Thompson, who manages the Special Collections room there, was a wonderful host and extraordinarily generous with her time. Marlene Giguere of the Brenau Library was also very helpful. I was overwhelmed by how nice the folks at Brenau were, and how willing they were to take the time to drag out the Stones and let an author look at them. I have many pleasant memories of my days there. The Chowan Stone and even the Eberhardt fakes constitute a wonderful treasure trove.

The entire staff at the North Carolina State Archives in Raleigh was most helpful when it came to researching C. C. Crittenden and the state's reaction to the Dare Stones. Let me also thank Walter R. Turner, the historian at the North Carolina Transportation Museum for information on U.S. Highway 17, the Ocean Highway. In Georgia, Christine Rodick of the University of Georgia River Basin Center provided details on the Chattahoochee River and its rocks. Betsy Boyden Eagles-Fouros, granddaughter of Boyden Sparkes and daughter of Joe Eagles Jr., provided additional information on the reporter. Matthew Schaefer at the Herbert Hoover Library in West Branch, Iowa, which holds the Boyden Sparkes Papers, gave a rundown on their Sparkes holdings. Dr. Barbara Brannon was extraordinarily helpful in the editing of the manuscript. And David A. Norris did a great job with the map.

Down at my home, the University of North Carolina Wilmington, folks there have continually helped me in numerous ways. A shout-out has to go to the entire staff of the UNCW's Randall Library Interlibrary Loan Department. Without their professionalism and help, this book would never have been completed. I certainly want to thank Dr. Lewis Walker of the Department of English for his help with Elizabethan words and language and the *Oxford English Dictionary*. Dr. Alan Watson of the Department of History is one of the top North Carolina historians, and he generously read articles and bits of manuscripts for me. I ask a lot of him and he asks nothing in return. I owe him much. A word of thanks also goes to Dr. Sue McCaffray, then my boss and the chair of the Department of History, who encouraged my writing and research. She is a good friend. Other friends and colleagues at UNCW who helped make this project a success were Dr. Will Moore, Dr. Chris Fonvielle, Dr. Bill McCarthy, and Dr. Paul Gillingham.

Outside the university, other friends who listened to my Dare Stone stories are Kevin Sands, David Fann, Raoul Sosa, Connie Nelson, Paco Strickland, Justine and Guy Ferreri, Lynne and Alan Williams, Chris Miller, Charles Pynch, and Mark and Jordyn Zimmerman. Naturally, I must thank my mother, Ann La Vere, and my sisters, Tracy and Rhonda La Vere; and I would like to remember my late father, Dick La Vere. Of course I owe much to my in-laws, Jack and Carol Mills. They are the greatest in-laws ever and true supporters of my writing. I dedicate this book to them. Of course, none of this would ever get done without the support of my loving wife, Caryn. She's the best and I love her very much.

Notes

Preface: A Colony Lost

(2) – "we found no man . . ." John White, "John White's Narrative of the 1590 Voyage to Virginia" in David Beers Quinn, *The Roanoke Voyages, 1584-1590. Documents to Illustrate the English Voyages to North America under the Patent Granted to Walter Raleigh in 1584.* 2 vols. London: The Hakluyt Society, 1955, 2:611, hereafter cited as White's 1590 Report. These are the North Carolina Outer Banks, a long string of barrier islands, broken only be narrow inlets, stretching from southern Virginia down to about Bogue Inlet in Carteret County, North Carolina. Though now North Carolina, in the 1580s England considered all this "Virginia." It is believed that in the 1580s, the Outer Banks were actually several miles further out east in the Ocean than they are today. Once behind the Outer Banks, one entered a almost inland sea formed by the Albemarle and Pamlico Sounds. The Roanokes called this inland sea "Occam." Roanoke Island, which sat amid the Occam Sea, is only about eight miles long and two miles wide. It may have smaller back in the 1580. Erosion over the last four hundred years has certainly moved both the Outer Banks and Roanoke Island.

(2) - "by the will of God . . ." White's 1590 Report, 2:611.

(2) - "so that they could neither stand nor swimme . . ." White's 1590 Report, 2:612.

(3) - "sounded with a trumpet Call . . ." White's 1590 Report, 2:613.

(4) - "I had safely found . . ." White's 1590 Report, 2:616. It is believed that Croatoan was located on what it today called Cape Hatteras, near the town of Buxton. It is the easternmost point of the Outer Banks. Archaeological excavations there have turned up a good-sized Indian town, but also evidence of English occupation in the form of a signet ring and other manufactured goods.

Chapter 1: A Stone on the Chowan

(11) - "Newshawks among the students . . ." James G. Lester and J. Harris Purks, Jr., "The Virginia Dare Stone." Address to the Faculty Club of Emory University, April 19, 1938, Folder 9, Box 1, Dare Stone

Collection, MARBL, Robert W. Woodruff Library, Emory University, Atlanta, Ga., 4, hereafter cited as Lester address.

(11) - "did not contribute . . ." Summary of Events Relating to the Hammond Stone. Folder 9 Box 1, Dare Stone Collection, MARBL, Robert W. Woodruff Library, Emory University, Atlanta, Ga., hereafter cited as Emory Archives.

(13) - "he has no business. . ." Lester address, 12.

(13) - "conducted himself with persistence. . ." Lester address, 12.

(13) - "Frankly, I believe the man . . ." Lester address, 12.

(14) - "ANANIAS DARE & VIRGINIA WENT HENCE. . ." The actual stone can be seen in the Trustee Library of Brenau College, Gainesville, Ga., but the transcription was published several times in Bulletins published by the college. See "The Dare Stone and the Lost Colony of Roanoke." *Brenau Bulletin.* Vol. 30, No. 3, March 1, 1939, Brenau College, Gainesville, Ga., hereafter cited as 1939 *Bulletin.*

(17) - "the coming of Eleanor Dare . . ." Paul Green to Chris. Crittenden, 11 Dec. 1937, Director's Office Material, General Correspondence, Roanoke Island Folder, June-December 1937, Box 117, R-Z, Department of Archives and History, State Archives, Raleigh, NC, hereafter cited as NC Archives. Paul Green (17 March 1894 - 4 May 1981), born in Lillington, North Carolina, was one of the state's most renown literary personalities. As a playwright, many of his plays were performed on Broadway. His play, *In Abraham's Bosom*, won the 1926 Pulitzer Prize for Drama. Green is credited with developing what he called "symphonic dramas," which were big productions, usually outdoor dramas of some historical event, full of music, pageantry, and period costumes. *The Lost Colony* is his most famous symphonic drama, but he wrote many more, including *The Stephen Foster Story*, which is still performed each summer at Bardstown, Kentucky. Green, though well known and highly respected in the New York theatre scene, would eventually move to Chapel Hill. He taught drama at the University of North Carolina there until his death.

(19) - "delicate frosting." Lester address, 7.

(19) - "He held the bit . . ." Lester address, 8.

(20) - "leave the evidence . . ." "'Lost Colony' Stone at Emory," *Atlanta Constitution*, February 13, 1938.

Chapter 2: The Experts at Emory

(23) - "we find a piece of the true cross . . ." Mark Twain, *The Innocents Abroad or the New Pilgrims'Progress* (Hartford, Conn.: American Publishing Company, 1869), 165.

(25) - "regular fellow" and "not particularly . . ." Confidential Report, Retail Credit Company, 18 December 1937, Folder 6, Box 1, Emory Archives.

(26) - "Conversation and correspondence . . ." Lester address, 12.

(26) - "exclusive right to publish . . ." Agreement between L. E. Hammond and Emory University, 9 November 1937, Folder, 7, Box 1, Emory Archives.

(27) - "a part of her petticoat . . ." Lester address, 10-11.

(27-28) - "planted by a person . . ." and "desiring to start. . ." Lester address, 13.

(28) - "that its authenticity . . ." Lester address, 14.

(28-29) – "Grave of Virginia Dare Believed Found in the State." All quotes here come from the *Raleigh News and Observer* story of November 22, 1937.

(29) - "I understand that you . . ." C. C. Crittenden to Haywood Pierce [sic], 19 Nov. 1937, Roanoke Island Folder, Box 117, NC Archives.

(29) - "the premature publicity . . ." Haywood Pearce Jr. to Crittenden, 24 Nov. 1937, Roanoke Island Folder, Box 117, NC Archives.

(30) - "on which the 'Lost Colony'. . ." Crittenden to Pearce, 27 Nov. 1937, Roanoke Island Folder, Box 117, NC Archives.

(31) - "In some places of the countrey . . ." Thomas Hariot, "A Briefe and True Report" in David Beers Quinn, *The Roanoke Voyages, 1584-1590. Documents to Illustrate the English Voyages to North America under the Patent Granted to Walter Raleigh in 1584.* 2 vols. London: The Hakluyt Society, 1955., 1:370.

Chapter 3: Pearce on a Mission

(36) - "photograph, measure, survey . . ." Permit [Emory University], Jan-May 1938, Roanoke Island Folder, Box 120, NC Archives.

(37) - "telegraphed me twice . . ." Crittenden to Roy Appleman, 1 March 1938, Roanoke Island Folder, Box 120, NC Archives.

(37) - "become the victim . . ." Crittenden to Appleman, 1 March 1938, Roanoke Island Folder, Box 120, NC Archives.

(38) - "plant an old metal chest . . ." G. G. Macintosh to Roy Appleman, 21 Feb. 1938, Roanoke Island Folder, Box 120, NC Archives.

(38) - "unethical writer . . ." and "Lost Colony episode . . ." Macintosh to Appleman, 21 Feb. 1938, Roanoke Island Folder, Box 120, NC Archives.

(39) - "Lost Colony" Stone at Emory, *Atlanta Constitution*, February 13, 1938; "Inscription May Solve Virginia Dare Mystery," *Raleigh (N.C.) News and Observer*, 30 Jan. 1938.

(39) - "We intend to publish . . ." "Lost Colony" Stone at Emory, *Atlanta Constitution*, February 13, 1938.

(40) – "chased from thence . . ." Richard Hakluyt, *Principal Navigations, Voiages, Traffiques and Discoveries of the English Nation*. London: G. Bishop and R. Newberie, 1589, 748.

Chapter 4: Searching for the Second Stone

(46) - "yet there is no circumstance . . ." and "if this is a forgery . . ." Thomas English to Dr. Randolph Adams, 26 January 1938, Folder 1, Box 3, Thomas Hopkins English Papers, Emory Archives.

(46) - "probably a fraud" and other quotes from R. C. Mizell to Legare Davis, 2 February 1938, Folder 7, Box 1, Emory Archives.

(49) - "make no claims . . ." 1939 *Bulletin*.

(50) - "With the second stone . . ." 1939 *Bulletin*.

(50) - "I believe . . ." Haywood Pearce Sr. to Jasper L. Wiggins, 3 Feb. 1939, Correspondence Folder, Box 3, Dare Stones Collection, University Archives, Trustee Library, Brenau University, Gainesville, Georgia, hereafter cited as BU.

Chapter 5: No Stone Unturned

(54) – "it is believed . . ." "Second Dare Stone May Leave State," *Elizabeth City Daily Advance*, 29 Mar. 1939.

(54) - "would be glad . . ." and others in that paragraph. Crittenden to Richard Dillard Dixon, 29 Mar. 1939, Roanoke Island Folder, Box 126, NC Archives.

(55) – "VIRGINIA DARE B. AUG 1587" "Surveyor Tom Shallington Has Ancient Ballast Stone Bearing Her Name; Dates," *Elizabeth City Daily Advance*, 30 Mar. 1939.

(55) - "I know that the old man . . ." W. O. Saunders to Crittenden, 27 Mar. 1939, Roanoke Island Folder, Box 126, NC Archives.

(56) - "shallow fracture marks" Harry T. Davis to Crittenden, 16 May 1939, Roanoke Island Folder, Box 126, NC Archives.

(56) - "consider the authenticity . . ." A Meeting, 17 May 1939, Roanoke Island Folder, Box 126, NC Archives.

(57) - "It seems to us evident . . ." and other quotes in paragraph. A Meeting, 17 May 1939, Roanoke Island Folder, Box 126, NC Archives.

(57) - "had accumulated . . ." and other quotes in paragraph. Jasper L. Stuckey to Crittenden, 18 May 1939, Roanoke Island Folder, Box 126, NC Archives.

(58) - "I believe we can say . . ." Crittenden to Edwin Bjorkman, George Andres, W. O. Saunders, W. S. Carawan, Paul Kelly, W. T. Crouch, 30 May 1939, Roanoke Island Folder, Box 126, NC Archives.

(58) - "some verbal tarring and feathering . . ." William T. Crouch to Crittenden, 31 May 1939, Roanoke Island Folder, Box 126, NC Archives.

(58) - "that the old man . . ." Saunders to Crittenden, 14 Jun. 1939, Roanoke Island Folder, Box 126, NC Archives.

(58) - "That is just what I wanted . . ." T. B. Shallington to Saunders, 11 Jun. 1939, Roanoke Island Folder, Box 126, NC Archives.

(60) - "considerable skepticism . . ." President [Pearce] to Stringfield, 17 May 1939, Correspondence Folder, Box 3, BU. The two replicas of the Dare Stone are mysteries in themselves. We're not sure how they were made, what they were made of, and what happened to them after the 1939 World's Fair was over with. However, Mr. Stephen Horrillo says that he inherited one of the replicas from his grandfather who found it under a trailer in New York about 1950 or so. See Horrillo's replica stone at http://www.angelfire.com/ego/iammagi/DARE_INDEX.htm. Also see the Roanoke Colonies Research Office website at http://www.ecu.edu/rcro/home_001.htm.

(60) - "We now have . . ." President [Pearce] to Stringfield, 11 July 1939, Correspondence Folder, Box 3, BU.

(60) - "more than 300 miles . . ." and other quotes in the paragraph. President [Pearce] to Stringfield, 11 July 1939, Correspondence Folder, Box 3, BU.

Chapter 6: A Diary in Stone

(66 and after) – The inscriptions on all the stones, both these and later ones, were eventually published by the Pearces in their Brenau *Bulletins*.

The last *Bulletin* on the Dare Stones contained the inscriptions of all the stones. See "The Dare Stones." Brenau Bulletin. Vol. 31, November 13, 1940, Brenau College, Gainesville, Ga., hereafter cited at November 1940 *Bulletin.*

(69) - "soap stones" and "good-luck stone." Boyden Sparkes, "Writ on Rocke: Has America's First Murder Mystery Been Solved?" *Saturday Evening Post*, April 26, 1941, 11.

(75) - "The soil there . . ." and "All the evidence . . ." President to Pres. Dice R. Anderson, 4 Aug. 1939, Correspondence Folder, Box 3, BU.

(75) - "Find 13 More 'Lost Colony' Grave Stones," and "If the authenticity . . ." *Atlanta Constitution*, 26 July 1939.

(77)- "Your part would be . . ." Laura Kingsbery to Pearce, 10 Aug. 1939, Correspondence Folder, Box 3, BU.

(77) - "wrote and produced . . ." Martha V. B. Mathis to Pierce [sic], 30 Aug. 1939, Correspondence Folder, Box 3, BU. Not much is known of Martha Mathis, certainly not how much she influenced the Pulitzer Prize-winning author. She was involved in the first production of Green's *The Lost Colony* in 1937. In fact, she seemed heavily involved in the pre-production phase. In June 1937 she had written Green that many of the play's cast members were very upset because they were being replaced by citizens from the town of Manteo, where the play was to be presented. In all, there is not much correspondence in the Paul Green papers between the two during this time. However, she certainly knew him and corresponded with him in a friendly manner. Martha B. Mathis to Paul Green, 21 June 1937, Box 6, Folder 417 and Martha Mathis to Paul Green, 4 December 1940, Box 8, Folder 545, Paul Green Papers #3693, Southern Historical Collection, Wilson Library, University of North Carolina Chapel Hill, Chapel Hill, NC.

(78) - "if you will take . . ." Pearce Jr. to Russell MacFarland, 7 Aug. 1939, Correspondence Folder, Box 3, BU.

(78) - "Sydnor – A well-known name . . ." G. R. Brigham to President Pearce, 22 June 1939, Correspondence Folder, Box 3, BU.

(79) - "18 others lye buried here." President [Pearce] to W. Lindsay Wilson, 17 Aug. 1939, Correspondence Folder, Box 3, BU. It is not known what happened to these stones. Mrs. Guy Vaughan of Spartanburg, SC, seeing a newspaper picture of the Brenau Stones, made the connection between them and the Inman stone. She actually went to the Hammett farm to compare the Inman stone with those Brenau had. She was convinced Inman's was a Dare Stone as well. She said she

wrote the Pearces offering to bring the Inman stone to Gainesville. But no word if she did or what happened. "Slab Found in County in 1935 Now Believed Relic of Lost Colony," *Spartanburg Herald-Journal*, Spartanburg, S.C., 30 Jul. 1939, Clipping Folder, Box 3, BU. Similarly with the Wilson stone, it's not know if he ever found it again or if the Pearces ever went rock hunting with him. Probably not as more Eberhardt stones were coming in and the conference was postponed a year. It is not known if Mr. Wilson attended the delayed October 1940 scholars conference.

(79) - "have never taken kindly . . ." Secretary to Randolph G. Ames, 30 Aug. 1939, Roanoke Island Folder, Box 129, NC Archives.

(79) - "New developments . . ." Pearce to Crittenden, 2 Sep 1939, Roanoke Island Folder, Box 135, NC Archives.

(80-83) – Stones 15 through 24. November 1940 *Bulletin*.

(85) - "The colony left 'Croatan' . . ." "The Dare Stones." *Brenau Bulletin*. Vol. 31, January 1, 1940, Brenau College, Gainesville, Ga., hereafter cited as January 1940 *Bulletin*.

(85) - "As our record . . ." and "the King . . ." January 1940 *Bulletin*. Exactly how many people were among the Lost Colonists has always been up to debate. John White returned to England and George Howe was killed, but two children, Virginia and the Harvie child, were born. The now accepted number stands at 117.

(86) - "It would therefore appear . . ." January 1940 *Bulletin*.

(86) - "'It may be,' . . ." "Excavation Planned," [Unknown Newspaper], c. Aug. 1939, Clipping File, Box 1, BU.

(86) - "The drama includes . . ." January 1940 *Bulletin*.

(87) - "50 miles . . ." John White, "John White's Narrative of his [1587] Voyage" in David Beers Quinn, *The Roanoke Voyages, 1584-1590. Documents to Illustrate the English Voyages to North America under the Patent Granted to Walter Raleigh in 1584.* 2 vols. London: The Hakluyt Society, 1955, 2:533., hereafter cited as White's 1587 Narrative.

Chapter 7: Pearce Rewrites History

(90) - "Mummy, why don't you . . ." Maude Fiske, *This Heritage: A Play Concerning Eleanor Dare and those English Colonists who went with Her from Roanoke after Landing there in July 1587* (Gainesville, Ga.: Brenau College, 1940), 54.

(91) - "You were told . . ." Fiske, *This Heritage*, 43-44.

(92) - "The Mulgraves . . ." Fiske, *This Heritage*, 46-47.

(93) - "Sails to the east . . ." Fiske, *This Heritage*, 52.

(93) - "Twas the King . . ." Fiske, *This Heritage*, 58.

(93) – "personal interest" and "his exposition . . ." Fiske, *This Heritage*, Acknowledgments.

(94) - "diary in stone." "Lost Colony's 'Diary of Stone' Displayed Here," *Atlanta Journal,* 10 Apr. 1940, Box 132, NC Archives.

(95) - "seen and studied . . ." and "Every facility . . ." "Three More Dare Stones Found," Brenau College Newspaper Release, 18 Aug. 1940, Clipping Folder, Box 1, BU.

(95) - "the former head . . ." November 1940 *Bulletin*.

(98) - "They robbed us . . ." John White, "John White's Account of the Abortive Voyage of the *Brave* and *Roe*" in David Beers Quinn, *The Roanoke Voyages, 1584-1590. Documents to Illustrate the English Voyages to North America under the Patent Granted to Walter Raleigh in 1584.* 2 vols. (London: The Hakluyt Society, 1955), 2:567, hereafter cited as "White's Abortive Voyage".

(98) - "without performing . . ." "White's Abortive Voyage," 2:569.

Chapter 8: Eleanor among the Indians

(101) - "We were shown . . ." November 1940 *Bulletin*.

(102-110) – Inscriptions from Stone 25 to Stone 46 are from the November 1940 *Bulletin*.

(102) - "if authentic . . ." in "Three More Dare Stones Found," Brenau College Newspaper Release, 18 Aug. 1940, Correspondence Folder, Box 1, BU.

(104) - "Farmer – Fisherman – Archeologist." "Virginia Dare Stone Finder Lives Simply," *Atlanta Constitution*, 21 Aug. 1940.

(106) - "the carver was . . ." Invitation to Meeting, Saturday, October 19 [1940], Correspondence Folder, Box 1, Folder 6, BU.

(109) - "found the half stone . . ." November 1940 *Bulletin*.

(111) - "I would to God my wealth . . ." John White to Richard Hakluyt, 4 February 1593 David Beers Quinn, *The Roanoke Voyages, 1584-1590. Documents to Illustrate the English Voyages to North America under the Patent Granted to Walter Raleigh in 1584.* 2 vols. (London: The Hakluyt Society, 1955) 2:715-16. John White is truly one of the tragic figures of American history. We know little of him before he appears on the Roanoke voyages. He was born into the English gentry sometime

between 1545 and 1550, probably in Truro, Cornwall and married Thomasine Cooper in 1566. The couple had a son in April 1567, but the child died the next year, December 26, 1568. Eleanor had been born sometime in early 1568 and she was christened on May 9, 1568. We know nothing more of White's wife, Thomasine. She did not accompany him to Virginia. We also know very little of White after his 1593 letter to Hakluyt. White said he made five trips to Roanoke. So he was probably on the 1584 Amadas and Barlow expedition. He was definitely with Lane's colonization attempt in 1585-86. He made a third as governor when he left his colonists on Roanoke in 1587. He made the ill-fated 1588 attempt in which his ship was attacked by French privateers and so never made it to America. And then his final 1590 expedition when he found his colony missing and was unable to go to Croatoan. White had been sent on the first couple of colonization attempts as an artist to record the area, plants, animals, peoples so Raleigh and potential investors could see what they had in Virginia. He drew and painted numerous pictures, not just items from around Roanoke, but also other places in the Western Hemisphere. In 1590, Theodor De Bry, a Belgian illustrator, used copies he made of Whites paintings when he and his sons published an illustrated edition of Thomas Hariot's *Brief and True Report of the new found Land of Virginia*. White's paintings are some of the very first images of American Indians to make their way back to Europe. They are a treasure trove of details and are some of the prizes of the British Museum. For an excellent book on John White and his paintings, see Kim Sloan, *A New World: England's First View of America* (Chapel Hill: University of North Carolina Press, 2007).

(113) - "This is a sharp Medicine . . ." See Edward Edwards, *The Life of Sir Walter Raleigh* (New York: MacMillan and Co. 1868), 705. The idea that the Lost Colonists' stranding by Simon Fernandez on Roanoke Island was sabotage by Sir Francis Walsingham comes from Lee Miller, *Roanoke: Solving the Mystery of the Lost Colony* (New York: Penguin Books, 2000), 180-84.

(113) - "A whole country of English . . ." found in Miller, *Roanoke*, 211.

Chapter 9: Preponderance of the Evidence

(115) - "If hoax it is . . ." Sparkes, "Writ on Rocke," 120.

(115) - "These lichens are . . ." and all quotes in that paragraph in Invitation to Meeting, Saturday, October 19 [1940], Correspondence Folder, Box 1, Folder 6, BU.

(117) - "perfect harmony . . ." November 1940 *Bulletin.*

(117) - "A geologist testified . . ." Crittenden to Fred M. DeWitt, 15 November 1940, Roanoke Island Folder, NC Archives.

(118) - "believes that the preponderance . . ." November 1940 *Bulletin.*

(118) - "certain doubts . . ." "'Dare Stones' Appear Authentic to Experts," *Raleigh News and Observer*, 21 October 1940.

(118-120) - "(1) The search for graves . . ." and the remaining points are found in Advisory Committee Recommendations, Thomas English to Crittenden, 12 November 1940, Roanoke Island Folder, Box 135, NC Archives.

(120) - "Scholars Study Authenticity of Dare Stones" *Atlanta Constitution*, October 20, 1940.

(120) - "Gainesville may well become . . ." "Cradle of History," *Gainesville (Georgia) Eagle*, 24 October 1940.

(121) - "disturbed" and "reconcile." H. J. Pearce, President to Crittenden, 28 November 1940, Roanoke Island Folder, Box 138, NC Archives.

(123) – Stone 48 inscription in November 1940 *Bulletin.*

(123) – "unrecorded." "Hint of Spanish Captives Given by Dare Stone," *Atlanta Constitution*, 29 December 1940.

(124) - "certaine men cloathed . . ." John Smith, *A True Relation of such occurrences and accidents of note, as hath happened in Virginia* in *The Complete Works of John Smith.* 3 vols. Edited by Philip L. Barbour. Chapel Hill: University of North Carolina Press, 1986), 1:49.

(124) - "The people cloathed at Ocanahonan . . ." Smith, *True Relation*, 1:55.

(125) - "to conduct two of our men . . ." Smith, *True Relation*, 1:63.

(125) - "to seek for the lost company . . ." John Smith, *The Generall History of Virginia, the Somer Iles, and New England, with the Names of the Adventurers and Their Adventures* in *The Complete Works of John Smith.* 3 vols. Edited by Philip L. Barbour. (Chapel Hill: University of North Carolina Press, 1986), 2:193.

(126) - "found little hope . . ." Smith, *Generall History*, 2:215.

(126) - "they were all dead." Smith, *Generall History*, 2:215.

(126) - "Peccarecamicke, where you shall . . ." *The Charters* in *Jamestown Narratives: Eyewitness Accounts of the Virginia Colony, The*

First Decade: 1607-1616. Edited by Edward Wright Haile. (Chaplain, Va.: RoundHouse, 1998*),* 23-24.

(127) - "some of our nation . . ." Virginia Council, "A True & Sincere Declaration of the purposes and ends of the plantation begun in Virginia" in *Jamestown Narratives: Eyewitness Accounts of the Virginia Colony, The First Decade: 1607-1616.* Edited by Edward Wright Haile. (Chaplain, Va.: RoundHouse, 1998*),* 367.

(127) - "Here Paspahegh . . ." and *"Here remaineth four men . . ."* and other names from Smith's Map are found in "Zuñiga map, depicting the James River (at bottom) and four waterways South: A) Chowan River; B) Cashie Creek; C) Roanoke River; and D) Tar River." See a reproduction of the map in Miller, *Roanoke.*

Chapter 10: A Blast from Tarheelia

(129) - "aroused . . ." Crittenden to Frank Stick, 25 October 1940, Roanoke Island Folder, Box 135, NC Archives.

(129) - "conducting a serious . . ." Crittenden to Stick, 25 October 1940, Roanoke Island Folder, Box 135, NC Archives.

(130) - "Every other explanation . . ." "Dare Stones A Hoax That Is Too Good," *Thursday (*Winston-Salem, NC), 24 October 1940.

(131) - "It was impossible . . ." "Crittenden's views on 'Dare Stones,'" Letter to the Editor, [Unknown paper], [no date], Folder 3, Box 1, BU.

(131) - "I believe neither . . ." "Crittenden's views on 'Dare Stones,'" Letter to the Editor, [Unknown paper], [no date], Folder 3, Box 1, BU.

(131) - "always looked upon . . ." Frank Stick to Crittenden, 23 October 1940, Roanoke Island Folder, Box 135, NC Archives.

(132) - "I feel reasonable confident . . ." Stick to Crittenden, 22 December 1940, Roanoke Island Folder, Box 138, NC Archives.

(132) - "obvious attempt . . ." Stick to Crittenden, 18 January 1941, Roanoke Island Folder, Box 138, NC Archives.

(132) - "continues her ridicule . . ." Pearce to Crittenden, 23 January 1941, Roanoke Island Folder, Box 138, NC Archives.

(133) - Quotes from Noel Yancey's story can be found in "Lively Argument is Swirling Over Whether 'Lost Colony' Belongs to North Carolina," *High Point (N.C.) Enterprise*, 9 February 1941.

(135) – "proud" and "insolent." William Strachey, *The History of Travel into Virginia Britannia* in *Jamestown Narratives: Eyewitness Accounts*

of the Virginia Colony, The First Decade: 1607-1617. Edited by Edward Wright Haile. (Champlain, Va.: RoundHouse, 1998), 664.

(135) - "comes to and fro amongst us . . ." Strachey, *History of Travel*, 619-20.

(136) - "the people have houses . . ." and "at Ritanoe the weroane Eyanoco . . ." Strachey, *History of Travel*, 596.

(136) - "The men, women, and children of the first plantation . . ." Strachey, *History of Travel*, 648.

(137) - "our nation without offense given . . ." Strachey, *History of Travel,* 664. Strachey's and Purchas's belief that the Lost Colonists relocated to the Chesapeake Bay, lived among the Chesapian Indians for twenty years, and then were killed by Powhatan was for decades the most accepted interpretation of the Lost Colonists' fate. One reason was that the Dean of Lost Colony scholarship, historian David Beers Quinn, in the 1950s and 1960s strongly backed Strachey's assertions. As Quinn saw it, between April 24 and 27, 1607, just days before Captain John Smith and the other members of the Virginia Company landed to establish Jamestown, they and the Chespians were attacked by Whahunsonacock's Pamunkey warriors. See Quinn's *Set Fair for Roanoke: Voyages and Colonies, 1584-1606* (Chapel Hill: University of North Carolina Press, 1985), 345, 360-63.

(137) - "how that from the Chesapeack Bay . . ." Strachey, *History of Travel*, 662.

(137) - "Powhatan confessed that hee had bin . . ." in John Smith, *The Proceedings of the English Colony in Virginia* in *The Complete Works of John Smith.* 3 vols. Edited by Philip L. Barbour. (Chapel Hill: University of North Carolina Press, 1986), 1:265n2.

Chapter 11: Dupes and Crooks

(139) – "genuine" and "some of them . . ." Sparkes, "Writ on Rock," 120.

(141) - "Haywood Pearce becomes resentful . . ." Sparkes, "Writ on Rocke," 121.

(142) - "I am not an Elizabethan scholar . . ." Sparkes, "Writ on Rocke," 121.

(142) - "broke off negotiations . . ." Sparkes, "Writ on Rock," 121.

(142) - "word of honor . . ." Sparkes, "Writ on Rocke," 121.

(143) - "He had the doggonedest . . ." Sparkes, "Writ on Rocke," 121-22.

(143) - "Jack DeLisle, publicity agent par excellence." Sparkes, "Writ on Rocke," 121-22.

(144) - "ballast stone . . ." William S. Powell, *Paradise Preserved: A History of the Roanoke Island Historical Association* (Chapell Hill: University of North Carolina Press, 1965), 143-44.

(145) - "that he never . . ." Sparkes, "Writ on Rocke," 121-22.

(145) - "without a shadow of doubt . . ." Anthony Buttitta to Crittenden, 21 April 1941, Roanoke Island Folder, Box 141, NC Archives.

(146) - "the authenticity of the stones . . ." "America's No. 1 Mystery!" *Cincinnati Enquirer*, 4 May 1941.

(147-155) All quotes on these pages come from Boyden Sparkes, "Writ on Rocke: Has America's First Murder Mystery Been Solved?" *Saturday Evening Post*, April 26, 1941, 9-11, 118-28. Boyden Sparkes is one of the more interesting characters in the whole Dare Stone story. His article, "Writ on Rocke," is a must-read for Dare Stone buff. Sparkes' papers are in the Herbert Hoover Presidential Library in West End, Iowa. As for his son-in-law, Joseph Colin Eagles Jr. would serve in the Navy in World War II. He would return to Wilson, North Carolina and serve a few terms from there as a state senator. He died in Wilmington, North Carolina on November 28, 1998.

(152) – "forced to believe less in the authenticity . . ." Hopefully Sparks got the report directly from Lester himself as a search through the archives at Emory University has not turned up Dr. Lester's report. Sparkes undercut his own argument here when he mis-dated Lester's report, saying it was made on June 26, 1939. This would have been impossible as Eberhardt "found" Stone Number 25 in August 1940. This mis-dating seems to be merely a typographical error.

(156) - "very shallow and most dangerous . . ." Ralph Lane, "Ralph Lane's Discourse on the First Colony," in David Beers Quinn, *The Roanoke Voyages, 1584-1590. Documents to Illustrate the English Voyages to North America under the Patent Granted to Walter Raleigh in 1584.* 2 vols. (London: The Hakluyt Society, 1955), 1:257, hereafter cited as Lane's Discourse.

(157) - "take a good store of men. . ." Lane's Discourse, 1:261.

(157) - "were seated far from him." Strachey, *History of Travel*, 664.

(157) - "out of his territory." Strachey, *History of Travel*, 648.

(157) - "confessed." Quote in John Smith, *The Proceedings of the English Colony in Virginia* in *The Complete Works of John Smith.* 3 vols. Edited by Philip L. Barbour. (Chapel Hill: University of North Carolina Press, 1986), 1:265n2. Wahunsenacawh's complicity in the destruction of the Lost Colonists is one of the most debated aspects of the mystery. Historian David Beers Quinn, in *Set Fair for Roanoke*, accepted Strachey's and Purchas's accusation that the Powhatan ordered it done. Quinn believed the Lost Colonists had relocated to the Chespian Indians on the south side of Chesapeak Bay and in early 1607 the Chespians refused to pay tribute to Wahunsenacawh. Once his scouts spotted John Smith's ships, the Powhatan felt this was the perfect time to wipe out both the English and the disloyal Chespians. David Durant in *Ralegh's Lost Colony* echoes Quinn. Historian James Horn in *A Land as God Made It*, believed the Colonists lived peacefully among the Indians for twenty years, slowly assimilating. However Horn, unlike Quinn, believes the Lost Colonists were living among the Choanoacs along the Chowan River. But just before the arrival of the Jamestown colonists, Wahunsenacawh sent his warriors to wipe out the Colonists. Horn reasoned that Wahunsenacawh feared the new Jamestown colonists would make an alliance with the Lost Colonists and Choanoacs against him. So Wahunsenacawh had to strike first. Only a few Lost Colonists survived and escaped into the interior of the country. Historian Michael Leroy Oberg, in *The Head in Edward Nugent's Hand*, posed several possible fates for the Lost Colonists, but whether they went to the Chesapeake Bay or the Chowan River, when they were attacked, it was at the hands of Wahunsenacawh, the Virginia Powhatan. Other historians have disputed this. Probably the strongest believer of Wahunsenacawh's innocence is author Lee Miller. In her *Roanoke: Solving the Mystery of the Lost Colony,* Miller attributes Strachey's and Purchas's accusation of the Indian leader as anti-Powhatan propaganda. What better way to deflate any sympathy for Wahunsenacawh back in England by accusing him of killing scores of English colonists. It would also justify making war on him and his chiefdom and taking Indian land. Instead, Miller believes the Lost Colonists made it to the Chowan River where they were eventually attacked by the Mangoaks to the west. Most Colonists were killed, while the survivors were captured and enslaved. In the end, this is what really divides Lost Colont scholars. There are those who think Wahunsenacawh killed them and those who think he did not.

Chapter 12: Acid and Extortion

(161) - "Father, Five are buried . . ." "Some of Stones Genuine; Tech
Geologist Believes," *Atlanta Journal*, 15 May 1941.

(162) - "which had been used . . ." "Some of Stones Genuine; Tech
Geologist Believes," *Atlanta Journal*, 15 May 1941.

(162) - "a good scolding." "Hoax Claimed By 'Dare Stones' Finder In
Extortion Scheme, Dr. Pearce Charges," *Atlanta Journal*, 15 May 1941.

(162) - "Pearce and Dare Historical Hoaxes." "Hoax Claimed By 'Dare
Stones' Finder In Extortion Scheme, Dr. Pearce Charges," *Atlanta
Journal*, 15 May 1941.

(163) – The two contracts are found in "Whole Thing Badly Discredited,
Dr. Pearce Admits in Stone Saga." *Atlanta Constitution*, 16 May 1941.

(164) - "I smelled a rat . . ." "Champion Stone Finder Prefers To Be Let
Alone," *Atlanta Journal*, 15 May 1941.

(164) - "in the rock business . . ." "Grocer Bruce Figures in 'Dare Stone'
Discoveries." *Atlanta Journal*, 16 May 1941.

(165) - "the Pearces recognized . . ." "Hoax Claimed on Famous Dare
Stones, Pearce Says," *Atlanta Journal*, 15 May 1941.

(165) - "established the authenticity . . ." "'Dare Stone' Sent to Noted
Metallurgist." *Atlanta Journal*, 16 May 1941.

(165) - "Easy To Be Fooled." T. W. Samuels Bourbon ad, n.p., 27
August 1941, Folder 6, Box 1, Emory Archives.

(166) - "The 'Lost Colony' Is Still Lost" and quotes in the next three
paragraphs come from Nell Battle Lewis's editorial "The 'Lost Colony'
Is Still Lost – Much To the Amusement of North Carolina." Probably
Richmond (Va.) Times-Dispatch, 1 June 1941, clipping in Roanoke
Island Folder, Box 141, NC Archives.

(168) - "several of their Ancestors . . ." John Lawson, *A New Voyage to
Carolina*. Edited by Hugh Talmadge Lefler. (1708; Chapel Hill:
University of North Carolina Press, 1967), 69.

Chapter 13: The Stones Roll On

(173) - "Inscribed Stones Revive Mystery of the Lost Colony,"
Providence (R.I.) Journal, 20 July 1941.

(174) - "stupid brother." Boyden Sparkes to Dean J. H. Purks, Jr., 7 May
1946, Folder 4, Box 1, Emory Archives.

(174) - "the man's face . . ." Sparkes to Purks, 22 January 1946 and
Comments, n.d., Folder 6, Box 1, Emory Archives.

(175) - "Since atomic physics . . ." Josiah Crudup to Cathy McCarthy, 4 October 1966, Box 3, BU.

(175) - "The [*Saturday Evening Post*] article . . ." Lucille Adams to Robert Furneaux, 11 May 1972, Folder 6, Box 1, BU; Adams to Carey E. Waldrip, 8 February 1973, Correspondence Folder, Box 3, BU.

(176) - "Frankly, I have not . . ." and all quotes from Dr. Stephenson over the next few pages are from "Report of Observations Regarding 'The Dare Stones,'" Dr. Robert Stephenson, 15 April 1983, Correspondence Folder, Box 3, BU.

(177) - "We did the best . . ." John E. Sites to Dr. Betsy Reitz, 12 November 1985, Correspondence Folder, Box 3, BU.

(178) - "The Dare Stones Mystery." Gerdeen Dyer, "The Dare Stones Mystery," *The Atlanta Weekly*, 19 April 1987, 6-23.

(178) – "Sparkes was interested. . ." All quotes in these next paragraphs and pages come from Robert W. White, *A Witness for Eleanor Dare: The Final Chapter in a 400 Years Old Mystery.* San Francisco: Lexikos, 1991, 62, 64-72.

(182) - "goodly high land." Lane's Discourse, 1:258-59. The division of the Lost Colonists into two parties – a small one to Croatoan and the majority of them going somewhere else, most likely the Chowan River – is now pretty much accepted by most Lost Colony historians. Miller, *Roanoke*, 228-29; Horn, *A Land As God Made It*, 145-46; Parramore, "The 'Lost Colony' Found," 67-83; Stick, *Roanoke Island*, 244-45.

Chapter 14: As Gullible as Mr. Pickwick

(187) - "Virginia Dare Novel in Stone Causes Georgia-Carolina Row, Associated Press, 8 February 1941.

(189) - "White's Colony . . ." Samuel A'court Ashe, *Biographical History of North Carolina.* 8 volumes. (Greensboro, N.C.: Charles L. Van Noppen, 1906), 4:15.

(190) - "one of the most plausible . . ." Hugh T. Lefler, *History of North Carolina.* 2 volumes. (New York: Lewis Historical Publishing Company, Inc., 1956), 1:28-29.

(193) - "in some townes . . ." Hariot, "A Briefe and true report," 1:379.

(193) - "without weapons . . ." Hariot, "A Briefe and true report," 1:379.

(193) - "Powhaton of Roanoke." *The Charters, Jamestown Narratives,* 24.

(196) - "four men, two boys . . ." Strachey, "History of Travel," 596.

(196) - "worth much labor." *The Charters*, *Jamestown Narratives,* 24.

(196) - "beat his copper." Strachey, "History of Travel," 596.

A NOTE ON THE SOURCES

For those seeking more information on the Roanoke Voyages and the Lost Colony, there are several primary sources. See "Arthur Barlowe's Discourse of the First Voyage"; Ralph Lane's "Discourse on the First Colony"; Thomas Hariot's "A Briefe and True Report"; and John White's paintings and his "Narratives" of his 1587 and 1590 voyages to Virginia. Fortunately, all these sources and more have been compiled and edited by David Beers Quinn in *The Roanoke Voyages, 1584-1590. Documents to Illustrate the English Voyages to North America under the Patent Granted to Walter Raleigh in 1584.* 2 vols. London: The Hakluyt Society, 1955.

Similarly, John Smith's reports of his men's search for the Lost Colonist can be found scattered throughout his many writings, such as "A True Relations of such occurrences and accidents of note, as hath happened in Virginia"; "The Proceedings of the English Colony in Virginia"; "The Generall History of Virginia." All these have been compiled into a three volume set of *The Complete Works of John Smith,* edited by Philip L. Barbour, and published in 1986 by the University of North Carolina Press. William Strachey's "A History of Travel into Virginia Britannia" can be found in *Jamestown Narratives: Eyewitness Accounts of the Virginia Colony, The First Decade: 1607-1617.* Edited by Edward Wright Haile. Champlain, Va.: RoundHouse, 1998.

Raleigh's Lost Colony of Roanoke remains America's Number One Historical Mystery and so leaves us with numerous questions. Where did they go? If killed, who killed them? If they assimilated with

Indians, which Indians? Did Wahunsenacawh have anything to do with their fate? Because of all these questions and the answers they generate, one of the most delicious things about the Lost Colony are the different interpretations arrived at by various historians. And there have been some excellent historians who have studied the Lost Colony. I relied on a host of these scholars for this book. For years, the top Lost Colony book was David Beers Quinn's *Set Fair For Roanoke: Voyages and Colonies, 1584-1606* (1985). It was Quinn who shaped so much of the Lost Colony argument by saying they had moved to the Chesapeake Bay and were killed by Powhatan. Today, the top scholar on the topic would be Michael Leroy Oberg. His most recent work is *The Head in Edward Nugent's Hand: Roanoke's Forgotten Indians* (2008), which looks at the English colonization efforts on Roanoke from an Indian point of view. Oberg is not sure whether the Colonists went to the Chesapeake Bay or the Chowan River, but believes they were eventually attacked by Wahunsenacawh. James Horn in *A Land as God Made It* (2005) about the founding of Jamestown believes the Colonists made it to the Chowan River only to be eventually attacked by Wahunsenacawh. In 2000, Lee Miller published a provocative interpretation of the Lost Colony titled *Roanoke: Solving the Mystery of the Lost Colony.* She said the stranding of the Colonists on Roanoke was a deliberate attempt to kill them by Sir Francis Walsingham in order to sabotage Sir Walter Raleigh's standing with Queen Elizabeth. She also has the Colonists being killed on the Chowan by the Mangoaks and the survivors being taken captive and essentially sold as slaves to other Indians at the Occaneechi trading town.

Other important books on the Lost Colony are Karen Ordahl Kupperman's *Roanoke: The Abandoned Colony;* lebame houston and Barbara Hind's *Roanoke Revisited: The Story of the First English Settlements in the New World and the fabled Lost Colony of Roanoke Island;* David Stick's *Roanoke Island: The Beginnings of English America;* David N. Durants, *Ralegh's Lost Colony*; and Thomas and Barbara Parramore's book *Looking for the "Lost Colonists"* and Thomas Parramore's article "The 'Lost Colony' Found: A Documentary Perspective" in volume 78, January 2001 of the *North Carolina Historical Review.* I'm sure there are plenty more that I am overlooking.

Interest in the Roanoke expeditions and the Lost Colony have gone far beyond just books. East Carolina University at Greenville, North Carolina has developed a Roanoke Colonies Research Office under the direction of Dr. E. Thomson Shields Jr. See their website at http://www.ecu.edu/rcro/home_001.htm. ECU has done much archaeological research on the Roanoke ventures under the auspices of Dr. David Phelps. The search for the Lost Colonists continues to this day.

As for the Dare Stones themselves, much of the information on Louis Hammond, the original Chowan River Dare Stone and Emory University's relationship with Hammond and the Stone can be found in the Dare Stone Collection, Manuscripts, Archives, and Rare Book Library (MARBL), Robert W. Woodruff Library, Emory University, Atlanta, Georgia. One may want to read Dr. James Lester's and Dr. J. Harris Purks's written transcript of their talk to the Emory University Faculty Club, "The Virginia Dare Stone." Address to the Faculty Club of Emory University, April 19, 1938, Folder 9, Box 1. Some of Boyden Sparkes's later searches for Louis Hammond can be found here. But there is plenty to read throughout the whole Dare Stone Collection.

The North Carolina response and antagonism to the Dare Stones, particularly from C. C. Crittenden, Frank Stick, and playwright Paul Green can be found in the correspondence left by Crittenden. This can be found in the Director's Office Material, General Correspondence, Roanoke Island Folders, Boxes 117-120, R-Z, Department of Archives and History, State Archives, Raleigh, NC. Similarly, much of the information on the Chapell Stone and Shallington Stones can be found here.

Just about all the information and quotes from the Pearces about their relations with all the Dare Stones and William Eberhardt are found in the Dare Stone Collection, University Archives, Trustee Library, Brenau University in Gainesville, Georgia. Between 1938 and 1940, the Pearces published four articles or bulletins on the Dare Stone. Many of the quotes by Haywood Pearce Jr. come from these: Haywood J. Pearce Jr., "New Light on the Roanoke Colony: A Preliminary Examination of a Stone Found in Chowan County, North Carolina." *The Journal of Southern History* 4 (May, 1938): 148-163; "The Dare Stone and the Lost Colony of Roanoke." Brenau *Bulletin.* Vol. 30, March 1, 1939, Brenau College, Gainesville, Ga.; "The Dare Stones." Brenau *Bulletin.* Vol. 31, January 1, 1940, Brenau College, Gainesville, Ga.; and "The Dare Stones." Brenau *Bulletin.* Vol. 31, November 13, 1940, Brenau College, Gainesville, Ga.

Boyden Sparkes did an amazing amount of research on the Dare Stones. His article, "Writ on Rocke: Has America's First Murder Mystery Been Solved?" *Saturday Evening Post*, April 26, 1941, 9-11, 118-28, is a must read.

Newspapers across the country ran stories about the Dare Stones during their four years of notoriety. Naturally, being closest to the action, the *Atlanta Constitution* and the *Atlanta Journal*, two competing papers back then now merged into one, ran the most in-depth stories. North Carolina newspapers, such as the *Raleigh News and Observer*, *Charlotte Observer*, *Washington (NC) Daily News*, and others were also interested in the story. Every now and again, papers throughout the nation ran articles.

Of course, the Dare Stones themselves can be found at Brenau University in Gainesville, Georgia. Whether fakes or authentic, they are valuable historical artifacts.

BIBLIOGRAPHY

PRIMARY SOURCES

Barlowe, Arthur. "Arthur Barlowe's Discourse of the First Voyage," in David Beers Quinn, *The Roanoke Voyages, 1584-1590. Documents to Illustrate the English Voyages to North America under the Patent Granted to Walter Raleigh in 1584.* 2 vols. London: The Hakluyt Society, 1955., 1:91-116.

"The Charters," in *Jamestown Narratives: Eyewitness Accounts of the Virginia Colony, The First Decade: 1607-1617.* Edited by Edward Wright Haile. Champlain, Va.: RoundHouse, 1998., 14-26.

"The Dare Stone and the Lost Colony of Roanoke." *Brenau Bulletin.* Vol. 30, March 1, 1939, Brenau College, Gainesville, Ga.

"The Dare Stones." *Brenau Bulletin.* Vol. 31, January 1, 1940, Brenau College, Gainesville, Ga.

"The Dare Stones." *Brenau Bulletin.* Vol. 31, November 13, 1940, Brenau College, Gainesville, Ga.

Dare Stones Collection, University Archives, Trustee Library, Brenau University, Gainesville, Georgia.

Dare Stones Collection, Manuscripts, Archives, and Rare Book Library (MARBL), Robert W. Woodruff Library, Emory University, Atlanta, Georgia.

Diaz, Pedro. "The Relation of Pedro Diaz" in David Beers Quinn, *The Roanoke Voyages, 1584-1590. Documents to Illustrate the English Voyages to North America under the Patent Granted to Walter Raleigh in 1584.* 2 vols. London: The Hakluyt Society, 1955., 2:786-95.

Director's Office Material, General Correspondence, June-December 1937, Box 117, R-Z, Department of Archives and History, State Archives, Raleigh, North Carolina.

English, Thomas Hopkins Papers, Manuscripts, Archives, and Rare Book Library (MARBL), Robert W. Woodruff Library, Emory University, Atlanta, Georgia.

Fiske, Maude. *This Heritage: A Play Concerning Eleanor Dare and those English Colonists who went with Her from Roanoke after Landing there in July 1587.* Gainesville, Ga.: Brenau College, 1940.

"Grant of Arms for the city of Raleigh in Virginia, and for its Governor and Assistants" in David Beers Quinn, *The Roanoke Voyages, 1584-1590. Documents to Illustrate the English Voyages to North America under the Patent Granted to Walter Raleigh in 1584.* 2 vols. London: The Hakluyt Society, 1955., 2:506-12.

Green, Paul Papers #3693, Southern Historical Collection, Wilson Library, University of North Carolina Chapel Hill, Chapel Hill, NC.

Hariot, Thomas. "A Briefe and True Report" in David Beers Quinn, *The Roanoke Voyages, 1584-1590. Documents to Illustrate the English Voyages to North America under the Patent Granted to Walter Raleigh in 1584.* 2 vols. London: The Hakluyt Society, 1955., 1:317-87.

Lane, Ralph. "Ralph Lane's Discourse on the First Colony," in David Beers Quinn, *The Roanoke Voyages, 1584-1590. Documents to Illustrate the English Voyages to North America under the Patent Granted to Walter Raleigh in 1584.* 2 vols. London: The Hakluyt Society, 1955, 1:255—94.

Lawson, John. *A New Voyage to Carolina.* Edited by Hugh Talmadge Lefler. 1708; Chapel Hill: University of North Carolina Press, 1967.

Oré, Luis Jerónimo de. "Relations of the Martyrs of Florida," in David Beers Quinn, *The Roanoke Voyages, 1584-1590. Documents to Illustrate the English Voyages to North America under the Patent Granted to Walter Raleigh in 1584.* 2 vols. London: The Hakluyt Society, 1955., 2:802-16.

Pearce, Haywood J. Jr. "New Light on the Roanoke Colony: A Preliminary Examination of a Stone Found in Chowan County, North Carolina." *The Journal of Southern History* 4 (May, 1938): 148-163.

"The Primrose Journal of Drake's Voyage, Florida and Virginia" in David Beers Quinn, *The Roanoke Voyages, 1584-1590. Documents to Illustrate the English Voyages to North America under the Patent Granted to Walter Raleigh in 1584.* 2 vols. London: The Hakluyt Society, 1955., 1:303-308.

Proceedings of the English Colonie in Virginia in *The Complete Works of John Smith.* 3 vols. Edited by Philip L. Barbour. Chapel Hill: University of North Carolina Press, 1986., 1:191-98.

Quinn, David Beers. *The Roanoke Voyages, 1584-1590. Documents to Illustrate the English Voyages to North America under the Patent Granted to Walter Raleigh in 1584.* 2 vols. London: The Hakluyt Society, 1955.

Smith, John. *Map of Virginia* in *The Complete Works of John Smith.* 3 vols. Edited by Philip L. Barbour. Chapel Hill: University of North Carolina Press, 1986, 1:121-90.

Smith, John. *A True Relation of such occurrences and accidents of note, as hath happened in Virginia* in *The Complete Works of John Smith.* 3 vols. Edited by Philip L. Barbour. Chapel Hill: University of North Carolina Press, 1986), 1:26-117.

Smith, John. *The Proceedings of the English Colony in Virginia* in *The Complete Works of John Smith.* 3 vols. Edited by Philip L. Barbour. (Chapel Hill: University of North Carolina Press, 1986), 1:203-89.

Smith, John. *The Generall History of Virginia, the Somer Iles, and New England, with the Names of the Adventurers and Their Adventures* in *The Complete Works of John Smith*. 3 vols. Edited by Philip L. Barbour. (Chapel Hill: University of North Carolina Press, 1986), 2:1-475.

Sparkes, Boyden. "Writ on Rocke: Has America's First Murder Mystery Been Solved?" *Saturday Evening Post*, April 26, 1941, 9-11, 118-28.

Strachey, William, *The History of Travel into Virginia Britannia* in *Jamestown Narratives: Eyewitness Accounts of the Virginia Colony, The First Decade: 1607-1617*. Edited by Edward Wright Haile. Champlain, Va.: RoundHouse, 1998., 563-689.

Virginia Council, "A True & Sincere Declaration of the purposes and ends of the plantation begun in Virginia" in *Jamestown Narratives: Eyewitness Accounts of the Virginia Colony, The First Decade: 1607-1616*. Edited by Edward Wright Haile. (Chaplain, Va.: RoundHouse, 1998), 356-71.

White, John. "John White's Drawings," in David Beers Quinn, *The Roanoke Voyages, 1584-1590. Documents to Illustrate the English Voyages to North America under the Patent Granted to Walter Raleigh in 1584*. 2 vols. London: The Hakluyt Society, 1955., 1:390-464.

White, John. "John White's Narrative of his [1587] Voyage" in David Beers Quinn, *The Roanoke Voyages, 1584-1590. Documents to Illustrate the English Voyages to North America under the Patent Granted to Walter Raleigh in 1584*. 2 vols. London: The Hakluyt Society, 1955, 2:515-38.

White, John. "John White's Narrative of the 1590 Voyage to Virginia" in David Beers Quinn, *The Roanoke Voyages, 1584-1590. Documents to Illustrate the English Voyages to North America under the Patent Granted to Walter Raleigh in 1584*. 2 vols. London: The Hakluyt Society, 1955, 2:598-622.

White, John. "The Arrival of the Englishmen in Virginia," [Map] and
"Engraving of the John White-Thomas Harriot2 Map of
Ralegh's Virginia" in David Beers Quinn, *Set Fair for Roanoke:
Voyages and Colonies, 1584-1606.* Chapel Hill: University of
North Carolina Press, 1985.

Newspapers

Alchemist
Associated Press
Atlanta Constitution
Atlanta Journal
Atlanta Weekly
Cincinnati Enquirer
Detroit News
Elizabeth City (NC) Daily Advance
Florence (SC) News
Gainesville (Ga.) Times
Greensboro (NC) News
High Point (NC) Enterprise
Indianapolis News
Newsweek
New York City Herald Tribune
New York Times
Patterson (NJ) News
Portland (Indiana) Commercial-Review
Providence (RI) Journal
Raleigh (NC) News and Observer
Richmond (Va.) Times-Dispatch
Spartanburg (SC) Herald-Journal
Thursday (Winston-Salem, NC)
Washington (NC) Daily News
Waynesville (Indiana) Press
Wilmington (NC) Star News

Secondary Sources

Ashe, Samuel A'court. *Biographical History of North Carolina.* 8
volumes. Greensboro, N.C.: Charles L. Van Noppen, 1906.

Ashe, Samuel A'court. *History of North Carolina.* 2 volumes. Greensboro, N.C.: Charles L. Van Noppen, 1908.

Brenau University Undergraduate and Graduate Catalog, 2002-2003. Gainesville, Ga.: Brenau University, 2002.

Connor, R. D. W. *History of North Carolina.* 3 volumes. Chicago: Lewis Publishing Company, 1919.

Demos, John. *The Unredeemed Captive: A Family Story from Early America.* New York: Alfred A. Knopf, 1994.

Durant, David N. *Ralegh's Lost Colony.* New York: Atheneum, 1981.

Edwards, Edward. *The Life of Sir Walter Raleigh.* New York: MacMillan and Co. 1868.

Green, Paul. *The Lost Colony: A Symphonic Drama in Two Acts.* Chapel Hill: University of North Carolina Press, 1937.

Horn, James. *A Land as God Made It: Jamestown and the Birth of America.* New York: Basic Books, 2005.

houston, lebame and Barbara Hind, eds. *Roanoke Revisited: The Story of the First English Settlements in the New World and the fabled Lost Colony of Roanoke Island.* Manteo, N.C.: Times Printing Co., 1997.

Hoving, Thomas. *False Impressions: The Hunt for Big-Time Art Fakes.* New York: Simon and Schuster, 1996.

Kelton, Paul. *Epidemics & Enslavement: Biological Catastrophe in the Native Southeast, 1492-1715.* Lincoln: University of Nebraska Press, 2007.

Kupperman, Karen Ordahl. *Roanoke: The Abandoned Colony.* Savage, M.D.: Rowan and Littlefield Publishers, Inc., 1984.

Lefler, Hugh T. *History of North Carolina*. 2 volumes. New York: Lewis Historical Publishing Company, Inc., 1956.

Mallios, Seth. "Gift Exchange and the Ossomocomuck Balance of Power: Explaining Carolina Algonquian Socioeconomic Aberrations of Power at Contact" in E. Thomas Shields Jr. and Charles R. Ewen, eds., *Searching for the Roanoke Colonies: An Interdisciplinary Collection*. Raleigh, N.C.: Office of Archives and History, 2003, 142-58.

Miller, Lee. *Roanoke: Solving the Mystery of the Lost Colony*. New York: Penguin Books, 2000.

Oakley, Christopher Arris. *Keeping the Circle: American Indian Identity in Eastern North Carolina, 1885-2004*. Lincoln: University of Nebraska Press, 2005.

Oberg, Michael Leroy. "Gods and Men: The Meeting of Indian and White Worlds on the Carolina Outer Banks, 1584-1586." *North Carolina Historical Review* 76 (October 1999): 567-90.

Oberg, Michael Leroy. *Dominion and Civility*: English Imperialism & Native America, 1585-1685. Ithaca, N.Y.: Cornell University Press, 1999.

Oberg, Michael Leroy. *The Head in Edward Nugent's Hand: Roanoke's Forgotten Indians*. Philadelphia: University of Pennsylvania Press, 2008.

Parramore, Thomas C. "The 'Lost Colony' Found: A Documentary Perspective." *North Carolina Historical Review* 78 (January 2001): 67-83.

Parramore, Tom and Barbara Parramore, *Looking for the "Lost Colonists."* Raleigh, N.C.: Tanglewood Press, 1984.

Perdue, Theda. *Cherokee Women*. Lincoln: University of Nebraska Press, 1998.

Powell, William S. *Paradise Preserved: A History of the Roanoke Island Historicaal Association.* Chapel Hill: University of North Carolina Press, 1965.

Potter, Stephen R. *Commoners, Tribute, and Chiefs: The Development of Algonquian Culture in the Potomac Valley.* Charlottesville: University Press of Virginia, 1993.

Quinn, David Beers. *Set Fair for Roanoke: Voyages and Colonies, 1584-1606.* Chapel Hill: University of North Carolina Press, 1985.

Rights, Douglas L. *The American Indian in North Carolina.* Winston-Salem, NC: John F. Blair, 1947.

Rountree, Helen C. *The Powhatan Indians of Virginia: Their Traditional Culture.* Norman: University of Oklahoma Press, 1989.

Sloan, Kim. *A New World: England's First View of America.* Chapel Hill: University of North Carolina Press, 2007.

Stick, David. *Roanoke Island: The Beginnings of English America.* Chapel Hill: University of North Carolina Press, 1983.

White, Robert W. *A Witness for Eleanor Dare: The Final Chapter in a 400 Years Old Mystery.* San Francisco: Lexikos, 1991.

Index

About the Author

David La Vere

David La Vere teaches American Indian History at the University of
North Carolina Wilmington. He is an award-winning author and public speaker.
Born in New Orleans, he was a Marine Corps infantryman before earning a
B.A. in History and Journalism from Northwestern State University in 1982. In
1989, he received a Master of Arts in History from the same university, and in
1993 received his Ph.D. in History from Texas A&M University. He came to
the UNC Wilmington Department of History in 1993 and has risen through the
ranks to full Professor. La Vere often lectures around North Carolina, and was
invited to attend the Oxford Round Table at Oxford University, England to
discuss diversity in society. La Vere has written five other books on American
Indian History, two of which (*The Texas Indians* and *Contrary Neighbors*) have
won multiple best book awards. David has also written numerous articles for
Our State North Carolina magazine and has been a contributing author to two
Our State Press publications: *North Carolina's Shining Moment: World War II
in North Carolina* (2005) and *North Carolina Churches: Portraits of Grace*
(2004).

Printed in the USA
CPSIA information can be obtained
at www.ICGtesting.com
LVHW020602041223
765568LV00002B/188